MORRISSEY IN CONVERSATION
—·— THE ESSENTIAL INTERVIEWS —·—

Edited by Paul A. Woods

PLEXUS, LONDON

British Library Cataloguing in Publication Data
A catalogue record for this book is available from the
British Public Library

  ISBN-13: 978-0-85965-443-2

Printed in Great Britain by Bell & Bain Ltd.
Book design by Rebecca Longworth
Cover design by Coco Wake-Porter
Cover photograph by Kevin Cummins/Getty

CONTENTS

MORRISSEY NEEDS NO INTRODUCTION
—·— BY PAUL A. WOODS —·—

'None of this should have happened, should it? . . . it was a mistake.'
– Morrissey, in conversation with Paul Morley

Britain's unlikeliest rock 'n' roll star in several decades is also its most essential. If popular culture is to comprise anything other than this year's spoonfed pablum, we'd best keep taking Steven Patrick Morrissey seriously.

Not that he was ever known by that moniker. Back in the earliest days of the Smiths, the alternately fey/aggressive, shy/histrionic young man with the Oxfam *couture* style devolved himself down to a single name – gatecrashing the ranks of Elvis, Bowie, or any other iconic artist evoked by a single word.

In the frothy world of mid-1980s pop music, the Smiths' gritty black-and-white aesthetic was all Morrissey's. In those captured moments of 1960s films/newspapers/TV, he held onto the world that had passed with his childhood: Terence Stamp as the repressed, lovelorn young man in *The Collector*, on the original cover of 'What Difference Does It Make?'; pools winner Viv Nicholson, spending her way out of poverty and back into it again for 'Heaven Knows I'm Miserable Now'; actress Yootha Joyce on 'Ask', unglamorous but stylish, working class 1960s womanhood personified.

His personal icons were all, like himself, characters trapped in worlds they never made: decadently epicene genius Wilde; doomed and brooding Jimmy Dean; ailing Brit rock 'n' roller Billy Fury, his time long past.

The Smiths brought realism to their romance, and tempered their angst with the lightest of touches. The times were personified in their frontman: rejecting all taints of rock 'n' roll machismo, he played up the social awkwardness of the misfit and the outsider, his gently haunting vocals whooping suddenly upward into a falsetto, clothed in outsize women's shirts, sporting National Health specs or a huge Johnny Ray-style hearing aid. This charming young man was, in the vernacular of the time, the very antithesis of a 'rockist' – always knowingly closer to the gentle ironicist Alan Bennett, or self-lacerating diarist Kenneth Williams, than a licentious Mick Jagger or drugged-out Jim Morrison.

In all this, erstwhile personal saviour Johnny Marr – who drew his songwriting partner out of an isolated bedroom existence that might have been scripted by Beckett – was the perfect collaborator. Together, the Morrissey/Marr axis epitomised rock 'n' roll in the eighties without falling prey to any of its redundant clichés. If 'This Charming Man' was an energising, obliquely English piece of post-Byrds powerpop, then a heartbreakingly sad piece like 'This Night Has Opened My Eyes' soundtracked life as it was – and still is – lived, as observed by the sympathetic outsider Morrissey. Drawing on the sounds and images of an earlier, more innocent era, Morrissey/Marr plunged deep into the kitchen sink of the soul.

As Morrissey remarked in the earliest Smiths interview in the national music press (with Dave McCullough, then at *Sounds*), his muse was born out of desperate times. In the post-post-punk climate of the early 1980s, the choking triumvirate of callous Thatcherite economics, Reagan's nuclear weapons on Airstrip One's soil and a war of attrition with the IRA gave very little cause for hope. While the zoot suit and ra-ra dress crowd partied like the last revellers on the Titanic, the nascent 'indie' scene (not that it was known as such then, becoming increasingly lame after the label had stuck) was either jangling away with the Postcard Records bands or consumed with its own insular pessimism.

If the lazy 'miserabilist' tag applied to the Smiths had been at all accurate, they would not have been fronted by one of England's last great mordant wits. Depression – seemingly lifelong, up until his current middle-aged resurgence – seems to have acted as a spur, a key to creativity, rather than an entry point into utter despair.

A true pop artist, Morrissey exists to articulate and poeticise what his audience can only feel. If the fits of melancholia described in many earlier interviews drove him close to self-destruction, then his bittersweet lyrical postcards from the brink were solace to many a despairing young soul. Whether Morrissey's words were empathetic enough to make the listener want to hold onto life, or whether they merely accompanied a sad passage from this vale of tears, they still *mattered.*

Today, his endurance makes nonsense of the suicidal tendencies one contributor (Irish journalist Neil McCormick) believed would make an end of him. A lifetime of melancholia, leavened by wit and humour, has produced one of the most interesting yet accessible repertoires in the history of the pop song. Only its creator can say whether it was worth sticking it out, but for the rest of us, we have a vocal commentator (or should that be commentating vocalist?) who well knows our strange little sadnesses and joys – albeit reflected through his own aloof viewpoint.

Morrissey is all but infamous for his estrangement from affairs of the heart and of the flesh. But his vacillation on his early sexual experiences (either non-existent, or so depressing that they led to years of abstinence) is no great contradiction. As the man himself said, back when he was an elderly boy, 'I wouldn't want to be thought of as Tarzan or Jane or whatever!'

For all the chimerical trails he has left regarding his sexuality, this variously (according to who is believed at what particular time) celibate/frustrated heterosexual/bisexual man illustrates the futility of the 'tick appropriate box' approach, when so many of us comprise Heinz' 57 Varieties.

Morrissey's much touted – and possibly much overplayed – celibacy aside, he has been far more directly vocal about the suffering inflicted on animals – principally by the meat industry, but also in recent years by medical tests and vivisection. 'If you agree with vivisection,' challenges this morally indignant but stylish man, not averse to leather shoes and belts, 'go and be vivisected upon yourself.'

Some have adopted his animal rights dogma slavishly, but to the observant Morrissey watcher it's emblematic of a personal religiosity cultivated in lieu of an absent God, with whom this lapsed Catholic conducts a fluctuating relationship. Lonely, he tells us, to the point of solipsism, only able to truly communicate with other people via song lyrics, the younger Morrissey never accepted the world on its own terms – while the older, stronger Morrissey refuses outright.

Some said he was just too sensitive to live, and it seems a wonder the neurosis that fuelled so much of his creativity hasn't destroyed him along the way. Many expected him to go under with the defection of Johnny Marr, his musical life raft.

But, having long since abandoned his northern hometown of Manchester, for years Morrissey hung onto the psycho-geography of his youth as a source of inspiration. British to the core, and patriotic (though non-jingoistic) to boot, our nation's traditional rainy bleakness and dark satanic mills were the lifeblood of this young Anglo-Irishman, the son of first generation immigrants. Even the most vicious criminals and nastiest crimes of the 1960s were lyrical succour to the melancholic songbird. (Think of 'Suffer Little Children', an extraordinary musical edit of Emlyn Williams' study of the 'moors murders' that blighted Morrissey's childhood, *Beyond Belief*, or the thumping glam-rocker 'The Last of the International Playboys', about Reggie Kray.)

While certain obsessions abide, there have been some interesting changes. Morrissey has fashioned himself into his own human creation, seemingly out of designer fabrics and healed emotional scar tissue. As his sartorial style began to reflect an unostentatious affluence, so Morrissey himself came to represent a quietly assured masculinity – worlds apart from the perceived wimpishness of the Smiths era, equidistant from the crass 1990s 'new lad' – becoming fascinated by the iconography of boxing, or praising the New York Dolls for their 'violence' on Jools Holland's *Later* show.

Perhaps one of the most remarkable aspects of his maturing into a more robust, burlier, beerier version of himself was his re-embracing of the early 1970s. Maybe in the Smiths era it was just too soon afterward to admit to its importance. But read this book's contents from back to back, and sense not only *A Taste of Honey* and the elusive soulfulness of Cilla Black, but the gaudy glitter of glam rock that burned through a near-bankrupt Britain's bleak skies.

Though dressed closer to a stylish Mafia lieutenant these days than the men in platform soles who once dominated the pop charts, Morrissey's extraordinary recent output is an outgrowth of 'glam'. Swaggering and flamboyant, with intricate little frills, it retains all the energy and economy of original fifties rock 'n' roll – but cut with the dramatic, almost flamenco flourishes that surely endear Morrissey to the young Mexican gangsters who love him, and whom he has elegised. The Smiths are fully exorcised and eclipsed.

It's telling that Morrissey's grand resurgence should be at a time when hollow, vapid 1990s concepts like 'Britpop' and 'Cool Britannia' are just empty memories. While other, much tamer artistes would drape themselves in the flag, it was deemed 'unacceptable' when this independently thinking (and speaking) bigmouth spoke of national identity, and its passing.

That this, and a couple of well observed songs on the Anglo-Asian predicament, should place him almost on the level of a war criminal was a measure of the politically correct times – and of a music press grown pious and stale, yet still self-important. The circumstances of his return to recording in the new millennium were also very typically English: having discarded one of our true greats, we were embarrassed to find he didn't belong to us anymore.

Almost as much as his mostly tightly honed and wittily confrontational songs, Morrissey has made an art form of the personal interview throughout his singularly turbulent career. So read on, but don't bother searching for staid consistency. In the early years the Smiths are described as a socialist co-operative, distinctly at odds with the internecine courtroom warfare between the songwriter and the rhythm section a decade later. Temporary showbiz friends become despised in the blink of an eye, after offending his raw-nerved sensitivity.

(Even his stage debut, with fourth division punk band the Nosebleeds, appears to have been historically suppressed – though Buzzcocks/Magazine founder Howard Devoto has a dreamlike impression of having seen it.)

Now Morrissey has refocused his perspective to face the world – not merely merrie old Englande, of which, as he admits, a little more ceases to exist every day. As the land that raised him began to fade into a pan-European cityscape, the neglected and vilified Morrissey upped sticks and vanished – first, oddly enough, to LA, land of sun-kissed vacuity and gang violence, then on a sojourn to Rome, where some kind of personal rebirth appears to have taken place. No more the little Brit in thrall to the *Carry On* films (whose refusal to treat sex as anything other than seaside postcard ribaldry must once have seemed so apt), the lowlife aesthete turns to the work of the late, great Pier Paolo Pasolini.

No longer 'a mess of guilt because of the flesh', Morrissey assures us he is now truly born. After all the tuneful tours de force he's made out of his and our own insecurities, seeking to know all the mucky little private details may seem somehow beside the point. The very existence of this capricious, perverse and quite brilliant pop artist is inspiring enough.

Paul A. Woods

MORRISSEY ANSWERS
—·—TWENTY QUESTIONS—·—

Steven Morrissey was born in Manchester on May 22, 1959. He's never had a job but has written two short books, one on James Dean, and the other on the New York Dolls. In early 1982 he met guitarist Johnny Marr and they formed the Smiths. A year later Rough Trade released their first single, 'Hand In Glove', an independent hit they followed up with their first chart hit, 'This Charming Man'. Since then Morrissey has enchanted, disturbed and annoyed with his laconically delivered lyrics, popularised bunches of flowers and being miserable and continued to indulge in his passions for Oscar Wilde, Billy Fury and Sandie Shaw.

1. *Were you bullied at school?*
I was never bullied at any point, I must admit. I was never picked on, never pushed around and that's that. It's not very interesting is it?

2. *When did you start wearing glasses?*
Seriously when I was thirteen. I needed to wear them much sooner but glasses had this awful thing attached to them that if you wore them you were a horrible green monster and you'd be shot in the middle of the street. So I was forced to wear them at thirteen and I've stuck with them ever since.

3. *What did your parents do for a living?*
Very spectacular jobs. One was a librarian and one worked in a hospital. Who did what? Elizabeth, my mother, is the librarian. Peter, my father, works in the hospital. Yes we still keep in touch, every day.

4. *Were you good at sport?*
Miraculous. It was the only thing I was good at and I used to love it completely. The 100 metres was my *raison d'etre*. Yes, I won everything. I was a terrible bore when it came to athletics. I was just the type of person everyone despises so I've carried on in that tradition.

5. *When did you leave home?*
I left spasmodically and I returned home spasmodically for years. I was never very good at it. I think the first time was when I was seventeen and the last when I was 23. I just went to the usual foul, decrepit bedsits that simply crush your imagination.

6. *Were you ever a punk?*
Not in the traditional sense. I did like lots of it. I did see most of the important

Saddled up in Salford: The 1980s pop scene is remembered for sparkly ostentation, but the young Smiths frontman embodied the austerity chic of the Thatcher years.

11

groups and I was incredibly aware at the time . . . but a punk as far as style goes I never was.

7. *What did you want to be when you grew up?*
Oh, I'm afraid I always wanted to be a librarian. To me that seemed like the perfect life: solitude; absolute silence; tall, dark libraries. But then they started to become very modern, you know, these little pre-fabs and they had no romance whatsoever. So suddenly the idea had no fascination for me. I also wanted to be what I am now, all the time, but I think when you want to sing and you want to enter popular music, you're convinced by everybody that it's an absurd notion, that it's childish, and it's a whim and it's diseased – which of course it is – and you're always badgered out of it. So I thought well, perhaps it is these things, but I'm going to try it anyway.

8. *What's the worst illness you've ever had?*
Probably being on the dole. I always consider that to be an absolute illness. A physical illness? I've not really had anything.

9. *Do you drink or smoke?*
I have spasms of wine but I don't smoke. But I'm afraid, yes, red wine occasionally.

10. *Are you gay?*
I feel that I am quite vulnerable and that's quite good enough because I wouldn't want to be thought of as Tarzan or Jane or whatever! I'd rather be thought of as someone quite sensitive who could understand women in a way that wasn't really sexual. I hate men who can only see women in a sexual way – to me that's criminal and I want to change that. I don't recognise such terms as heterosexual, homosexual, bisexual and I think it's important that there's someone in pop music who's like that. These words do great damage, they confuse people and they make people feel unhappy so I want to do away with them.

11. *Favourite shop?*
Rymans, the stationers. To me it's like a sweetshop. I go in there for hours, smelling the envelopes. As I grew up I used to love stationery and pens and booklets and binders. I can get incredibly erotic about blotting paper. So for me, going into Rymans is the most extreme sexual experience one could ever have.

12. *Favourite joke?*
The funniest thing – I mean I'll say this now but it won't seem the least bit funny, it'll seem completely damp – was when this famous social gadfly came up to Oscar Wilde at this celebrated event in Paris and said, 'Isn't it true, Oscar, that I'm the ugliest woman in the whole of Paris?' and he said, 'No, my dear, you're the ugliest woman in the whole of the world,' which I thought was quite funny.

13. *Who does your laundry?*
Me, I'm afraid. Every Friday night you'll find me leaning over the bathtub, immersed

in Persil. I simply cannot go to the launderette and I don't have a washing machine and I don't have time to get one. It's quite passionately romantic leaning over the bath, scrubbing one's shirts.

14. *Are you in love?*
If I said no, that would seem too stark. I have to be. I think everybody has to be, otherwise where do you get the energy from to go on, in life, and strive for certain things? The things that stir me are schools and buildings and I'm quite immersed in the past and in the history of this country and how things have evolved and I get quite passionate about certain people in desperate situations.

15. *Are you frightened of growing old?*
No, not to any degree. I was never happy when I was young so I don't equate growing old with being hysterically unhappy. To me old age doesn't mean doom, despair and defeat. There are lots of people I know in considerably advanced years that I find fascinating.

16. *Do you socialise with the rest of the Smiths?*
Well, I see them every single day, but we don't go out to clubs, so no, we don't socialise in that way. We haven't fallen into that throng of people who need to be seen – we're quite private in that respect.

17. *Are you a socialist?*
I am. I don't belong to any particular party but if I were to be stripped down, as it were, I would be shoved in the socialist box. Why? Just the very obvious things of coming from a working-class background, being exposed to hardships and the reality of life. I think all socialists are absolute realists.

18. *Do you believe in an after-life?*
Not really. I can't think of any reason why I should. You're born, you live, you die and that's the end.

19. *If you were an animal what would you be?*
I'd probably be a cat, I think. Mainly because I'm very fond of them and they can lead a relatively luxurious life. They're also very independent beings – not like dogs who need persistent attention. I'd like to be an ordinary scrubber, an alley cat . . . no, a tabby.

20. *The best thing about being a pop star?*
The best thing is, one way or another, that people respect you. It just boils down to fame. No matter what you've done in the past – people will forgive you. People in the past who've spat at you are quite forgiving. It's two-faced, of course, but it gives me a great deal of satisfaction because it's an enormous sense of achievement. It can't be surpassed, really.

Star Hits Collection, 1985

THE MORRISSEY COLLECTION
—·—·— BY IAN BIRCH —·—·—

OSCAR WILDE 1854-1900
Victorian wit, novelist, playwright and poet.
My mother, who's an assistant librarian, introduced me to his writing when I was eight. She insisted I read him and I immediately became obsessed. Every single line affected me in some way. I liked the simplicity of the way he wrote. There was a piece called 'The Nightingale and the Rose' that appealed to me immensely then. It was about a nightingale who sacrificed herself for these two star-crossed lovers. It ends when the nightingale presses her heart against this rose because in a strange, mystical way it means that if she dies, then the two lovers can be together. This sense of truly high drama zipped through everything he wrote. He had a life that was really tragic and it's curious that he was so witty. Here we have a creature persistently creased in pain whose life was a total travesty. He married, rashly had two children and almost immediately embarked on a love affair with a man. He was sent to prison for this. It's a total disadvantage to care about Oscar Wilde, certainly when you come from a working class background. It's total self-destruction almost. My personal saving grace at school was that I was something of a model athlete. I'm sure if I hadn't been, I'd have been sacrificed in the first year. I got streams and streams of medals for running. As I blundered through my late teens, I was quite isolated and Oscar Wilde meant much more to me. In a way he became a companion. If that sounds pitiful, that was the way it was. I rarely left the house. I had no social life. Then, as I became a Smith, I used flowers because Oscar Wilde always used flowers. He once went to the Colorado salt mines and addressed a mass of miners there. He started the speech with, 'Let me tell you why we worship the daffodil.' Of course, he was stoned to death. But I really admired his bravery and the idea of being constantly attached to some form of plant. As I get older, the adoration increases. I'm never without him. It's almost biblical. It's like carrying your rosary around with you.

JAMES DEAN 1931-1955
Moody idol of the Fifties who died in a car crash aged 24 after making only three films, including *Rebel without a Cause*.
I saw *Rebel without a Cause* quite by accident when I was about six. I was entirely enveloped. I did research about him and it was like unearthing Tutankhamun's tomb. His entire life seemed so magnificently perfect. What he did on film didn't stir me that much but as a person he was immensely valuable. Everything from his birth in a farming town to coming to New York, breaking into film and finding he didn't really want it when he had enormous success. At school it was an absolute drawback because nobody really cared about him. If they did, it was only in a synthetic rock and roll way. Nobody had a passion for him as I did – for that constant

uneasiness with life. Even though he was making enormous strides with his craft, he was still incredibly miserable and obviously doomed. Which is exactly the quality Oscar Wilde had. That kind of mystical knowledge that there is something incredibly black around the corner. People who feel this are quite special and always end up in quite a mangled mess.

BILLY FURY 1941-1983
Born Ronald Wycherly, made name in late Fifties as tough rock and roll rebel (Britain's answer to Elvis Presley). Re-emerged in film *That'll Be the Day* in '73. Died of heart trouble.

Billy Fury is virtually the same as James Dean. He was entirely doomed too and I find that quite affectionate. He was persistently unhappy and yet had a string of hit records. He was discovered working on the docks in Liverpool, was dragged to London, styled and forced to make records. He always wanted to make very emotionally overblown ballads but he found himself in the midst of the popular arena. He despised almost every aspect of the music industry and was very, very ill from an early age. This album [*Sound Of Fury*] is the rarest I have. It was his first. Albums made in those days were thrust out to appeal to a mature audience. They talked about 'chandeliers' and 'cocktail dresses'. Singles were for teenagers and I'm afraid I always preferred the singles. I was the kind of child who'd bound out of bed on a Saturday, leapfrog down to the local shop and just stay there inhaling the air for hours and smelling all the vinyl and caressing the sleeves. I'd leave about mid-day and go to bed and consider that a completely successful day. I was really quite poor so whatever record I could buy was like a piece of my heart. Something I couldn't possibly exist without. Billy's singles are totally treasurable. I get quite passionate about the vocal melodies and the orchestration always sweeps me away. He always had such profound passion.

Smash Hits, 21 June – 4 July, 1984

HANDSOME DEVILS
—•— BY DAVE McCULLOUGH —•—

Desperately scrambling for something 'new', the music business and the music press don't (as is normal) realise that something new *is* happening. It might appear quiet, low lying, polite and very obscure, but it isn't.

First there was punk, then post punk, the funny name groups like Echo and Teardrop, groups who used traits of psychedelia nicely. And who only now, three years too late, are being (successively) ripped off by Tears For Fears et cetera. The funny names keep coming and they are useless and way out of time.

This year already you've had a new crop of groups, the Wake, the Smiths, the Box and a recharged Go Betweens, who present a new urbanity, a new sensibleness amid the attempts to shock and the attempts to block (the future).

Music *beyond* punk rock.

Smiths say: 'Don't mention punk in this piece. We feel that is far behind everything we're about. It's ancient history . . .'

This polite, sensible and unflash approach shouldn't hide these groups' true allegiance to '76 and all that, nor, especially in Smiths' case, the very *impolite* state of their art.

Smiths are no ordinary name in a paper.

Smiths look tremendous, they have the cool. Guitarist Johnny Marr plays a red Rickenbacker type machine gun in best early Jam fashion. He looks a *handsome* Costello but denies the resemblance strongly.

Singer Morrissey has a history stretching back to '77 punk and writing for fanzines. He is reputed to be the 'last great Devoto figure out of Manchester'. He has the cool down to a tee, flinging flowers about on stage and writing lyrics which deal with sex as you've never heard apparent 'confessors' like the mixed-up Marc Almond write about it.

The subject of child molesting crops up more than a few times in Smiths songs. They are hilarious lyrics, more so because they will suddenly touch on the personal.

Smiths have a grand 'Freebird'-like finale to their live set. This and the Costello and child molestation claims they will reject out of hand, this is all part of the Smiths plan. Gonna be huge.

Smiths are signed to Rough Trade, a nice angle this, not only because those Smiths' lyrics must therefore be brought into question *vis a vis* Will Geoff Travis *approve?* but because it raises the question, will Rough Trade be able to make this exceptional new group the stars they can very likely be?

Morrissey is a wonderfully arrogant pig ('I crack the whip and you'll skip, but you deserve it, you deserve it'). Quite simply, funnily, they *know* the talent that the Smiths possess.

How good are you?

Morrissey: 'I tremble at the power we have, that's how I feel about the Smiths. It's there and it's going to happen.'

Are Rough Trade the best label for immediate stardom?

Morrissey, enigmatic smile on handsome face: 'What we want to achieve *can* be achieved on Rough Trade. Obviously we wouldn't say no to Warners, but RT can do it too.'

I know Factory wanted you. Wouldn't they have been cooler?

Johnny: 'We'd be stuck in the "Manchester scene" then. What we're thinking of isn't even in terms of national success. It's more like world wide . . .'

Morrissey: 'Factory aren't really interested in new groups. Factory have been good, but they now belong to a time that is past. Look, we had a great social life, Factory has been great, but let's leave all that behind us now.

'Look, the quote that best sums up the Smiths is from Jack Nichols' book *Men's Liberation*: 'We are here and it is now.' I feel really strongly about *now*. I don't want to wait around, I don't care about two years time, things have got to happen *right now* for the Smiths. And I think they will.'

Let's sort this sexual thing out.

I get a traditionalism from Smiths that is almost HM (that Skynyrd finale). It's certainly an aggressive sexual stance they've got. Morrissey goes Oscar Wilde:

'I'm in fact very anti-aggression. Obviously I'm interested in sex and every song is about sex. I'm very interested in *gender*. I feel I'm a kind of prophet for the fourth sex.

'The third sex, even that has been done and it's failed. All that Marc Almond bit is pathetic. It sounds trite in print but it's something close to "men's liberation" that I desire.'

The fourth sex! Excuse me, but I'm still in a metaphysical state about it. It will come. With every Smiths appearance it comes closer. Off stage, in bed, in bed alone. It's coming . . .

'I just want something different. I want to make it easier for people. I'm bored with men and I'm bored with women. All this sexual segregation that goes on, even in rock 'n' roll, I really despise it . . .'

Smiths share with this year's best new groups an anti-boredom stance, an aura of breaking through to completely new territory. A sexual neutralism that rejects the Bowie/macho/wimp norms. It is hard to identify because it is so radically different.

Everything I call the Smiths is wrong because I still place them in an old context: hard when they are soft, immoral when they are moral:

' . . . We do not condone child molesting. We have never molested a child.'

Traditionalist macho, when they . . .

Morrissey: ' . . . I just so happen to be completely influenced by feminist writers like Molly Haskell, Marjory Rose and Susan Brown-Miller. An endless list of them!

'I don't want to *go on* about feminism but it is an ideal state. It will never be realised beyond that because this society detests strong women. You just have to look at the Greenham women. This is a society that only likes women who faint and fawn and want only to get married. I'm not neurotic about it, but it is an integral part of the way I write.'

Why the importance in carrying flowers?

Morrissey: 'They're symbolic for at least three reasons. We introduced them as an antidote to the Hacienda when we played there; it was so sterile and inhuman. We wanted some harmony with Nature. Also, to show some kind of optimism in Manchester which the flowers represent. Manchester is so semi-paralysed still, the paralysis just zips through the whole of Factory . . .'

Your finale tells that '(Love Is Just A) Miserable Lie'. Do you believe it, that people are totally separate, even from an ultimate state of love?

'Yes. Unfortunately. But there's an optimism in admitting it . . . Explain? Oh I could tell you of years of celibacy when I just couldn't cope with physical commitment because it always failed. I suppose I'm unnatural in the general scheme of things, because I have these feelings.'

Morrissey is a self-publicising weirdo, in other words a lover.

'I want a new movement of celibacy. I want people to abstain . . . explain? Howard Devoto I know quite well and I know he formed a group in order to make friends (he'd never had any). I can only say I'm the same, and gather from that what ye will.'

Johnny mentions the Ramones in passing. There is a Ramonish tint in Smiths that is only the beginning of what they are about. A nihilism, the molesting scam that soon leads into a fierceness and a morality-despite-it-all that is more Fall-like.

Morrissey: 'These are desperate times. But I don't think we should join in with the desperation. We should conquer it. I'm fed up with this depressive attitude people have.'

What about your humour?

'There are many really desperate characters from literature who had amazing senses of humour. Stevie Smith wanted to kill herself at nine. That's wonderful. I can relate to that. Sylvia Plath, just before she killed herself, had this incredible sense of humour in *Letters Home* . . .'

Is having or not-having a job important in Morrisseyland?

'Not in the least. Jobs reduce people. One of our lines goes, "I've never had a job because I don't want one": jobs reduce people to absolute stupidity, they forget to think about themselves. There's something so positive about unemployment. It's like, Now We Can Think About Ourselves. You won't get trapped into materialism, you won't buy things you don't really want . . .'

Smiths are an anti-stance group in the grand Fall tradition. An Alka Seltzer to a binge of Heaven 17s.

Morrissey: 'We're fed up with people who won't talk about the press, all this New Order crap. They probably *really* haven't *got* anything to say. I believe that's the truth . . .'

Johnny: 'We're unique because we really rate the press. Putting out papers every week when there is so obviously very little good music around except the Smiths must be really hard . . .'

Morrissey: 'The British music press is an art form.'

Garry Bushell?

'There is always an exception to a rule, Dave.'

Is it crucial being H.A.N.D.S.O.M.E. in Smithland?

Morrissey: 'Absolutely.'

Johnny: 'We find it just finishes off the package nicely. It just so happens we're handsome. We didn't rope in good-looking chaps on bass and drums, it just happened that way . . .'

Doesn't this rule out 95 per cent of the world from Smithland?

Morrissey: 'Probably. But we genuinely want a handsome audience above everything else. I can predict that in six months time they'll be bringing flowers to our gigs . . .'

But what happens if you're ugly as sin?

Morrissey, waving a vague finger about: 'Oh I'm sure they can arrange it somehow. They can, ah, learn to *look* handsome. With great training of course!'

Of course. Expect a plastic surgery boom in '83.

Sounds, 4 June, 1983

THE SMITH HUNT!
—•— BY DAVID DORRELL —•—

It's no exaggeration to say that it came as a shock, a numbing body-slam to the nervous system.

But then what would you feel if you opened a daily newspaper and discovered you had been all but directly accused of molesting children?

The Smiths know: they feel reviled . . . and confused.

Only a few days before, they had finished a session for *The David Jensen Show*. Their first single 'Hand In Glove' had achieved positive press criticism, and they'd hoped that their follow-up, 'Reel Around The Fountain', would build on that success. Everything was great.

Morrissey was singing in excelsis, Johnny Marr's guitars and harmonica were precisely etching the very face of the session, and Mike Joyce and Andy Rourke had lifted the rhythm of their drums and bass until it hammered at the ceiling and crashed to the floor. On a temporal stage the Smiths know it's Heaven when they're up there.

And they smile with devilish intent.

And as for notoriety . . . well is one thrashing a bouquet of golden daffodils onstage anything more than poetic licence? Or is the sensitive profile of a naked man on a single sleeve aspiring to subversion?

But two weeks ago, *The Sun* ran a news story by their showbiz correspondent, Nick Ferari, which alleged that BBC Radio chiefs were to hold an emergency meeting to decide whether a 'song about molesting' should be broadcast on *The David Jensen Show*.

According to the garbled and inaccurate article the track in question was entitled 'Handsome Devil' – and it contained 'clear references to picking up kids for sexual kicks'. When questioned by *The Sun* about his 'controversial lyrics' Morrissey is reported as saying, 'I don't feel immoral singing about molesting children.'

What man would sign his own death warrant thus? That 'Handsome Devil' had not been recorded for the session did not affect the paper's verdict on the band; nor did any of the other flagrant fabrications (including the interview). What did matter was the crash of breaking glass as a thousand lonely housewives dropped their milk-bottles . . .

Following the spot-the-pervert accusations in *The Sun*, *Sounds* ran a damning indictment of the band in their gossip column 'Jaws' – penned by none other than Garry Bushell, a fervent enemy of the Mancunian quartet.

Bushell has been blamed by the Smiths' record company, Rough Trade, for giving *The Sun* its derogatory and misleading information in the first place. Bushell, when asked, denied such claims and in turn accused his arch rival Dave McCullough – who is an ardent fan of the Smiths – of misinterpreting the band's lyrics in a feature that he wrote: thus instigating the whole story.

The 1980s indie-pop star: Wearing outsize women's shirts and National Health specs, Morrissey played up the social awkwardness of the misfit and the outsider.

As Morrissey says: 'It's really their affair and we're just bait.'

Since then Rough Trade's solicitor has dispatched letters to both *The Sun* and *Sounds* asking for a retraction. If no such retraction and apology appears legal action is likely to be taken.

So there, condensed and shrink-wrapped, you have the none too pleasant tale of how the Smiths, a wan and wonderful phenomena from Manchester, crossed the great divide between independent fame and national infamy. How do they feel?

'Well, we're still in a wild state of shock,' an ashen Morrissey replies. 'We were completely aghast at *The Sun* allegations, and even more so by *Sounds*. We really can't emphasise how much it upset us because obviously it was completely fabricated,' he claims. 'I did an interview with a person called Nick Ferari – and what developed in print was just a total travesty of the actual interview. It couldn't possibly be more diverse in opinion.

'To me it's about somebody else, they're writing about another group . . . it's so strange. It's tragically depressing . . .

'Quite obviously we don't condone child molesting or anything that vaguely resembles it. What more can be said?'

What more indeed? Since the deplorable rape of a six year old Brighton boy, *The Sun* has picked up a new word for its meagre vocabulary: 'paedophilia'. And now that word has been used as a wedge to open the door for an onslaught on anything that doesn't fit into its own Moral Bible.

Paranoia or persecution? If this strikes as a symptom of the former, then take heed: it's as likely to be a concrete encroachment from the latter. Nothing, not even Bingo, can boost a reactionary tabloid's sales like a jingoistic war cry or a McCarthurian witch hunt. Are we so pathetic as to believe that Fleet Street's crusaders march out with unsoiled hands?

As guitarist Johnny Marr states: 'It seems on the surface of it as the obvious hatchet job against a new, rising band who are getting a certain amount of publicity. But on every level the whole thing's got completely out of hand . . . and it's affecting us personally now.

'I've got a younger brother who is eleven, who on the day it was in *The Sun* went to school and was hassled by kids, hassled by teachers.'

Morrissey continues: 'It's really difficult to conceive such . . . savage critique. Because it's not just "bad" it's about as bad as you could possibly, humanly get it. And there is so much hatred from *Sounds* . . .'

Wasn't it possible that the *Sounds* piece was a joke?

'Well, they might be "jokes" but they're really not funny,' Morrissey soberly replies.

'I'm sure,' says Johnny, 'that if the mother of the young lad in Brighton was to read the statement concerning us, or anybody who has strong feelings about the case, then they're not going to see it as a joke.

'I think if there is that ambiguity there, then it was there with that purpose: for whoever wants to believe it. I think there are more people that are gonna take it seriously than do regard it as a joke. It's more than ambiguous.'

And *The Sun*'s piece?

Morrissey: 'It's quite laughable coming from a newspaper like *The Sun* – which is so obviously obsessed with every aspect of sex. So it's all really a total travesty of human nature that it's thrown at us, such sensitive and relatively restrained people. I live a life that befits a priest virtually and to be splashed about as a child molester . . . it's just unutterable.'

However fatuous and fantastic *The Sun* article was, it did succeed in its dirtying the Smiths name (for reasons unknown). It also ensured that the session, which wasn't being 'investigated', was censored and that a six minute version of 'Reel Around The Fountain' was removed. According to Mike Hawkes, the producer for David Jensen's show, the specially commissioned track was removed purely as a precautionary measure. As for the article itself, all the BBC press office could offer was that veritable cliché, '*The Sun* got it wrong again.'

Unfortunately Morrissey was saddened to hear that Aunty had decided to drop the track because, 'The record itself is protection because of its innocence.

'Curiously though, at the end of the day, the BBC did pledge their allegiance to us. So I think that's more important than anything else.'

And for the Smiths that's probably true. The BBC have not banned their material and plan to play the single when it is released. In fact, their sad treatment at the hands of the Bingo Barons and other writers of prurient pap may well be the foundations for their success.

What obviously attracted the flies to the meat was Morrissey's blunt but beautiful lyrical style. For many of the songs the *leit-motif* is that of an ageless, genderless love; and an unrequited love at that. Unfortunately the nebulosity of each song's protagonist does inject a certain sense of ambiguity into the storyline. And that was a red flag to *The Sun* . . .

Morrissey: 'It's completely taken out of context – but it depends on where the individual's mind lies. If you want to read something in particular lyrics you will – whether it's there or not.'

What – 'A boy in the bush is worth two in the hand, I think I can help you get thru your exams'?

Morrissey: 'Yes. If you read the rest of the lyrics then it completely complies. And the message of the song is to forget the cultivation of the brain and to concentrate on the cultivation of the body. A boy in the bush . . . is addressed to a scholar. There's more to life than books you know, but not much more – that is the essence of the song . . .

'So you can just take it and stick it in an article about child-molesting and it will make absolutely perfect sense. But you can do that with anybody. You can do it with Abba.'

To meet Morrissey is to meet somebody of unsettling calm. Broad, square and white, he is imbued with the same sense of enormity that marks the great men of religion. He is – in varying measures – bashful, sarcastic and serene. Thankfully his often caustic wit and his elastic ego are countered by his zealotry and passion. At times he is both missionary and heathen. And at times he writes the best love songs since the Buzzcocks.

His partner in contempt of crime is Johnny Marr, a nervous, effusive creature who hides behind dark glasses and plays great scores.

'I live a saintly life,' Morrissey laughs. 'He lives a devilish life. And the combination is wonderful. Perfect.'

'Hand in glove/The sun shines out of our behinds' – 'Hand In Glove'
Of course to hear is to believe. And with their debut Troy Tate-produced LP set for imminent release, more will hear and more will believe.

An American distribution arrangement has been agreed with WEA and their hopeful conquest of the Atlantic shores will come as no surprise. Though, no doubt, the question of their lyrical content will surely be mooted by that country's more puritan forces.

Not that it matters.

Morrissey: 'I'm certainly not going to change the way I write because I think it's essential. If I have to be accused of anything, it's because I write strongly and I write very openly from the heart . . . which is something people aren't really used to. They're used to a very strict, regimented style – and if you get too personal, and I don't mean offensively personal but just too close then it's what a "strange" person, let's get him on the guillotine.'

Will that hinder your commercial success?

'No,' he continues vigorously. 'At the end of the day the truth comes through and we shall find the highest success.

'Our egos are not so fragile that we are shattered by anything some mini-streamroller at *Sounds* could write. We're not that fey – good grief. Neither were we really affected that much by *The Sun*. It's just the rest of the world you have to worry about – you have to take their feelings into consideration – which is a great burden.

'It really proves that you don't have as much control over your destiny in this business as you think you do. There are people who like you and there are people who hate you. So why should you give the people that hate you precedence? Really we should stamp on it. It's history already.'

Throughout, Morrissey speaks of himself and his band in elevated tones almost as if he holds a certain disdain for the soiled and grubby cameo that the rest of us portray as life. He sees the body as the Taoist temple of the mind: he doesn't drink, he doesn't smoke and he doesn't swear. Above all, he is celibate and has been for a long time. He sees himself as more than a rival to Cliff Richard.

Yet undeniably his penmanship constantly returns to the throes of Love: in all its tempered glory. And through it comes the weakness and forced purity that underlies the solidity of his work. When he sings his voice is that of an angel in purgatory. And his stigma is the anguish of the damned.

'You can pin and mount me like a butterfly/But take me to the heaven of your bed/Was something that you never said' – 'Reel Around The Fountain'
Are you removed from love?

Morrissey: 'I'm physically removed, but there are so many aspects of it. Much of what I write about is unrequited.

'I feel that I do have a unique view of it because obviously it dominates every individual's life – which I've observed for quite a time. I feel I have a particular insight, which sounds terribly pompous and terribly ostentatious. It's funny though that most people that get enchained to the idea of "absolute love" are usually totally irresponsible and self-deprecating individuals.'

Isn't that a sterile view of love?

'No. I'm not a bitter and twisted individual with a whip crashing down on lovers in the park!'

All in all it smacks of an almost religious devotion to an ideal; an ideal that is clouded somewhat by its own grandeur but is basically akin to the awe-inspiring moments that make the Bunnymen so crystalline in their magnificence.

Yet Ian Mac is firmly rooted in his own background and belief, and therefore bows to the world and possesses humility. Morrissey, on the other hand, is quite content to let his lofty aspirations get the better of him and as such fails to win on a human level. His songs are all from a birds-eye view and until he admits to his own weaknesses the best part of the Smiths' creed will remain frozen and other-worldly.

Is this man, you ask, an egotist?

Morrissey: 'It's not really ego. If you have something and you know that you're good why be shy and hide behind the curtains? There's no point . . .'

What does all of this mean to you?

'It's more essential to me than breathing – it's more natural to me than breathing. I don't know why I'm here, it's like being hurled on an escalator and you go up and you don't have any say in the matter. That's all really . . .

'The whole thing really is a matter of life and death. And that's how serious we are . . .'

Aren't you worried that people might not take you seriously?

'Some people won't, some people will and the fact that some people will and do already, means that it's been valuable, it's been worthwhile . . .'

Do you feel that you have to be a threat to be successful?

'No, not in the least. If the whole threat thing means you have a brain and you use it, then we're a threat. But if it means anything other than that, well, I don't really see how we're dangerous in any way. I don't think we'll disturb anybody – and I don't think it's coy to say that.'

In less than a year the Smiths have forged a resilient beauty. Their candour, their confidence, has blossomed into the most melodic of spiritual sounds. There is a rawness in their music that belies their musical age; a fresh, ethereal ability that captures more than just the routine of 'making' good songs. In a great Smiths song there is an overview that simply towers above the congregating mortals in the popforum. And for that I'll say a little prayer.

'The good people laugh/Yes, we may be hidden by rags/But we have something that they'll never have' – 'Hand In Glove'

New Musical Express, 24 September, 1983

ALL MEN HAVE SECRETS . . .
BY NEIL McCORMICK

Morrissey of the Smiths has taken the place of both Duran Duran and the Thompson Twins, single-handedly wiping them out, at least on my one (increasingly used) cassette. When I told him whose conversations we were taping over he said, 'Good. I'll talk louder then.' Not a man to be taken lightly.

'Behind Joy and Laughter there may be a temperament, coarse, hard and callous. But behind Sorrow there is always Sorrow. Pain, unlike Pleasure, wears no mask. There are times when Sorrow seems to me to be the only truth. Other things may be illusions of the eye or the appetite, made to blind the one and cloy the other, but out of Sorrow have the worlds been built, at the birth of a child or a star, there is pain.' – Oscar Wilde, *De Profundis*

'Heaven knows I'm miserable now.' - Morrissey (the Smiths' new single)

Outside, while not quite twilight, the day is edging towards gloom. Morrissey sinks into an armchair in the dullest corner of his living room. Bare, cold light falls on one side of his face, somehow emphasising a jaw that seems oddly out of line. There is something awkward in his presence, he rarely looks you in the eye. There is none of the casual confidence that decorates the manner of most pop stars.

He is dressed as you would expect to find him, a sartorial disaster in a thinning, off-white aran sweater and faded jeans. His hair juts up in an awkward and uncomplimentary quiff. All that's missing is a bunch of ragged daffodils. 'Regardless of what you do or what you wear or what you say, if you fall into the public eye however you look appears as an image,' he says. 'If you have no image, if you become popular and people begin to mimic you, how you dress can seem to be something that's quite manufactured and contrived, which of course it never ever was. I think the image trap is just there and everybody goes into it. It strangles most people.'

Morrissey's flat is certainly not the pad pop star dreams are made of. It is mutely coloured, very tidy, elegant in an almost old world manner. His living room has a table with a typewriter and neatly stacked paper on it. There is a pleasant three-piece suite (sofa, two armchairs) arranged around an empty fireplace. A tightly packed row of books stands on the mantelpiece, including numerous volumes on Oscar Wilde ('I've read everything he wrote and everything written about him and I still find him totally awe-inspiring') and on James Dean ('It's not his acting, actually I think he was a bit of a ham. I get quite embarrassed when I see those films. But I'm fascinated by the way he seemed to represent his time and his generation'). Both are tragic figures, which Morrissey admits he finds appealing.

Above the mantelpiece there is a moody portrait of Mr. Dean. 'He had that strange quality that he could look good anywhere, in anything,' says Morrissey. There are also around the room three framed photographs of Morrissey, but he makes no such claims for himself. 'I'm ugly.'

The profile that launched a thousand caricatures: With that prominent chin and the alarmingly vertical quiff, it can only be the young Morrissey.

His voice is soft with an almost imperceptible light North of England flatness. He is a second generation Irishman, Manchester born and raised. 'I find Ireland fascinating. Maybe I shouldn't say this,' he laughs, considering the fact that he's going to be quoted in an Irish paper. 'Oh, I'll say it anyway, it's one of the most Catholic countries in the world but it's also one of the most repressed, and I think it's quite sad. But to me it's an immensely attractive place, obviously, with having Irish parents as everyone in the group has, we're all deeply imbedded there. I mean most of the people that I ever cared about in literature came from Ireland, for some totally unfathomable reason.'

He recently, with the success of the Smiths, moved out of Manchester and his 'little Ireland' community and came to live in London. 'I quite love it here,' he says, 'but I also liked it in Manchester. People in Manchester are really quite short-sighted and dim on the subject because they feel if you leave the place you defect and you're worthless and you've turned your back on the starving thousands in the back streets of Manchester, and so they spit on you. But really, when I was living there I can't remember anybody that helped me, anybody in the diminutive music industry there, anybody on the club circuit or whatever. Nobody helped me so I literally do not owe anything to anybody in Manchester, which is a very pleasant way to be.

'I still have endless enthusiasm and affection for the place, however, and I'm quite sure I'll return. But for me now London is really quite perfect. I mean, I regret to say it really is as exciting living here as some people who are always considered to be misguided say that it is. I think when you visit London and you only stay for a few days you get a completely obscure vision of the place and it seems impersonal and hateful and synthetic. But when you stay here for a long time, you realise the enormous advantages. It's really quite simple: there are just endless things to do here, and mobility is so easy. In Manchester the entire place closed at 8 pm and you were just totally paralysed, but here you can go wherever you want to, whenever you want to, and do whatever you want to.'

So what kind of things does he do?

'Nothing,' he says lightly, laughing with self-ridicule. 'I really don't do anything. But if I wanted to do something I could. I don't feel any restraint.'

There is a melancholy about Morrissey, it's not just a trick of the fading light. He laughs frequently but it's a quiet, almost embarrassed laugh, usually directed at himself and what he is saying. When he sings 'What Difference Does It Make?' on *Top of the Pops*, he fills the phrase with casual despair. His lot in life he feels is not a happy one. 'I used to think success and fame and fortune would make me happy, but now I realise it comes from too deep inside you to be changed by any of that . . . Not that I've made any money yet.'

That laugh again.

The Smiths came rapidly out of nowhere, the first group in some time to cross that pop/independent barrier. 'I wouldn't like to appeal to one sector and not the other,' says Morrissey. Not so long ago he was a solitary individual who read so much that he tried to give it up because, 'I wasn't actually living. I was just creased up in a chair twenty hours of every single day,' and who wrote constantly, but only for himself: 'I tried to be a journalist, but failed miserably. I used to write songs but with only neb-ulous tunes because I couldn't play an instrument.'

Then he met up with guitarist Johnny Marr and joined forces not only because Johnny could write music but also because 'he was very aggressive. I could see this was someone who was going to get things done quickly.'

The Smiths appeared with a basic, uncluttered guitar band sound like a breath of fresh understatement in the synthesised melodrama of the charts. 'I always felt that we only really needed basic utensils anyway. It wasn't really a severe calculation, it just so happens that as we got together it was just four individuals and this is what we played. It was never really a question of expansion or deduction, the balance seemed quite perfect. But I do think it was quite crucial to strip down most elements of the popular group: having very traditionalist instruments, being called the Smiths, hav-ing no pretensions whatsoever, being very forthright and deliberate. So it all really slots in quite neatly.'

They have caught the imagination of both the loyal independent audience, where their album tops the charts, and the fickle pop fans, where they have top ten hits with shining songs of sensitive unhappiness. There is a disturbed, sometimes disturbing beauty to the Smiths, a poetic depressiveness that makes them the true sons of Joy Division, coupled with a vigour and earthiness, a slightly comic plainness of language and a sincere spirit of delivery, that would ally them more with the Undertones. They've bridged a huge chasm.

'All men have secrets and this is mine
So let it be known
We have been through hell and high tide,
I can surely rely on you?'
'What Difference Does It Make?'

'One would get the impression listening to your songs that you haven't had a very happy love life,' I observed. 'I haven't had any love life,' said Morrissey with one of those uncertain laughs. 'Yeah, it's been quite ridiculous, and it's something I'm asked to cover quite a lot in interviews, and people who don't like me always get the impres-sion that I just constantly sit and moan for hours on end – but it's quite difficult when you're asked these questions and if you want to give honest replies, which I always want to do, then I have to say yes, I'm quite miserable. So why am I laughing?'

I read somewhere that you decided to be celibate, is that so, I asked, rather gin-gerly. Morrissey looked embarrassed. 'Mnn, yeah, I have,' he replied. 'That's been quite a long time. Initially it was involuntary, but eventually I realised that . . . ehm . . . it was quite interesting. I thought, "I'll hang on to this." It's entirely nonsensi-cal really.'

Why is it entirely nonsensical?

'I dunno, it's just really . . . It's just the way things are. I can't really analyse it. It's just *there* and it's happened. So why am I laughing again?'

Pop stardom usually puts an end to that, I suggest.

'It usually does,' agrees Morrissey, 'but I must be the exception to the rule.'

'Too many pop stars are not good figureheads. Young people need figureheads, I know I do, and popular music is the only thing left for them. They don't read books, they don't believe in movies. Popular music is all there is, and too many pop stars are shallow and worthless as figureheads, or else content to be obscure and mysterious. We would never be obscure, we could never be obscure, because I use very fundamental language in my lyrics. I use very simplistic words, but hopefully in quite a powerful way. And by that I mean saying things that people in daily life find so very hard to say, like, "I don't want a job," "I don't want to be loved," or, "I am ugly." I mean things that are really quite simple words but things that people can never really say. I mean if you say to your friends or to your parents, "I am very unhappy," it's like scraping open nerves . . . it's too close and it just can't be said. So I want to say these things instead of being very esoterical and other worldly and mysterious, because I think it's more effective and . . . I don't think it's ever been said in popular music. I really don't.'

So if you are a figurehead, what are you a figurehead for?

'It's quite curious but I seem to get masses of letters, people writing to me telling me their problems. They write telling me of trouble they're having at school, or in love or with their parents, or saying they identify with some song. It seems as though people who have quite difficult lives see me as some kind of a kindred spirit, or a person who has some of the answers which of course isn't true. But, ehm, it's much more interesting than just simply the usual fan letters where they just want to know what size shoes you take. So it's quite curious but I do get the impression people treat me quite seriously instead of just being a popular figure, a nonsensical pop star, which of course, I wouldn't want to be.'

Do you answer these letters?

'Religiously, every day. Of course you have to be careful, and sometimes it's important not to take them seriously. I get suicide letters which you never really know how to deal with. It would be laughable to suggest you could solve anyone's problems with a scribbled note on the back of a postcard.'

It seems you're being cast in the role of agony aunt to a new generation! As someone who seems to feel your lot in life is an unhappy one, what qualifies you to advise others?

'I can't think of anyone more qualified. (*laughs*) I've been through it and I understand it. I don't think a happy person could ever really understand it, they think you'll grow out of it. Unhappiness is too deeply ingrained just to be solved by getting a mere job or having a whirlwind romance. But I think what you can do is just simply learn to cope with it and learn to master it on a day to day basis.'

That doesn't seem a very appealing basis for survival.

'Well I think this is the basis that most people survive on. I don't think everyone's as happy as they would like to think.'

How do you feel about suicide?

'I have to be very careful what I say about this, but . . . having been quite close to it myself on a number of occasions, I can quite admire someone with the strength to do it. People who have never been close to it cannot hope to understand it, and the idea that it was illegal until recent years is of course laughable, but I think to me it's

This charming man: Alternately fey and aggressive, shy and histrionic, so-called 'miserabilist' Morrissey's early Smiths performances were a joyous experience.

quite honourable in a way, because it's a person taking *total* control over their lives and their bodies. By not thinking about suicide, or considering it, or examining it, it means that we ultimately just do not have control over our destinies and our bodies and our brains. And I think people without that sense of control are quite shallow, thin individuals. But I'm not saying that simply by having control over your body, the ultimate destination is suicide. But I admire it in a way.'

Are you afraid of death?

'No. To me it's totally necessary. I could not imagine life without death. I think that would really be quite ridiculous. The very idea of living forever . . . I mean, I always remember as a child being raised in a quite severe Catholic upbringing, where it was impressed on you that you would go to heaven and live forever and ever and ever, and I always remember the very idea of living forever petrified me because I couldn't imagine *life without end!* I think it's quite necessary and I think it keeps us all on our toes. And if there was no such thing as death we'd never do anything. We'd just lie down and eat cakes. (*laughs*)'

Do you have any spiritual or religious beliefs?

'I do, but not quite as dramatic as I should have by that absurd Catholic upbringing. I could never really make the connection between Christian and Catholic. I always imagined that Christ would look down upon the Catholic Church and totally disassociate himself from it. I went to severe schools, working class schools, where they would almost chop your fingers off for your own good, and if you missed church on Sunday and went to school on a Monday and they quizzed you on it, you'd be sent

31

to the gallows. It was like, "Brush your teeth NOW or you will DIE IN HELL and you will ROT and all these SNAKES will EAT you." And I remember all these religious figures, statues, which used to petrify every living child. All these snakes trodden underfoot and blood everywhere. I thought it was so morbid.

'I mean the very idea of just going to church anyway is really quite absurd. I always felt that it was really like the police, certainly in this country at any rate, just there to keep the working classes humble and in their place. Because of course nobody else but the working class pays any attention to it.

'I really feel quite sick when I see the Pope giving long, overblown, inflated lectures on nuclear weapons and *then* having tea with Margaret Thatcher. To me it's total hypocrisy. And when I hear the Pope completely condemning working class women for having abortions and condemning nobody else . . . to me the whole thing is entirely class ridden, it's just really to keep the working classes in *perpetual* fear and feeling *total* guilt.'

Do you think you are the product of that most Irish of complaints – Catholic repression?

'To a certain degree yes. But though I came from a monstrously large family who were quite absurdly Catholic, when I was six there were two very serious tragedies within the family which caused everybody to turn away from the Church, and quite rightly so, and from that period onwards there was just a total disregard for something that was really quite sacrosanct previous to the tragedies. So yes, I experienced the severe, boring fear, but then I also experienced the realities of life.'

Do you think your unhappiness stems from your background?

'Well, I think it obviously does because if I had a fabulously wealthy and fabulously adventurous background I can't imagine that I'd have most of the anxieties that I have today. But we were always quite poor and everything was impossible. I was unemployed for years and years and years and years, voluntarily so, because I never wanted to work anyway, and I don't think you can go through years of unemployment and dealing with the DHSS and all that depression and just simply step out of it one day and be somebody else. So I think yes, there's correct and quite severe reasons why I'm like this.'

You talked earlier about man exercising control over his own mind and destiny – does that not also mean controlling your state of mind?

'Ehm, no I don't think it does, because we don't raise ourselves and we don't orchestrate the conditions which we're raised in. They're just like circumstances that befall us, obviously, but I think . . . to a point you can, but to a point that is much more important you can't.'

You don't seem to be a happy person, so what makes you think you are, or would be, a good figurehead? What makes you think your opinion is of value?

'Because it is! It's an incredibly easy question and it's impossible to give the answer. I don't ring up journalists and plead with them to come round and speak to me, they want to speak to me. So it's not as if I'm going door to door. But for years and years I wrote in total anonymity and so many people thought I was entirely insane, and now that I have a *record* contract and I release *records* and I more or less say the same things that I've been saying for ten years anyway it seems to have kind of *legalised* my insanity. And it really gives you a license to be as open as you like, and it will be accepted.

'And I really do want to be an influence. I really do want people to listen and people to respond because I can't see anybody in popular music who's saying anything or who's attempting to say anything. I'm not saying I'm an irreplaceable Messiah on a hilltop or anything but . . . everybody seems entirely mute to me.'

Just an ugly streak of misery? Or a brother under the skin, sweeping away the cobwebs of advice agony aunts spin around young people? There is something in Morrissey's vulnerability, in the Smiths' contemporary sense of tragedy that an increasingly large audience like or relate to. It is a million miles from the illiterate unhappiness of country music, singer songwriter self-pity or post-punk bitterness. It is something delicate, proud, funny and alive, and it is making the Smiths the new order on the name dropping circuit (credibility-wise).

'I think people can recognise the integrity of the group,' says Morrissey. 'I'm quite determined that we'll never lose it. Not as long as I'm holding the reins.'

Does the integrity come from you? I ask.

'Quite largely,' he replies, glancing down to watch the tape recorder wind on. 'Because I am the spokesperson for the group and I am thrust forward and other group members very rarely give their comments, and when they do they're much less serious than mine anyway. They don't really share my lyrical viewpoint. Most of the time they quite like it, but they certainly don't share it. But I don't mind. I mean there's lots of things they do that I don't share.' He smiles mischievously. 'But we won't dwell on those seedy aspects of the Smiths. Of which there are many . . .

'I suppose my input is more serious. And much more crucially personal. I think that at the end of this experience, if or when the Smiths break up, I feel sure that the other three group members could walk on to something else, but I don't think I could because I fear this is absolutely *it* for me, and my neck is in the noose, almost. The other three *can* step back and they *can* claim disinvolvement. But I never could.

'I'll risk anything.'

His light, uncertain laugh drifts into silence.

Hot Press, 4 May, 1984

MORRISSEY
—•— BY ELISSA VAN POZNACK —•—

The Morrissey that greets me in the doorway of his genteel Kensington abode is without his familiar voluminous D. H. Evans outsize shirt and beady accoutrements. He is also more than 275 miles away from the ebulliently effusive creature I'd met last January in his group the Smiths' former Manchester HQ, but he was six months younger then, six months less famous. In a tight white jumper, he looks tremulously thin and the ultra-high pollen count is making him struggle for breath, in spite of which the front room he leads me into is crowded with flowers.

'Get rid of them? How can I,' he sighs, 'they're an extension of my body!' Ah yes, the flowers . . .

Seldom has a nation capitulated so swiftly and so adoringly. And to what? A quartet of couth Mancunian youths as classical as a string ensemble; elfin guitarist Johnny Marr, drummer Mike Joyce and bass player Andy Rourke, all nineteen or thereabouts. And Steven Morrissey, the 24-year-old wordsmith, possessor of the voice and flinger of flowers.

Suddenly, after years of teenage trauma and monastic introversion, alone in his room with the Compleat Works of Oscar Wilde and every Sixties kitchen sink drama ever filmed, not to mention a self-imposed celibacy, everybody wants to be Morrissey's friend. Last Christmas in Manchester, Morrissey couldn't open his door for carollers singing 'This Charming Man', the Smiths' second single on Rough Trade, the independent label to which they have plighted their troth. That single with its 'cover star' Jean Marais – Cocteau's youthful lover, gazing aesthetically into an Orphean pool – was the turning point. It also spotlighted the dreamy, often sexual, ambiguity of Morrissey's lyrics which drop in disconcerting metaphysical imponderables without so much as ruffling a hair on Morrissey's finely-tuned James Dean quiff.

A bunch of lotus-eating narcissi pounced upon in the heat of the moment or something greater? Methinks the latter. So does Morrissey, who is usually the first to say so. Yet, all this charmingness has taken its toll.

'He's far too accommodating,' says friend and confidante, writer Jim Shelley. 'The other day he gave 24 interviews, topping his previous record of sixteen and sometimes I think he just invites me around to answer his phone.'

'He's exhausted,' says manager Scott Peiring, recounting a typical gruelling week of business meetings, let alone appearances on Pop Quiz *and* Eight Days a Week. *Rolling Stone have been and gone;* Penthouse (Penthouse!) *are waiting in the wings; the new single, 'Heaven Knows I'm Miserable Now', has gone straight into the charts at nineteen and* Top of the Pops *must be countenanced once more. The platinum disc for 300,000 copies sold in the UK of the debut album, simply titled* The Smiths, *should be arriving any moment to join the gold one on Morrissey's mantelpiece.*

By the time you read this, the Smiths will have headlined a 10,000 capacity festival in Finland, where they've trekked despite a morbid fear of flying, followed by the GLC Jobs

For A Change rally in London on June 10, followed by the even newer single, 'William, It Was Really Nothing'. Give this man a holiday!
Instead, he gets another interview, possibly his last for a long while . . .

You once quoted Fran Lebowitz: 'Polite conversation is no conversation.' Are you prepared to talk dirty and tell the truth, the whole truth . . . ?
I am and promise to throw myself upon the mercy of the courts.

You seem a little subdued today, are you miserable now?
Mmmmmmm . . .

Your phone is constantly engaged or unobtainable.
Yes, it has been quite strange these last three weeks. Perhaps it's broken, let me listen now. (*picking up the phone*) No, it's alright but it definitely has its moods and that suits me fine because I've had to change the number. So many people phoned that I was on it 24 hours a day. (*The phone pings momentarily and Morrissey visibly stiffens.*)

Sorry, that was my bangle hitting the phone. Do you do all your interviews here, you seem a bit agoraphobic?
Yes-no. Initially I did but then there was such a flux of journalists coming in and out, I suddenly felt naked. Everyone would come in and bound all over the place. People were beginning to get too close and know too much which must sound paranoid and neurotic but . . . Richard Jobson, who lived here before me, told me that he never allowed anyone connected with the music industry in. I couldn't really understand then. Now I do. I don't do most interviews here. In fact I'm thinking of stopping them completely.

Last week you had 24 interviews lined up for just one day, including one with Penthouse!
Yes, though we haven't actually done it yet and I can't see *Penthouse* wanting a straight interview. They're probably quite brutal and get straight down to the 'Were You A Horny Teenager?' thing.

Were you a horny teenager thing?
Oh definitely (*giggle*), can't you tell?

Would you pose naked if offered enough money?
Probably. I have nothing whatsoever to hide.

Who last saw you in your natural state?
Almost certainly the doctor who brought me into this cruel world.

When was that?
Some 24 or so years ago.

You looked a little uncomfortable wedged between Tony Blackburn and Wham's George Michael on telly the other day.
Yes. It was quite painful. *Eight Days a Week* was considerably easier than *Pop Quiz* for some unknown reason.

What did you have stuffed into your ear on Eight Days a Week*?*
I'm afraid it was the old prop, the old hearing aid implement to gain audience sympathy, if such a thing is possible. I did feel that ultimately the whole thing was pointless; three individuals talking about films and books they hadn't read or watched.

Didn't you do your homework?
I tried but most of it was so strenuously bad that I was unable to proceed beyond the first five minutes, then I was expected to give an absolute critical essay on the whole thing, which is so unfair. *Pop Quiz* was unbearable. I realised it was a terrible mistake the moment the cameras began to roll.

Why did you do it?
I had this groundless idea that modern faces in music should really break through these barriers and change things. I realised that *Pop Quiz* was ultimately impenetrable. You can't change it, everything is cemented, the jokes are rigid, the movements are so severely staged that nobody could make any difference. I just squirmed through the programme. I went back to my dressing room afterwards and virtually felt like breaking down, it had been so pointless. I felt I'd been gagged.

Isn't it a bit like the charts in general; where do the Smiths fit in?
I'm not sure we do. Ultimately we're misfits, though *Pop Quiz* have asked me back, which is rather perplexing.

Were you at all surprised at the Smiths being voted the best new group in the New Musical Express *readers poll?*
Not really, it all seemed quite natural, I would really have been surprised if we were still playing in Dingwalls.

With all these interviews and media attention, do you feel you've been overexposed?
It seems I've been extremely overexposed because of the nature of the interviews. They get very personal, even if you do just one big interview where it gets embarrassingly personal, you seem entirely overexposed. It's a dilemma, I don't know quite what to do.

Isn't it an object lesson: to be less personal in future?
I can't be interviewed and talk in light, wispy terms. In throwaway interviews where people ask me basic things, I feel an absolute sense of worthlessness. You can do a hundred interviews and explain absolutely nothing about yourself but I tend to get asked very serious questions and to give very serious replies. When I talk about my childhood, it always comes across as being severely humorous or so profoundly black that it's embarrassing drivel but it always has a strong effect on people. Some unwritten law

states that you're not supposed to admit to an unhappy childhood. You pretend you had a jolly good time. I never did. I'm not begging for sympathy, but I was struggling for the most basic friendships. I felt totally ugly. (*Morrissey is sniffing loudly.*)

Oh don't cry.
No, actually I'm dying of hayfever.

So, it's not a heavy coke habit?
Not yet, I'm working towards that.

Did you read Julie Burchill's piece in the **Sunday Times** *in which she argued that youngsters were a bunch of ungrateful whingers who had no right to expect life's mod cons on a silver platter?*
No and I don't agree. I always found young people to be uncommonly satisfied and placid. If I ever got angry and dissatisfied as a child it was because there was never any angst from anybody. Personally I was very unhappy but in general, the reason I felt strange was because no-one else was saying, 'I'm really miserable, I can't stand being nine years old, when are things going to change?'

You joked that Dorothy Parker, the acerbic wit, was your spiritual mother.
Oh, I wish she was.

How does your real mother feel when you talk about your unbearable childhood?
She takes it very seriously and reads my interviews religiously. I know it upsets her sometimes but it's not something she doesn't already know about. We have ploughed through it several times, many years ago. But I really can't help it, if somebody asks me a question, I answer it, I can't lie.

What do your parents do?
They've always had very straightforward jobs.

You never talk about your father.
My parents got divorced when I was seventeen though they were working towards it for many years. Realising that your parents aren't compatible, I think, gives you a pre-mature sense of wisdom that life isn't easy and it isn't simple to be happy. Happiness is something you're very lucky to find. So I grew up with a serious attitude, but my parents weren't the basis of my neuroses.

You spent a lot of time cloistered in your room, what was it like?
Quite strange really. I had a very small bedroom and I remember going through periods when I was eighteen and nineteen where I literally would not leave it for three to four weeks. I would be in there day after day, the sun would be blazingly hot and I'd have the curtains drawn. I'd be sitting there in near darkness alone with the typewriter and surrounded by masses of paper. The walls were totally bespattered with James

Dean, almost to the point of claustrophobia, and I remember little bits of paper pinned everywhere with profound comments.

Such as?
Oh, newspaper clippings like 'Fish Eats Man'. Probably the most important quote was from Goethe: 'Art and Life are different, that's why one is called Art and one is called Life.' But strangely, whenever I've returned to the house and the room I just couldn't make the remotest connection between how I felt, how I was and the room. It sounds dramatic, but at one point, I thought I could never possibly leave the room. It seems that everything I am was conceived in this room. Everything that makes me is in there. I used to have a horrible territorial complex. I would totally despise any creature that stepped across the threshold and when somebody did, or looked at my books, or took out a record, I would seethe with anger. I was obsessive: everything was chronologically ordered – a place for everything, everything in its place. Total neurosis. My sister only ever popped her head around the door. But now, it's totally foreign. It's strange how things that seem to mean so much, ultimately don't matter.

Did your mother ever manage you in the Smiths' early days?
No, but she was instrumental in engineering the way I feel about certain things. She instilled Oscar Wilde into me and when the Smiths began, she was very strong-willed and business-minded. Frankly, she always let me do what I wanted. If I didn't want to work she said fine. If I wanted to go somewhere she said here's the money, go. If I wanted a new typewriter, she'd provide it. She always supported me in an artistic sense, when many people around her said she was entirely insane for allowing me to stay in and write. It's this working class idea that one is born simply to work, so if you don't you must be of no value to the human race. Because I didn't work, it was a cardinal sin. But everything has worked out well – it's all proved to have some value and she feels as great a sense of achievement as I do. It's nice to have the last laugh.

Did you keep your poetic inclination quiet at school or were you laughed at?
No I didn't keep it quiet and yes, to a large degree I did get hooted at. But the one thing that saved me in spite of my uncommon perversions, liking Cilla Black and Oscar Wilde – being a working class person from Manchester it really doesn't help being obsessed by Oscar Wilde – was my ability at athletics. I was a model athlete and they are the treasured students who can get away with anything.

Did anyone fancy you at school?
Not demonstratively. There were whispers but since I was such an intellectual idiot, people were convinced that if they talked to me I'd quote Genesis and bolts of lightning would descend from the sky. So I never was kissed behind the bicycle shed.

When did you lose your virginity?
I wasn't aware that I had.

So, is virginity a state of mind?

Well (*chuckling*) let's just say that you helped me out of that one.

Did you enjoy being that obscure wretch Steven Morrissey, whose sole mission seemed to consist of sending letters about the New York Dolls to the* New Musical Express?
No, that was a horrible period and I hate the Dolls now. I was sixteen or seventeen and went through this mad period of trying to break into music journalism. I also wrote to everyone. I'd receive about 30 letters a day from no-one in particular. I'd enter competitions. I spent every solitary penny on postage stamps. I had this wonderful arrangement with the entire universe without actually meeting anybody, just through the wonderful postal service. The crisis of my teenage life was when postage stamps went up from 12p to 13p. I was outraged.

Are you dismayed that your James Dean book has been re-pressed by Babylon Books?
I hate it, it's a cash-in. The book's been reissued in a way that could only attract Smiths' fans. It has a new cover and a Smiths' picture of me which does sour the whole thing. I'd rather leave the book, if it can be called such a thing, in the past.

Is Steven Morrissey dead?
Yes. When the Smiths began it was very important that I wouldn't be that horrible, stupid, sloppy Steven. He would have to be locked in a box and put on top of the wardrobe. I needed to feel differently and rather than adopt some glamorous pop star name, I eradicated Steven which seemed to make perfect sense. Suddenly I was a totally different person. Now when I meet pre-Smith people who call me Steven, I sit there and wonder who they're talking about. I always despised the name Steven, though being spelt with a 'v' rather than a 'ph' made life slightly more tolerable. But it was very important that Steven be drowned nonetheless.

What's Steven's middle name?
(*barely audible*) Patrick. What use does one make of a middle name? Paddy?

What would you have preferred to have been named?
Oh something like Troy or Rock, those plastic machismo Fifties names. Rip Torn, imagine calling your son Rip.

***I see that you're the proud owner of Gaute and Odell's* Murderer's Who's Who.**
Mmmmm. Yes, but I'm never interested in those murders where the wife poisons the husband and the husband suffocates the wife. Very extreme cases of murder have to be a constant source of bewilderment; where the police burst into a flat and find seven bodies in the fridge. It's not amusing, though you titter, it's a magnificent study of human nature although I wouldn't want to be so close to the actual study that I'm squashed in the fridge. (*chortle*)

Have you had your palm read?
Yes. It said that in February 1985 I would be in severe trouble with the police.

Did you cry when Billy Fury died?
Persistently. Loudly.

Were you dismayed when Terence Stamp, another hero, kicked up a fuss about being the cover star of 'What Difference Does It Make?'
I was indescribably unhappy. I was even more shocked when Albert Finney refused to be the star of the next single sleeve because he's always been immensely dear to me and he refused, wouldn't have anything to do with it.

Why use Joe Dallesandro out of Andy Warhol's **Flesh** *for the album sleeve?*
Well, I feel a twinge of sadness about that. Up till then everything had an icy Britishness to it, then I succumbed to the whole Warhol thing – like those modernites who crave the Factory thing and everything from late Sixties New York which surely was a depressing waste of time.

Valerie Solanas thought so, she tried to assassinate Andy Warhol.
Yes, he made a misogynistic comment and she took umbrage, loaded her pistol and aimed it at Andy's delicate little brain.

Do you admire that in a woman?
I do because then she wrote a book about it, which was quite riveting. I mean how obstreperous can you get? Shooting Andy Warhol, then going straight home, getting out the typewriter: *Why I Shot Andy Warhol* by Agnes Gooch. It's captivating.

If I put you in a room with Robert Smith, Mark E. Smith and a loaded Smith and Wesson, who would bite the bullet first?
I'd line them up so that one bullet penetrated both simultaneously. (*chuckle*) Mark E. Smith despises me and has said hateful things about me, all untrue. Robert Smith is a whingebag. It's rather curious that he began wearing beads at the emergence of the Smiths and (*eyes narrowing*) has been photographed with flowers. I expect he's quite supportive of what we do, but I've never liked the Cure . . . not even 'The Caterpillar'.

Were the Buzzcocks, and Pete Shelley in particular, near and dear to you?
Mmmmm. Yes. They had an endearingly confused quality . . . really Northern, dim and appealingly camp.

Are the Smiths making nostalgia for an age yet to come?
I hope so. I wouldn't want the Smiths to be seen as some kind of deranged pantomime, or just a laugh like Chas 'n' Dave. It has to be a little bit more meaningful than that. I hope intellectually aware people put the right connotations on what we do.

Are you a Male Feminist?
Well, I wouldn't stand on a table and shout, 'I'm a Feminist' or put a red stamp across my forehead, but if one tends towards prevalent feminist views, by law you immediately become one. Likewise, if you have great sympathy with Gay Culture

you are immediately a transsexual. I did one interview where the gay issue was skirted over in three seconds and when the interview emerged in print, there I was emblazoned across the headlines as this great voice of the gay movement, as if I couldn't possibly talk about anything else. I find that extremely harmful and simply don't trust anyone anymore.

Does it bother you that writers always try and probe into your sexuality?
Yes. The interview I just did with *Rolling Stone* begins: 'Morrissey is a man who says he's gay,' which upset me because of course I didn't say anything of the kind. People make assumptions but there's no point complaining about it. I came into this business willingly and I know the pitfalls so I accept them. At the end of the day, sexual terms just segregate people, it's all monotonous and an insult to their individuality. I don't mind effeminacy, it's better than being a bottle-it-up type or a Tetley Bitter Man. Men who drop their defences don't necessarily march about the street crying and reciting Wordsworth.

How did your dream date with the Associates' Billy Mackenzie fare?
He walked off with one of my James Dean books, which is a persistent cause of anxiety to me. I was quite speechless, I watched him walk out the door. It wasn't my favourite book but these things are sacrosanct. Billy has got this sense of uncontrollable mischief though I think that's exactly how he wants to be seen.

Were you happy with the Sandie Shaw collaboration?
No, I was never happy with the press. I was never happy, because she never said anything good about me which was worrying.

Was it a case of a private infatuation going public and losing something in translation?
Yes. I always felt like a spotted schoolboy, dribbling and getting nowhere. Previous to the Sandie thing, all the press I was getting, and the Smiths, was immaculately serious and very good. The Sandie publicity reduced me to a quivering jelly.

Is pop music trivial?
How can it be? Songs rule people's lives. People are just waiting for a voice, someone to say something. There's so much depth in the Smiths' music that when people say to me, you sang that song and I cried, I'm not surprised. I understand completely, it's happened to me. I've purchased records that are Biblical; you think, 'This person understands me, nobody else does.' It's like having an immovable friend.

What is the most Biblical record in your collection?
Undoubtedly, Klaus Nomi's last single before he died. It's called 'Death' and it's incredibly moving. The lyrics go, 'Remember me, but forget my fate.'

What would you find in Room 101, the room in Orwell's 1984 *where Winston Smith is confronted by his worst fear?*
Could anything be more horrifying than garlic and onions? I have this pathetic pho-

bia about them, everything, especially the smell, frightens me to death.

If eternal youth were for sale, would you buy it?
No. I've always found people of an advanced age most alluring. The older I get the calmer I become.

So you don't see any parallel between yourself and Dorian Gray?
Not really. I've always been old before my time.

Will the Smiths, so opposed to making promo videos, make a feature film?
You mean, like *A Hard Day's Night*? Yes, it's appealing. *A Hard Day's Misery*. But I don't want to stray from the initial burning desire to make wonderful records. It's not enough to make one or two wonderful records. I want an endless stream of priceless singles for people to caress to their bosoms.

There is a mysteriously bathetic line in 'Miserable Lie' that goes, 'What do we get for our trouble and pain/Just a rented room in Whalley Range.' Does Whalley Range really exist?
I'm afraid so. It's the little suburb of Manchester bedsit land and everyone who lives there is an unrecognised poet or a failed artist. Anyone who wishes to pursue their destiny ends up there and never gets out.

But you escaped and now live in the heart of Kensington, even though you declared that you'd never move to London.
I know, it's the sorrow of my life. I had to move to cut down on my phone bills. If only Rough Trade had moved to Manchester. Still I lived in Whalley Range a miraculously short time and it was nice to be immersed in the low life, living the life of pained immaculate beauty, walking around the park inhaling the riches of the poor as it were, but the sense of being entrapped by the DHSS was worrying.

When did the Smiths stop signing on?
We stopped signing on about a year ago. The Smiths had been going a few months but we weren't earning any money. As soon as 'Hand In Glove' began to sell, it became too dangerous. And of course, the DHSS feel that if you've made one record you're just an enormous international massively rich person, even if your record's 38 in the independent chart and you owe your record company £30,000.

Were the Smiths hyped in America?
No. We just played one performance, at Danceteria, and the record jumped twenty places. Sire haven't promoted the group anyway. They released 'What Difference Does It Make?' instead of 'This Charming Man' totally against our wishes and of course it will fail. I thought 'This Charming Man' the most obviously instantaneous release imaginable.

Are you now a member of the middle class?

Oh no. Really we're all the same people, money doesn't change anything. And we haven't much anyway.

You mean, you haven't got £50,000 in your bank account, like Phil Oakey?
(*laughing*) To be honest, I don't have a bank account.

Where do you keep it, under the mattress?
No, truthfully, the Smiths have a group account. We're a cooperative and everything I earn goes into that.

Once you've said you're miserable what's left for you to write about?
Ooh. There's so much buried in the past to steal from, one's resources are limitless. I'm not saying everything I write has been written before but most of the way I feel comes from the cinema. I fed myself on films like *A Taste of Honey*, *The L-Shaped Room*.

Have you now got what you were hoping for all those years in your room?
Not completely, but Oscar Wilde had a few words to say, of which you should take careful note: 'When the Gods wish to punish us, they answer our prayers.'

The Face, July, 1984.

A SUITABLE CASE FOR TREATMENT
—·— BY BIBA KOPF —·—

The recording of the new Smiths LP has been one of the season's better kept secrets.

Your appointed Hitman would have liked it to stay that way a while longer, for it certainly would have made his task easier.

Having nursed an inexplicable grudge as swollen as his preconceptions about a group who've been within permanent earshot throughout 1984 he was quite prepared to jab at them blind, rough them over a bit, let them know they'd been here – you know the routine – as he was contracted to do.

Does that sound unfair? Come on! There must have been a point when you, too, yelled enough at the thought of another Smiths single, adding a further variation to Morrissey's growing catalogue of misfortune.

I mean, the year ended almost the way it began – with a second Smiths LP almost the same as the first and full of all the 45s that preceded it. Add to that the ever present sight of Morrissey's permanently pained expression in print accompanying more strained milkings of his hypersensitivity, and didn't you at least once wish he'd fall under his own misery-go-round?

No? Well, OK wise guy you have obviously been paying closer attention than your friendly neighbourhood Hitman, catching all the shades and nuances he's been missing; spotting things like Morrissey's statements buried deep in a *Melody Maker* about how disappointed he felt when the IRA, for once finding a suitable target for their wrath, missed Thatcher.

Now this is hardly the sort of thing you'd expect from Morrissey's perceived persona of either a beatific idiot – 'Oh it's true!' he will later tease – or the patron saint of poet sufferers everywhere. Well, maybe that's true, too, but without the connotations of preciousness the description might carry.

Morrissey, thin and frailbodied though he may be, is obviously made of firmer stuff – not to mention funnier.

'I'm not totally averse to violence,' he says. 'I think it's quite attractively necessary in some extremes. I would say that violence on behalf of CND is absolutely necessary, because all sorts of communication via peaceful methods are laughed at and treated with absolute violence by the government. Therefore I think it's now time to fight fire with fire and attack very strongly. I don't think that is terrorism, it's more a self-defence.

'Obviously CND care about the people and that's why they do what they do. That's patriotism. In some cases I think violence is profoundly necessary – when the consequences of no violence are frightening, then the consequences with violence.'

Their just finished third LP – second LP proper – is called, incidentally, *Meat Is Murder* after a song dealing with animal slaughter.

The Hitman's resolve was softened before he got to hear *Meat* . . . however.

Playing the compilation *Hatful Of Hollow*, it quickly becomes obvious that he's not dealing with a fey, fashionably unfashionable reed blowing in the wind as he lazily suspected.

Most immediately apparent is the humour at the very conception of the Smiths, in the splendid contrast of the deadpan, doleful but surprisingly malleable Morrissey voice and his guitarist co-writer Johnny Marr's extraordinary ability to compose songs almost entirely from middle eights. Better, once the similarity of the surface jangle of the two singles that did seem to repeat each other – 'Heaven Knows I'm Miserable Now' and 'William, It Was Really Nothing' – dissipates, the variation of tempo and attack within the songs is readily remarked.

The humour is carried through in Morrissey's words. He will construct a most poignant declaration of love from a comic book image – 'Heavy words are so lightly thrown/But still I'd leap in front of a flying bullet for you' – and later compound it with something far more commonplace, devoting to both the furrowed intent the sentiment of the song ('What Difference Does It Make?') deserves.

Unlike with Woody Allen, the humour in Morrissey's work is not an apologia for being serious. One reinforces the other, creating a mood at once perfectly in keeping and at odds with Marr's irrepressible tunes. What's more he has written some of the most unashamedly lovely and erotic songs recorded this year. But with 'William . . .' the ambiguity of some Smiths songs finally sunk in at the BBC, resulting in severely limited airplay and TV invitations.

This has not shaken their resolve any, as evidenced in their new LP *Meat* . . ., released on Rough Trade in February. The songs are so plump and richly textured that it's difficult to catch what most are about on the few listenings permitted. One interestingly plumbs Morrissey's schooldays – 'the teachers were so brutal I really did think I'd get a purple heart when I left,' remarks Morrissey – and others, like the title song's plea for vegetarianism, see Morrissey rewardingly looking to sources outside of himself for inspiration.

If an image of Morrissey left by recordings is of a freshly shorn back and sides schoolboy not sure whether to laugh or cry at his own awkward reflection, Morrissey in person is more assured. He turns up with Johnny Marr at the Hitman's usual haunt – Konditerei Kopf – and immediately calls his bluff.

'I understand you neither like nor dislike the Smiths,' he inquires, peering from beneath the rim of a large hat. Suddenly feeling naked the Hitman blushes and responds with a question of his own.

Rather than writing about yourself in the abstract, your new songs seem to isolate particular instances . . .
Morrissey: Yes, it is the first time that I've written in the third person, spectating on things, which is good for me. I needed to do that, for something I abhor in modern music is the 'I' syndrome – 'I' did this, 'I' went here, 'I' did that. Well, *I* hate that and try to avoid 'I' as much as possible, though in turn I still try to write from an individual standpoint.

I still like the idea of songs being virtual conversation pieces – 'tell me, why is your life like this?' dictating . . . ha ha, well not really. But I like the idea of being the sympathetic vicar.

Do you know Stringer Davis? He's in a lot of Miss Marple films. He's her good friend. Very sympathetically he'd listen to all her japes and problems. Well, like him.

Maintaining a conversational tone is difficult to pull off without sounding banal or stilted.
Morrissey: Well, that comes from using very basic language, very fundamental language. I try to dodge metaphors. I try to dodge being oblique or obscure. There's no point. Time's too precious.

People have to hear a record and instantaneously know what's happening, though obviously lots of records that have appealed to me in the past I've never understood, but responded to with a gut reaction – good heavens, that voice. In which case what the voice was saying was immaterial. It's just like the pangs of desire are in force, a spontaneous feeling, a sense of rejoicing, overflowing emotions.

Now I don't want to do it. I appreciate it in others, but I think there's enough people like that.

Very few people achieve a conversational tone in songs. Lou Reed springs to mind as one . . .
Morrissey: Trouble is there's a gap of a decade between each good song.

Yours maintain a fine balance, humour emerging from the proximity of banality and profundity within the space of lines.
Morrissey: This is down to using fundamental language mentioned earlier. For me – and this sounds kind of chic – but for me one of the greatest lyricists of all time is George Formby. His more obscure songs are so hilarious, the language was so flat and Lancastrian and always focused on domestic things. Not academically funny, not witty, just morosely humorous and that really appeals to me.

I hate academic writing as regards themes. I mean writing about love in an academic way that it never should be. I do think that without wanting to sound like George Formby that a lot of what I write is humorous in a deadpan way. But nobody's ever noticed or recognised the fact. Perhaps it's not working! It's certainly there, more so on this new record, but I thought 'This Charming Man' was incredibly humorous in a lyrical way. Whether people see it or not I don't know.

Maybe people were distracted by the constant use of words like 'miserable', 'suffer', and 'ill' in your titles, suggestions planted that this is serious stuff, it can't be funny.
Morrissey: That's probably true. Then, I think the way I write is very Northern. I'm not in the least infected by London or the South, not that it's possible to divide language by district – this word belongs to the West Country etc. – but I feel that mine is Northern . . .

What is it about the North that takes you back there?

Morrissey: The reasons why aren't very tangible. It's just a state of mind. It's not because I'm terribly insecure and have to be stood in a pit in Salford in order to feel some sense of security. I don't feel that. It's more a lack of desire to travel. How it can be explained I don't know. It's not that I want a security blanket though.

But drawing on those sixties realist films for Northern Imagery, associating yourselves with them through stills on your sleeves – they always seemed to represent ambitions denied, dreams limited. (Not to mention this bleak peak in British cinema had been superseded by televison.)
Morrissey: I think that's good in a way, because previous to the period films made in England about working class situations featured actors with brilliantly theatrical voices, the most fabulously eloquent English imaginable heard in this alley in the middle of Birmingham. Why those films we like were treasurable is because for the very first time people were allowed regional dialects, were allowed to be truthful and honest about their situation. And regardless of what colour the truth is, it's always gratifying to have it.

Johnny Marr: And since we've been running the pictures on the sleeves I sometimes wonder whether those films wouldn't have been ignored if it weren't for Morrissey's lyrics. I'm quite surprised at the interest they've stirred.

I mean, it's alright for people interested in film, but sixteen and seventeen-year-old record buyers would probably have never thought about Salford in '60-'64 if it hadn't been for what we're generally associated with. I sometimes wonder whether we're the last dying breath of that sixties grim working class thing! I often feel like we're that one solitary clog left in the middle of the Arndale Centre! [A modern Mancunian shopping mall, apparently.]

But why is it important to hold onto that? Surely the same circumstances do not exist?
Morrissey: I think it applies overall that we treat what we do seriously and in non-glamorous terms. Pop music had got to the state where it had become very scientific. Romance was still a province in the heart of London, still the most glamorous place, still leaving on a jet plane etc. Because we never really did that we never understood those things. It's not a matter of being down, depressing, miserable or morbid.

Granted, given the contrasting vigour of the music, but haven't the Smiths succeeded, where the narratives of those films often represented crippled ambitions?
Morrissey: But they're the roots of the group and you can't really get away from that, regardless of what happens in your adult life.

Johnny Marr: To be honest I don't think it's a matter of rising above it. To lose the thread of it would be quite dangerous. It's part of our lives. We can't lose it. I don't want to not be associated with it.

Combining your taste in films and the sixties as the source point of your music, your harking back to a golden age has never been adequately explained. Before I listened properly I suspected a Luddite tendency.

Johnny Marr: We've always had that thrown back at us: if it weren't for Roger McGuinn's Rickenbacker or the Sandie Shaw collaboration – well, again it was just lazy journalism.

The idea of taking that spirit of optimism and of possible change and trying to use it in '84 I don't see anything wrong with at all. But more important than that are the images we grew up with: smokey chimneys, backstreets, the impressions I get from Morrissey's lyrics. It isn't just nostalgia, it's a Northern spirit, a working man's spirit – and here I'm trying to not sound like Gary Kemp doing the working class bit. But we're more about the working class values in the sixties than Rickenbackers and Brian Jones haircuts . . .

Certainly we don't feel restrained musically in any way by the period. What I'm saying is we do not confuse roots with formula. The formula we're prepared to slash away at, musically try things we've never done before. But the roots are the reason why we're here. That's something I'll never get away from. I'm always aware of why we started and I think that's a good thing. Those reasons are still valid.

Morrissey: . . . I find people who're quite artistic and creative crawl from dreadful conditions, where people who're cushioned in life tend not to produce anything dramatically artistic. To me popular music is still the voice of the working class, collective rage in a way, though seldom angst ridden. But it does really seem like the one sole opportunity for someone from a working class background to step forward and have their say. It's really the last refuge for articulate but penniless humans.

One level of sophistication would deem that viewpoint somewhat passe, a clichéÈ passed down with the Smiths.

Morrissey: Maybe it has, but what has replaced it petrifies me. It is totally lacking in sensitivity, nothing to do with people in their ordinary everyday lives . . .

The Smiths are probably the oddest expression of that working class rage, yet it obviously makes sense. Where do the Smiths stand in relation to those self appointed vents of working class spleen? Redskins? Seething Wells?

Morrissey: Well, I don't want to be that extreme, though all the causes they stand behind I almost always agree with. I think audiences get bored with groups introducing strong hardcore politics into every song. You don't have to be madly blunt in a political sense. To me that lacks a certain degree of intellect. And although we haven't made any abrasively bold political statements in a lyrical sense, I think people can gauge where we stand.

Would your vanity tolerate total subordination to a particular line?

Morrissey: Yes, I think it would. But I'd get bored. I think things can be slyly slipped in through the backdoor.

The title track of your new LP **Meat Is Murder** *seems to be pretty direct.*

Morrissey: Hmm, yes, it is a direct statement. Of all the political topics to be scrutinised people are still disturbingly vague about the treatment of animals. People still seem to believe that meat is a particular substance not at all connected to animals playing in the field over there. People don't realise how gruesomely and frighteningly the animal gets to the plate . . .

Ah, I see you've been shopping at Boots. They have a record in the country for testing out products on animals, murdering all these animals every single day. These people have to be attacked because they won't recognise communication between the Animal Liberation Front and themselves. So . . . boycott Boots!

Do you ever get the urge to talk so directly about sexuality, champion gay rights in the same way you've done with **Meat Is Murder***?*
Morrissey: No, not really. That can be very dull. The age of consent doesn't interest me, nor that kind of self advertisement.

But as far as sexuality is concerned I do feel very strongly about it. Therefore I have a very non-sexual stance, seeing people as humanist. There's so much segregation in modern life the last thing we need is a massive chasm between the sexes, which gets wider as the year passes.

All the so called liberators spout excessive hatred. On the one side feminists scream men are the enemies, they're killing us, on the other extreme it's the Tetley bittermen machismo thing. I refuse to recognise the terms hetero-, bi- and homo-sexual. Everybody has exactly the same sexual needs. People are just -sexual, the prefix is immaterial.

The prefixes preclude too much. Would you say your humour partly arises out of the human comedy of coupling?
Morrissey: Yes. But it's not entirely ridiculous. People need their bonds.

One memorable couplet from your new record: 'A double bed, a stalwart lover for sure/These are the riches of the poor.'
Morrissey: That came from a sense I had that, trite as it may sound, when people get married and are getting their flat – not even their house, note – the most important thing was getting the double bed. It was like the prized exhibit; the cooker, the fire, everything else came later. In the lives of many working class people the only time they feel they're the centre of attention is on their wedding day. Getting married, regrettably is still the one big event in their lives. It's the one day when they're quite special . . .

Isn't that a mite condescending?
Morrissey: Yes it does sound condescending, but it's a fact I've observed.

I do know people who have no money, marry and live in very threadbare conditions and have threadbare requirements. I'm glad I'm no longer in that situation myself. It sounds very snotty but what can I say?

Being from a large family, wasn't one of your first urges to get a place of your own in order to get some space?

Morrissey: That's a very familiar pattern. I tried to do a lot of things but they didn't actually work until I had money, mainly because I didn't make any attempt whatsoever to thrive in very horrendous hovels. I couldn't really face the gasfire that didn't work, the eight blankets on the bed, or the frost on the windows. I wasn't quite that resilient.

Do you want to be rich?
Morrissey: Yes! I do but more importantly I don't want to be poor. I suppose anybody who's made a good record feels this, but I feel like we deserve it because we work hard. There's a lot of imbeciles in this business who are obviously richer than I am from making records that have no degree of human value. So, yes, I do want to be rich.

What's the point, having told Jim Shelley in Blitz *that you really didn't have much to live for?*
Morrissey: Well, then I just think of money – yes, there's one reason to go on! Ha ha. Of course I'm not serious. These are separate things.

What did you say that to Jim for? Effect?
Morrissey: Well, I was serious and what was remarkable to me was that everyone laughed! Which was quite a hammer blow!

The trouble is with me, people get the punchlines confused, they find the punchlines rooted in the depression! But I did really feel like that at the time. Then I didn't really seem to have any reason for being. For me life was never easy, but it wasn't even acceptable until the release of 'Heaven Knows I'm Miserable Now'. I liked that record and good times seemed to happen to me then. I'll look back on them as pleasant days.

But before then I'd never felt it. I was making records that though successful weren't really quite clicking with me. It was like I'd still had this hangover from the years of nothingness, of being on the dole, having to live in that horrible atmosphere of communicating with the DHSS, people saying why are you writing this absurd song. 'Heaven Knows I'm Miserable Now' seemed to me an enormous release...

Weren't you digging your own grave with all those interviews of that period, for which you seemed to step into the professional, long suffering sensitive Morrissey role?
Johnny Marr: Whose opinions were exactly the same every day. The impression I got was he didn't seem to be allowed to say he felt different today, as long as he had these rigid personal policies he'd adhere to exactly, be in the same frame of mind every morning. Knowing Morrissey, I knew it was unreal. It's unreal to expect that of any human being anyway.

Morrissey: It had got to the point where I was this totally separate character from the group. I was never asked about them or the music. I'd feel there was always this desire to create a caricature of me – a repressed priest, insane pseudo axeman, or whatever .

Vegetarian pop stars don't tend to be very militant types – Paul McCartney, Limahl, etc . . .
Yes, very effete figures, non-political figures who would never raise their voices which, of course, is pointless. Whenever vegetarianism has been covered in the popular press, it's been whispered, nothing ever very forceful. Nobody really concentrates on the reasons why people don't eat meat, instead this person eats blah blah blah . . .

Yes. Brown rice and here's how to cook a nut cutlet in your **Habitat** *kitchen . . .*
Yes, so the brown rice becomes the centrepiece of this person's stand – when, of course, it isn't.

Why do you think being vegetarian is almost considered effeminate? Ozzy Osbourne, Ted Nugent, so-called 'macho' people like that have to be real red-blooded meat-eaters.
Yes, I've never really thought about that. I can't think of any reason why vegetarians should be considered effeminate. Why? Because you care about animals? Is that effeminate? Is that a weak trait? It shouldn't be and I think it's a very sad reflection on the human race that it often is.

What about your heroes? I'm sure Oscar Wilde enjoyed a nice leg of mutton.
Or a big rump steak. Yes. He was a hideously fat person so I'm sure he did indulge quite often – in fact he did but he is forgiven.

And James Dean probably enjoyed a tasty hamburger.
I'm sure he did. But we all have our weaknesses.
So it's alright, is it?
No, it isn't. Certainly not.

How far can you take this? What do you want to achieve?
Well, I'm very nervous about it because I'm deadly serious. It isn't, you know, catchphrase of the month. It isn't this year's hysteria. I'm madly serious about it.

Did you have any pets when you were young?
Yes, I had a pet which I still have, in fact. I have a cat that is 23 years old, which makes him something like a thousand in cat years. He's actually older than the other members of the Smiths, which is remarkable.

What's his name?
His name – and I'm not responsible – is Tibby. It could be worse but I think that was a very popular cat name in the early Sixties. It's quite extraordinary because we have family photographs of me when I was a day old and I'm clutching this cat and there he is today still hobbling around the house.

What do you feed him on?

Regrettably, cat meat. Sad as it is, he eats meat but nothing can be done now because he won't eat anything else. Certainly if I bought a pet today, I'd feed it on non-meat products like Smarties and baked beans. It's a shame that Tibby is glued to meat, as it were, because – in effect – he's eating other cats.

But cats are natural carnivores. Wouldn't it be a bit selfish to impose your views on a cat and turn it into a vegetarian?
No, because cat food is an animal. It's a horse or it's a cat or it's a dog or whatever. So how can I be selfish by not allowing an animal to eat another animal? I'm simply looking after it. Animals can live without meat. We get violently upset when animals eat human beings, it's horrific, it's dreadful. So why shouldn't we feel horror when human beings eat animals?

I do.
You do what? Eat humans?

No, eat animals. Which human would you most like to eat?
Well, now. This is tricky because I spent the last eighteen months criticising people, putting them down, destroying them, and I've reached the point where I realise that there's not any point. Because you meet these people and you find that some of them are really quite affable. Some of them are quite nauseating.

Is Limahl affable?
No, he's certainly not in that category. But I've got a new policy. I'm not going to drag people down anymore. Everybody within this curious profession has to do their own thing, however obnoxious that may be. And nothing I can say is going to change that. Besides, I've too many enemies. It's quite distressing. It's a bit of a strain because one is welcome almost nowhere. I don't want to go to parties or go skiing with Spandau Ballet or anything but still it's become quite tiresome, this constant barrier of hate. Silence is the safest thing.

What do you eat?
I have a daily intake of yoghurt and bread.

Do you think that this might be responsible for your present state of ill-health? A good McDonald's quarter-pounder would put you back on your feet in no time.
I sincerely doubt it.

If you died tomorrow, went up to Heaven and met Colonel Sanders of Kentucky Fried Chicken fame, what would you say to him?
Words would just be useless. I think I'd resort to the old physical knee in the groin – 'This is on behalf of all those poor animals who died simply because of you.'

That was a trick question. You should have said Colonel Sanders wouldn't be in

Heaven.
Oh.

OK. That's the end.
Of what?

Of the interview.
Thank heavens for that. You didn't ask me about Band Aid.

What about Band Aid?
Band Aid is the undiscussable, I'm afraid.

You brought it up!
Yes, and *I* finished the sentence. Full stop.

Smash Hits, 31 January, 1985

THIS CHARMING MAN
BY SIMON GARFIELD

If there is any space at all for subversion in the pop charts, then that place is occupied by Manchester band the Smiths. If there has been any creative advancement at all in the music industry in the last year, then that progression has been forged by the Smiths. If there's been one debut album that can safely lay claim to being 'a complete signal post in the history of popular music', then it was *The Smiths* by the Smiths. And if there's been only one band since the Sex Pistols to upset the cosseted old Biz and genuinely excite young record buyers again, then it's the . . .

All Morrissey's views these, and what you'd have expected from the Smiths' lead singer and lyricist. What you wouldn't have expected – not two years ago anyway – is that 1985 would find so many people agreeing with him. Worse than that, they're actually worshipping him. Not hard to imagine happening to a Boy George or Simon Le Bon, but this man? A man who unashamedly calls himself a genius, who writes ceaselessly about that darkest well of despair and loneliness, who expresses a hatred for the royal family and the Band Aid project, who sings of the Moors Murders and animal slaughter, a man who admits to being a helpless James Dean and Oscar Wilde nut? Yes, we do, it seems want this stuff.

We want it enough to buy more than 100,000 copies of the Smiths' second official album *Meat Is Murder* and put it in at Number One in its first week of release. Enough to vote the Smiths best rock 'n' roll band in the world in the music press polls. Enough to set the champagne corks flying at their fiercely independent and often fiercely disorganised Rough Trade label, a company that's finally achieved the sort of success that many swore was impossible. Enough indeed to put Morrissey in audacious and searing form on a high landing in the feverishly refurbished Britannia Hotel in his cold hometown.

His media forays thus far have coupled a charming, winning eloquence with a seemingly endless list of controversial sentiments, and have consequently ensured that his interviews have sold probably more records than his lyrics. 'I'm not so shallow that I'd be happy hiding behind slogans,' he says, half uneasy at the way he's become not only the group's spokesman, but also that of yet another lost generation of British youth. It used to be Joe Strummer, Bob Geldof or Paul Weller. Morrissey isn't happy being compared to any of them . . .

'By rights the Smiths shouldn't be here,' he suggests. 'People want to throw a blanket over even the slightest mention of the Smiths, and the industry spends all its time denying that we're a phenomenon. I think it's because we have this grain of intellect, and when you as a band are trying to lay down the rules you're actually spoiling things for so many middle-aged mediocrities who control the whole sphere of popular music. Let me tell you, the music industry absolutely *detest* the Smiths.'

Industry darling or not, Morrissey has just reached that thin rung on the success ladder that he'd always dreamed he'd attain, but always hoped he'd never have to deal with. For a lot of people success comes easy: you hire a 24-hour gorilla, you buy that ranch, you stick a rolled fiver to your nose, and you put out one album a year in a vile cover. But Morrissey and his fans know that the Smiths could never move comfortably within the realms of affluence, and he hopes he's recently taken one step further away from it by moving from Kensington to a new house in Cheshire to maintain closer touch with the forces that shaped him.

For the man exudes one thing above all else – integrity. 'I will die for what I say,' he boasts, and it's totally convincing.

The Smiths have enjoyed a rise both phenomenal and strange. Formed by the (then) teenaged guitarist and co-songwriter Johnny Marr, the band first lined up as a guitar-based four-piece in September '82 and stirred interest almost immediately.

They stood out about ten miles. For one thing it was the time of the Human League and the synthesizer, and guitar bands were out (in the same way that four-groups were out when the Beatles auditioned at Decca). Further, it was a time of softnesss, of saving face, of dumb-dumb baby-baby lyrics that stood almost a generation apart from the brutal and realistic sentiments expressed by Morrissey. The Smiths had love songs too, but they were anguished and clever and believable. In fact they were often anguished to the point of absurdity, and frequently appeared ludicrously contrived.

John Peel and his producer John Walters enthused, several majors expressed interest, but the band characteristically signed to Rough Trade for a relatively small advance, and their first single appeared just under two years ago. 'Hand In Glove' was a great song, but it did bugger all. In not working it as hard as they might have done, Rough Trade had seemingly let the Smiths down. Morrissey was aware that both Aztec Camera and Scritti Politti had deserted Rough Trade for majors, and he began to understand why. 'But they had to do something with us – we were really their last vestige of hope. I'm convinced that if the Smiths hadn't occurred, then Rough Trade would have just disappeared.'

The realisation seemingly hit both parties at once. Rough Trade pushed harder, Morrissey talked his effeminate white beads off, and their fortunes took off together. The subsequent singles charted high, and the often extremely petty, but always intriguing, controversies surrounding the band doubled, trebled, quadrupled in number and stature.

Did Morrissey really have a flower fetish? Just why did he throw £50 of gladioli into the audience every night? Why did he insist on prancing around on *Top of the Pops* with a hearing aid and a bush down the back of his jeans? Was he really celibate? And was he really gay, as *Rolling Stone* hinted? Did really wear women's shirts from the Evans outsize shop? Was their first single truly to be recorded by Sandie Shaw? Where did the names Morrissey and Johnny Marr come from anyway? Was it just coincidence that they were respectively a murder victim and the hero of Cornell Woolrich's novel *Rendezvous in Black*? Was Morrissey honestly the desperately lonely teenager who never left his damp Whalley Range room, a room covered from floor to ceiling in James Dean pictures? Did long-time Morrissey hero Terence Stamp really object to being used on one of the band's single sleeves? And did WH Smith really ban the band's eponymous debut album because it contained a song called 'Suffer Little Children', about the Moors Murders, even though Morrissey claimed he got on swimmingly with the parents of the victims?

Some of it was garbage, but yes, most of it was true. The first album went gold (over 100,000 copies sold) and the mini-scandals sure must have played some part in its success. 'No more scandals!' said Morrissey when the worst of them were over. But the tabloids didn't believe him.

'They hound me,' he says, 'and it gets very sticky. What makes me more dangerous to them than anybody else is the fact that I lead somewhat of a religious lifestyle. I'm not a rock 'n' roll character. I despise drugs, I despise cigarettes, I'm celibate and I live a very serene lifestyle. But I'm also making very strong statements lyrically, and this is very worrying to authoritarian figures. They can't say that I'm in a druggy haze or soaking in alcohol and that I'll get out of it. They probably think I'm some sort of sex-craved monster. But that's okay – they can think what they like. I'm only interested in evidence, and they can't produce any evidence to spoil my character.'

Dangerous? This 25-year-old man in black blazer, lime-green cotton shirt, heavily creased beige pegs, brown shoes and a James Dean quiff – a sex-craved monster and corruptor of youth?

In truth, there is something very unsettling about being in his presence – he's almost too soft, too gentle, too nervous, and he's not a million miles from that pathetic archetypal Monty Python accountant. He bows when he shakes your hand, and that's something you don't expect from a rocker with a Number One album.

'The main reason I'm dangerous is because I'm not afraid to say how I feel. I'm not afraid to say that I think Band Aid was diabolical. Or to say that I think Bob Geldof is a nauseating character. Many people find that very unsettling, but I'll say it as loud as anyone wants me to.

'In the first instance the record itself was absolutely tuneless. One can have great concern for the people of Ethiopia, but it's another thing to inflict daily torture on the people of England. It was an awful record considering the mass of talent involved. And it wasn't done shyly – it was the most self-righteous platform ever in the history of popular music.'

But it's another of Morrissey's handlebar flyers – the hyperbole and cries of 'conspiracy!' are hard to resist if he knows that they'll at least double the impact of what he is actually bold enough to say. Which is either a whole pile, or not much at all, depending on the richness of your idealism and the length of your memory. Pick the albums and singles to pieces and you find songs that are stirring, occasionally funny, often moving, but, like the man who sings them, far from dangerous or alarming. Indeed they are more an incitement for lethargy than rebellion.

Sentiments are often obscure, abstract and even cowardly in what they don't say. Is a Morrissey line that runs 'Let me get my hands on your mammary glands' really any more risqué than a Tony Blackburn radio jingle that has him 'whipping out his twelve-incher'? Well no, it's a mixture of the innocent, the embarrassing and the comic. It's a nice rhyme too.

Or often it's just a case of the old Dylans – keep 'hot' songs vague and you're

The Smiths at Newcastle City Hall, 1984, as seen on The Tube*: For all his asceticism, Morrissey believed his old band could have been 'at least as big as Queen'.*

bound to get more people believing that you're gunning for them. But Morrissey's most threatening weapon is sub-textual – his dour, parochial obsession with Manchester. His languorous depictions of Rusholme, Whalley Range and the Manchester that in his rhyme always seems to have 'so-much-to-answer-fer', are frank impressions of Northern industrial squalor and decay that show slightly more of the world than the perfumed works of the Wham!s, Durans, Madonnas and Princes.

And as for Johnny Marr's music, well that's nothing earth-shatteringly original either . . . and perhaps that's part of its appeal. For someone in his very early twenties, Marr certainly displays an enormous and well-executed guitar range; ethereal, semi-classical acoustics, fine-picked chiming and spiky electrics, and taut, chopping block-chords often working quite apart from the vocals. But at its best it's good old countrified garage stuff delivered with a wink to the same old guitar greats. The new album track 'Rusholme Ruffians', say, sounds a great whack like the 1961 Elvis Presley recording of the Doc Pomus and Mort Shuman composition '(Marie's The Name Of) His Latest Flame'. But it sounds pretty terrific all the same.

Strange, then, that both Morrissey and Marr often seem like desperate men hugging an invaluable patent, hanging on to that magic ingredient that very occasionally makes rock music so special. 'It's just that you have to hold on to what you want to say very tight,' Morrissey explains, 'because there are so many people in this industry trying to trip you up and push you over and catch you out and unveil you.

'The industry is just rife with jealousy and hatred. Everybody in it is a failed bassist.

Everybody wants to be on stage – it doesn't matter what they do, they all want to be you. But the mere fact that you have that and nobody can take it away from you, is your ultimate weapon. It's just really awash with jealousy and sourness and bitterness.'

Revenge for not being asked to participate, maybe? Getting his own back, in true flamboyant and petty rockstar style, for what others have previously said about him? Morrissey says that several of the people involved have publicly admitted absolute hatred towards him. Including Geldof, of course. 'He said it on the radio the other day, and it was totally unprovoked. It was as if he was really quite anxious and desperate to put me down. The fact that Bob Geldof – this apostle, this religious figure who's saving all these people all over the globe – the fact that he can make those statements about me yet he seems quite protected, seems totally unfair. But I'm not bothered about those things . . .'

Just as the new album shows Morrissey not to be at all bothered by child beating, animal slaughter or the royal family. But the man is away now, in unstoppable flow. Pick a topic and watch Morrissey curl a dry tongue around it . . .

I ask Morrissey about one of the verses on the album that apparently runs: 'I'd like to drop my trousers to the Queen . . . /The poor and the needy are selfish and greedy on her terms.'

'Actually I despise royalty. I always have done. It's fairy story nonsense' – and all this in the decadence of the *Britannia* Hotel – the very idea of their existence in these days when people are dying daily because they don't have enough money to operate one's radiator in the house, to me is immoral. As far as I can see, money spent on royalty is money burnt. I've never met anyone who supports royalty, and believe me I've searched. Okay, so there's some deaf and elderly pensioner in Hartlepool who has pictures of Prince Edward pinned on the toilet seat, but I know streams of people who can't wait to get rid of them.

'It's a false devotion anyway. I think it's fascist and very, very cruel. To me there's something dramatically ugly about a person who can wear a dress for £6,000 when at the same time there are people who can't afford to eat. When she puts on that dress for £6,000 the statement she is making to the nation is: "I am the fantastically gifted royalty, and you are the snivelling peasants." The very idea that people would be interested in the facts about this dress is massively insulting to the human race.'

In short, Morrissey belongs to that old protest school with guts – the one where the singer names names. There are a few like him – Billy Bragg and the Redskins come to mind – but the Band Aid project, he feels, was certainly not one of them. 'The whole implication was to save these people in Ethiopia, but who were they asking to save them? Some thirteen-year-old girl in Wigan! People like Thatcher and the royals could solve the Ethiopian problem within ten seconds. But Band Aid shied away from saying that – for heaven's sake, it was almost directly aimed at unemployed people.'

And, as a result of naming names, Morrissey feels he's unearthed a deep prejudice against the Smiths, an industry plot against independence. He claims his records have been ignored 'by every single media channel in existence'. Actually, he's quite wrong; every single media channel in existence has grabbed eagerly at the band's music, if only as a way of getting to their audacious leader. In fact he's currently turning down interview requests by the bucketload.

Morrissey, by contrast, is currently awash with magnanimity, sweetness and forgiveness. An hour gone, and he's still in full glorious swing. He's hoping the near future will hold a book of his own journalism – he's already interviewed Pat Phoenix and has designs on pools scooper Viv 'Spend Spend Spend' Nicholson (the cover star of an early Smiths single). 'I've got lots of questions,' he says, 'and lots of people I want to probe, especially in the dark.'

Morrissey *knows* the Smiths will be here for a long time yet. 'We're not just fashionable – in fact I don't know what fashion is. It's quite simple: before we came there was no outlet for emotion – people couldn't tear their coat and jump on somebody's head.'

And if the Smiths do bust up tomorrow, modest old Morrissey already reckons he's done enough for the history books. 'I don't mind how I'm remembered so long as they're precious recollections. I don't want to be remembered for being a silly, prancing, nonsensical village idiot. But I really do want to be remembered. I want some grain of immortality. I think it's been deserved. It's been earned.'

Really? In two years?

'Oh yes! Oh yes! In two days! In two days!'

Time Out, 7-13 March 1985

BIGMOUTH STRIKES AGAIN
—·•·— BY MAX BELL —·•·—

Once upon a time, during the early days of glam rock, a teenager called Steven went to the Manchester Apollo to see Roxy Music. Loitering round the backstage door beforehand, Steven was rewarded with a vision that shaped his entire life. What he saw wasn't Roxy Music in their decadent glory but Roxy's tour bus, and hanging from its door – Brian Eno's psychedelic ostrich feather cape. Morrissey, for the lad was he, recalls the incident with a tremor.

Thirteen years later Morrissey, now turned 27, comes across Roxy singer Bryan Ferry in a studio, only this time the parties are more equal. 'I didn't bother asking him for his autograph. I'd had it since I was fourteen.' To finish the tale, Ferry asked Johnny Marr to play guitar on his new LP only weeks after Rolling Stone Keith Richard had called up the mop-haired wonder boy; proof that if you're a good boy and eat all your spinach one day you can emulate your heroes.

S. P. Morrissey is something of an intellectual squirrel. While he doesn't keep a diary he remembers everything from his past and stores it away, not just the musical artefacts of youth like his front row David Bowie ticket ('seven shillings and six pence!') and his records, but aspects of his own upbringing which most of us would conveniently file away under Out Of Date.

There are several versions of Morrissey's story. The one about 'never being a teenager. I was the one with the furrowed brow and the rolled up *New Statesman*. I've caught up now with my teenage years and it is a great social embarrassment I can tell you,' is familiar.

But of course there is more to Morrissey than the boy who hung around parks and cemeteries reading poetry. There's also the pop fan. In the golden age of the glam *Top of the Pops* Morrissey got girlfriends to make him David Bowie costumes.

1986 is just beginning for the Smiths. Bigmouth is back and on form with a new LP, *The Queen Is Dead*, indicating that Morrissey is not overkeen on the Royals.

'They are so staid and uninteresting. Has Diana ever uttered a sentence of any vague interest or use to the world?

'The establishment – the Monarchy and the government – don't care as far as I can see. Many of them are of advanced years but they do nothing for old people. People in Britain are dying from poverty and cold because they can't afford heating. Others will never ever work again. But if you say these things people stare at you as if you're mad. If Live Aid had been about English poverty it would never have got off the ground, never received a minute's airplay. Because it was far away and somehow glamorous you could get lost in the charitable hypnosis.'

The Smiths in 1985 had troubles of their own. Bassist Andy Rourke had 'personal problems. He was ill and it seriously invaded the Smiths, it infested our place. He rejoined because his leaving seemed more wrong than his staying. It was too easy to turn like a pack and say, "You're useless! Get Out!" Now Craig Gannon has also joined we sound more formidable as you'll hear on the next single "Panic", so perhaps

Andy's brief departure was a benefit.'

Rourke's troubles weren't helped by legal battles between the band and their company Rough Trade which prevented *The Queen Is Dead* from being released in February. Last year's album *Meat Is Murder* also ruffled too many prickly consciences and the Smiths felt the backlash on a trio of singles, 'Shakespeare's Sister', 'That Joke Isn't Funny Anymore' and 'The Boy With The Thorn In His Side'.

In *The Queen Is Dead* Morrissey still protests loudly but he is more relaxed.

On the inner sleeve of the album the band are standing outside the Salford Lads Club in the real Coronation Street and Morrissey is smiling!

'We took our lives in our hands getting that photo. While we were setting up a gang of ten-year-old girls came and terrorised us. Everyone in the street had a club-foot and a vicious dog!'

Morrissey chose that location because he associates it with another hero, the actor Albert Finney, star of the magnificent Sixties film *Saturday Night and Sunday Morning.*

'Finney was the Northern boy made good which is why I can relate to him even more.

'I find that mood of a Northern person going to London and then returning home very poignant. You can't describe how you feel when you go from South to North, stopping at the service stations. It hits a deafening note. The beauty of Finney was his natural quality as an actor. Even when I'm asleep I can't look natural.'

While Morrissey says he hates nostalgia he admits that not much excites him about the 1980s. The closer he feels the 21st Century breathing down his neck, the more he panics.

Morrissey is so far removed from the jet setting image of the happy-go-lucky pop millionaire that people assume he is an old misery guts. When you meet him this isn't true at all. He is extremely funny and delivers many statements knowing they should be taken with a hefty pinch of salt.

'My self view is that I'm more cynical than romantic and I do appreciate the value of sarcasm. I'm not a jolly character, a life and soul of the party type and I suppose I asked for the misery tag. I just didn't expect such a generous response! However I dispute that I'm the Ambassador of Misery.

'I'm still embedded in a fascination for suicide and intensified depression. I feel a great deal inside me that must be tapped. I have to sing about what is ensnared in me.'

Suicide, depression, death! All good grist to Morrissey's mill. His current favoured form of relaxation is visiting London cemeteries with old Manchester pal Howard Devoto (ex-Buzzcock).

'It's a most gripping pastime I can assure you. Gravestones have a very dreamlike quality. It's a private pleasure that Howard and I share because we're such boring people.'

Conversation turns from the morbid to the macabre. He goes on to talk about the Moors Murders case, the Chalk Pit Murders, mass murder in the past 100 years and is an expert on the cannibal Albert Fish ('You passed on just one Mr. Morrissey') but then he starts spluttering. 'I can't imagine this boosting record sales! I must stress I have no personal interest in murder, I'm not nurturing any plans but I may give it some thought in the future. It's a good job for you I don't have a back garden. Any minute now I shall press a button and your armchair will disappear through the floor.'

No. 1, 28 June 1986

THE BOY IN THE BUBBLE
—— BY STUART BAILIE ——

It takes all number of hitches, provisos and cancellations, but eventually our first interview with Morrissey in a year and a half is finalised. Indeed, sometimes along the way it seemed that negotiating for global disarmament would have made an easier, more thankful task. And then by way of a final dramatic flourish, we encountered a photo session that was unusual even by *Morrissey* standards.

The transparencies which arrived (most of which were later vetoed by the singer) showed him pancaked and pouting, with a 'tattoo' pencilled on his forearm. The plan, apparently, had been to look like Elvis Presley, but he came out of it looking more like Coco the Clown. Just what was he getting up to? This, combined with his legendary isolation, and speculations about his emotional balance, begged the question once again. Was he developing into some sort of homegrown Michael Jackson, our very own boy in the bubble? In short, had Mozzer finally gone wacko?

Thankfully, the young man I come across the following week seems fully possessed of all his faculties. Maybe he's just a little bit cautious, but given his turbulent relationship with the press, that's quite understandable. I pump his hand, present him with some bottles of stout (a colleague's peace offering) and ask him about these curious outtakes from the photo session.

'I was really pleased with the session at the time,' he explains ruefully, 'but when I saw the slides, I just looked like . . . a ponce, really. I had too much make-up on, I just looked like the pop star in the studio. So I thought no, not really.'

The photos made you look like you had put on some weight, didn't they?

'I mean, time does pass; I'm not a teenager any more, which may surprise you. I'm not really a teenager, I have grown quite old recently, especially with all the worry,' (he laughs) 'and the financial hardship.'

So do you always insist on approving photographs of yourself?

'Yes, but not because I want photographs which make me look unnaturally young or anything like that, but just because there are certain profiles that have to be banished from the public eye, as you can imagine. And so they are.

'You'd do the same thing if you had photographs taken that were supernaturally ugly. You wouldn't say, "That one would make a nice front cover"; you'd say, "Hide that one, and find a nice one."

'It's not vain to want to look acceptable, not really. Vanity doesn't enter into it. But even if it did, it's not too bad to want to look reasonable, is it?'

The idea was for you to look like the Elvis photo on the cover of 'Shoplifters', wasn't it?

'Not really, I mean that would be too much to strive for.'

But didn't you choose that picture of Elvis because it looks slightly like you?

'I wish that were even *vaguely* true. No, it doesn't, not to the clear-sighted.'

Say it with flowers: Morrissey's thrashing gladioli were one of his least 'rock'n'roll' accoutrements, but were adopted like a fetish by devoted Smiths fanatics.

There is some resemblance, you must admit that.

'Well, I'm deeply, deeply, deeply flattered.'

I didn't actually say which bits were the same, though!

'Yes . . . I thought you'd have to go and spoil it. It was the bow tie, wasn't it?'

'Shoplifters Of The World Unite' is the thirteenth Smiths single in four years, and whatever your views on the band (people will differ wildly here) they are unquestionably the most consistent English singles band to emerge this decade. The last four singles, for example, have all differed in style, pace and lyrical attack, and it is no longer enough for their opponents to write them off as being simply 'miserable'. Having said that, 'Shoplifters' is less immediate than 'Ask' or 'Panic', and the diehards have been either wailing 'Another "Shakespeare's Sister"!' or holding out in the hope that it will be a grower in the 'How Soon Is Now?' mould.

Lyrically, 'Shoplifters' is an obscure affair, and the author is typically unhappy about expanding on the song's meaning.

'Well, I never really like to say, I never really like to pin it down. Do you understand that? I mean, there's someone in Huddersfield who might have a fascinating, fiery explanation, and then I go and shatter it by saying it's about greyhound racing. Their *life* collapses.'

That's putting it a bit strongly, isn't it?

'Well, you never know, it happens. I mean, I could talk about nuclear weapons, but it gets quite tiresome, doesn't it? Everyone gets quite bored with it. I often wonder why shoplifting can be such a serious crime when making nuclear weapons isn't. That should really be a crime, I think, but it isn't. We live in a very twisted world, with a very twisted morality.'

Yet in the midst of all this unpleasantness, Morrissey confesses that the continued support for the Smiths 'lightens one's step'. He gratefully acknowledges the *Record Mirror* poll results which gave the Smiths the best band award, the best album (*The Queen Is Dead*), the best single ('Panic'). And as for the man himself taking the runner-up slot in the 'Best Buttocks' category? 'It was perfectly justified,' he immodestly remarks. But going back to 'Panic' for a moment, didn't some say it was slightly similar to T.Rex's 'Metal Guru'?

'Well, it *was* whispered somewhere in the corridors of the British Isles, I can't remember where, but . . . I don't know, everything has its reference points, I suppose. Like the clothes we wear have their reference points . . .

'I thought the song was extremely funny, I really did. And I thought it was extremely funny to hear it on national daytime radio on the few occasions it was actually played in the mish-mash of monstrous morbidity . . . I think it was quite amusing – a tiny revolution in its own sweet way.

'After that it was quite crucial to release a single that was a slight antidote to "Panic", because if the next single had been a slight protest, regardless of the merits of the actual song, people would say, "Here we go again." That's why we put out "Ask". The idea there is . . . Well, restraint is a decent thing really, but it's nice to throw caution to the wind as well – to jump in at the deep end.'

Morrissey's conviction that 'restraint is a decent thing' has of course been well documented in the past, as has the notion that his records can 'ease the paranoia of being celibate'. But another area in which the Smiths have been highly influential has been in creating a better climate for the newer breeds of indie bands.

Many of the shambling-type bands, for instance, owe a debt to the Smiths in providing an audience for softer, more articulate music. It is now much easier to sing about 'affairs of the heart', and the pressure to fall back on rock and roll stereotypes is no longer so pressing. Witness the success, for example, of Talulah Gosh, who share with Morrissey a love of Sixties all-girl groups and an affinity with singers like Twinkle.

Does Morrissey himself feel that it's easier now for bands to be musically, er . . . 'wet'?

'I don't know about *wet*: a lot of people drag that word out, and I don't actually approve of that term. Because it might be "wet" as far as cavemen logic goes, in very traditional, brusque terms. I quite enjoy the history of British music, and I think that was a very scarce feeling within recent years. People would not see Twinkle or suchlike as an intelligent reference point.

'People didn't understand what Sandie Shaw meant, or even Billy Fury perhaps. I think there was a great wealth of creativity in those seemingly simplistic English small town approaches. I mean, I never cared for James Brown and Chuck Berry.

'As far as the term "wet" is concerned, I don't know many top ten groups who would call their LP *The Queen Is Dead* – there'd be too much to lose. The Smiths certainly take risks; I don't think we've ever made life easy for ourselves.

'So I don't really believe that the groups who appreciate the Smiths are fey individuals. I think they must have some degree of strength.'

Have you been impressed by any of the Matt Johnson records?

'I have accidentally heard some of it. It hasn't stirred me in any great way – in the same way that the Christians or the Primitives have.

'The difference, I suppose, and the thing that makes the Smiths so unique, is the fact that in certain territories we have reached a stadium level. And on reaching that level, the temptation to be respectable and just sail along is very great, and I don't think the Smiths have acknowledged that in any way. I don't know how Matt Johnson would write if he was playing in front of an audience of 15,000 people.'

And what about the Housemartins?

'I'm not really sure. I can't really work it out, to be quite honest. I do appreciate their presence, and the fact that they have views, I think, is quite revolutionary. And I know they're receiving blockages from certain directions because of their viewpoints, which I think is really admirable.

'I'd rather have them in that position than anybody else. They seem to take over from where Madness left off, which is good because it can be enlightening for the younger section of the record buyers. Their record has gone platinum, I believe.'

This is the side of Morrissey that some people find unbearable; the pompous, opinionated persona that he has adopted to counter his shyness and insecurity. But he wears this arrogance badly, and his intolerance for non-Smiths disciples is especially annoying when you consider how many of his songs appeal for open-mindedness. In the course of our short conversation, he decides that I must be 'a Saint and Greavesie man', accuses me of liking 'Oi' music, and pooh-poohs my going for a chocolate biscuit instead of his fruit shortcake selection. Some of us, after all, just aren't cut out for fruit shortcakes.

On the other hand, he perks up at the mention of St Valentine's Day, and the prospect of 'tons and tons of cards with fluff on them, and big yellow hamsters'. On the subject of the Moors Murderers, and the recent turn of events, he is genuinely concerned about the parents of the dead children, and is upset that the public attitude to Myra Hindley has become 'dangerously civil'. He enthuses about the TV show *Golden Girls*, and raves about a book called *Jealousy* by Nancy Friday.

'Do you know Nancy Friday? Her most famous book is *My Mother, Myself*, which you've surely stumbled across; it's been everywhere for years. You've not read it? I'm stunned!

'So this book is about jealousy, and it's remarkable, I'm just underlining everything. What's it about? I don't know how to describe it, let's just say that I'm learning so much from it.' (*NB: Nancy Friday is a feminist writer;* My Mother, Myself *is about mothers and daughters.*)

Would you say that you were a jealous person?

'Oh, desperately. But I tend to find jealousy where it doesn't exist, within circles of people, which is a great barrier. But I think everyone has their particular traits, and I don't think jealousy is particularly negative. But I only learned that through reading Nancy Friday.'

The holier-than-thou aspect of Morrissey's public profile has naturally enough tempted numerous journalists to try and bring him down, though none have met with any great success. Some have unsuccessfully tried to brand him as a racist, picking up on his 'burn down the disco' sentiments on black music.

The other line has been to probe for a story on the man's sexuality, taking their cue from the camp artwork on Smiths record sleeves and from lyrics like 'I'm the eighteenth descendent of some old queen or another.' Perhaps the most 'creative' of these investigations involved putting Morrissey together with his friend Pete Burns and 'documenting' the outcome.

'Well, I never talk about this really.'

Were you pissed off about it?

'Yes, completely, and I don't have anything vaguely humorous to say about it. It had no reflection of what actually occurred and it made me out to be a bit poncified . . . Pete was less annoyed, even though I said to him, "You never said that, you never called me Joan Collins." His attitude was, well, forget it, but that's not really my attitude. I think it was absolutely and pathetically stupid.'

You were portrayed as two queens camping it up, weren't you?

'Well, of course, that's what certainly came through. But it was a really sombre day – we were just sitting around on the settee being quizzed. I find that most journalists, when they create an overblown, camp atmosphere in interviews, they tend to have some alternative interests. And more than that, I shall not say.

'Like there's this journalist in America, I've been interviewed twice by him, and he's a leading voice in the gay movement in America. And on the two occasions when I've had rather damp conversations with him, he's transcribed these as "the dawn of gay

lib" and "the Smiths are the gay voice of the world". Which to me is absolute crap –
I really resent that kind of thing being written.'

And the speculations about Andy Rourke's involvement in drugs?

'I can't really deny anything. I don't really know that it's my place to speak on
Andy's behalf, because it is quite personal. And that's that, really.'

Are there any further thoughts about the band signing to EMI?

'Let's just say that it's a necessary progression. It's a very touchy issue and I'd rather
just get on with it rather than discuss it.'

And so the Smiths will surely continue to 'get on with it' in their prolific and highly
individual way, mapping out the last frontiers of rock music with intelligence and
taste. The Morrissey/Marr team is without rival in this department, based on what
the singer sees as a well-defined structure. 'I often feel that whereas I can lay eggs,
Johnny can make omelettes.'

The end of this month sees the release of a compilation album, *The World Won't
Listen*, a companion to *Hatful Of Hollow* with its assortment of singles and B-sides,
plus the tandoori-flavoured 'You Just Haven't Earned It Yet Baby', which was once
planned as a follow-up to 'Panic'. Unlike *The Queen Is Dead* however, this album
doesn't have the unity of feeling and the mixture of the comic and serious that made
the last LP such a great success. Side two of this new release, in particular, makes for
some very depressing listening.

Setting that aside though, what *are* we to make of this character Morrissey? Is he some
kind of contemporary poet, a visionary outcast who is pointing the way towards a
more civilised consciousness? Or shall we believe the cynics who reckon he's an ego-
tistical twit with a whole lorry load of hang-ups? An hour and a half in the man's company confirms that he's anything but an ordinary Joe, but successfully reinforces all
the other confusions. Let's just say that the jury's still out on this one.

Record Mirror, 14 February, 1987

MR SMITH: ALL MOUTH AND TROUSERS?
—————— BY DYLAN JONES ——————

Oh, how they love to hate Steven Patrick Morrissey. Ever since the Smiths hit paydirt in 1983, the critics have taken Morrissey to task for being a miserable 'celibatarian aesthete', wallowing in his own shambolic melancholy. But much as the critics despised this supposedly morose creature, Morrissey became a popular spokesman for those disillusioned with the rampant permissiveness of modern pop.

The Smiths themselves have made some of the finest rock music of the Eighties, sixteen singles and six LPs worth of Manchester tenement operas – everything from maudlin ballads and relentless modern thrash to psychedelic music-hall and sparse, simple pop. Their new LP *Strangeways, Here We Come* is released this month.

Of course the Smiths' success has always relied on the abrasive collaboration between Morrissey and Johnny Marr. In the last five years they've been elevated to the ranks of the great double-acts: Jagger and Richard, Laurel and Hardy, Grand Marnier and Lucozade, Morrissey and Marr – Morrissey playing the librarian, Marr the rock 'n' roll groupie.

That partnership was recently severed. Johnny Marr officially left the group at the end of July, due to the legendary 'musical differences'. Both Morrissey and Marr say the split was amicable, but this seems unlikely: Marr apparently formed his own band in October 1986, and they were all set to play a showcase gig at the Marquee until Morrissey talked him into returning. Sources close to the group say Marr's already recorded his debut LP, well on his way to becoming the next Eddie Van Halen.

There are some strange stories about Morrissey and his bedroom B-movie of a life: apparently he shares the same part-time bodyguard (called Jim) as the Irish Prime Minister; some say that he isn't as celibate as he makes out, and that he has a rather well-known 'friend'; others say that Morrissey has a mother fixation. This might be the case but he certainly hasn't much time for his father: When the Smiths became more than local heroes in 1984 Morrissey's dad (a drunken ne'er-do-well according to friends of the family) would invade the stage at their concerts along with the overzealous fans; Morrissey had to ask him to stay at home.

Other stories will probably soon come to light seeing as at least five people closely associated with the band are now trying to sell their stories.

Whether or not the Smiths will be able to withstand the loss of Marr is doubtful; but regardless, Morrissey remains one of the country's best lyricists. He may have the unfortunate manner of a dotty old aunt, and he may be full of camp conceits, but Morrissey has the wit and wisdom of a true British vaudevillian. Like Pete Shelley in his Buzzcock days, Mozzer has the sense to inject a large dose of irony into much of what he writes. Oddly enough, he refuses to acknowledge Prince, yet he would kill to be able to write something as remarkable as 'If I Was Your Girlfriend'.

'There's more to life than books, but not much more': Rock 'n' roll is an illiterate's medium, but Morrissey has been a devotee of authors ranging from Wilde to Plath.

His equals? Well, the only other media personality who professes to practice and enjoy the same sexual habits as Morrissey (total abstinence) is Kenneth Williams.

In general, do you think that British music is better than any other kind?
Yes, it certainly has been. I'm not really quite sure about now, but the history of British music is better than anyone else's history. In the Seventies America hardly existed in musical terms – it was a total anathema. In the Sixties it was passable, but that was mainly due to Elvis Presley. There *must* be a reason why it's still important for international recording artists to be successful in Britain; and it's taste really – they know that British people have more taste . . .

What records have you bought in the last year?
Not many, but there have been some – the Primitives, the Christians, A-ha [this is pronounced Ah-haaaaaaaaaaaaaa] . . . mainly mainstream pop. Nothing on import or anything like that. I'm never impressed by modern lyricists, I know that sounds unbelievable, but it's true.

You don't listen to people on Rough Trade?
Good heavens no! Nothing has touched me at all.

What do you think of Prince? He's a lot sexier than you . . .
He's clinical and impersonal . . . but sexy? I don't know, I don't think so . . . On a lyrical level I don't find him desperately interesting. His beat isn't very good either. But I don't dislike him, I find him quite funny and arrogant and confrontational. At the end of the day though, he's s-l-i-g-h-t-l-y overrated.

Many people say the same thing about the Smiths . . .
I know, but it isn't true!

There was a story in a music paper last year which appeared to accuse you of racism. You were very upset about it at the time, but in hindsight you just seemed to be saying you weren't particularly interested in dance music. No big deal really . . .
I don't think my opinions were particularly wayward. After that a lot of people rang me up and wrote to me, saying, 'At last someone is saying this – we're tired of all this stuff . . .' But the journalist made me sound demonstrative, and it's certainly not a crusade by any means. But I've never completely embraced dance music. I never ever went to clubs, I never danced, or anything like that. I went to concerts, I went to see groups in gig situations. But I do possess records by people who just happen to be black. It has happened!

How have your attitudes changed towards London? You live in Chelsea now . . .
Initially I had those very typical views about the South, and I really viewed London as enemy territory. But once I'd stayed here for a long period of time all those things dispelled. I still have a healthy obsession with Manchester, but it's difficult to feel part of the daily life because I'm never there.

Where do you go, when you go out?
I *never* go out publicly. I never go to clubs or things like that. I hover around Sloane Square occasionally and I go shopping, but that's about it. I like the Kings Road because it has a lovely catwalk feel. I don't travel very far and wide, and I certainly don't hike to any trendy spots. But I do like watching people in the Kings Road, all the ones who have perfect symmetry . . . the ones whose clothes all fit perfectly. It makes me quite envious . . . all those people who look so neat and so clean, they inspire me. I especially like footwear. Only occasionally do you see people who are so abstract that they look absurd.

I don't suppose you go on public transport now . . .
I go on trains every now and again, because I have to, but I haven't been on a bus for four years. I don't miss it.

How does Morrissey relax? Is there something he does immediately when he gets home?
[A raised eyebrow and a knowing smile here . . .] *Well,* TV certainly helps me relax; not mentally, I mean I don't watch *Terry and June,* but it takes the edge off me. I do have a vast collection of video tapes though. Anything pre-1970, generally Fifties and Sixties English films. I like *Carry On* films, early British comedy, things like *Hobson's Choice, Far from the Madding Crowd, The Family Way . . . The Leather Boys . . .*

What sums up Britain for you?
I quite like the rather dark side of Britain. Rain and fog and the countryside, the theatre district of London. I don't like anything particularly advanced. Having a television and video is completely at odds with these feelings, but you can't have an old fashioned video, now can you?

But you're constantly living in the past.
Well, it's cheaper, it was much cheaper in those days! I think I do to a certain degree, but no, it's really only a matter of taste. I just find that things buried in the past are so much more interesting than anything around today. I hate things like McDonalds – I prefer the world of tea rooms and mysterious little chip shops to the world of fast food. Unfortunately it's difficult to find many interesting old tea rooms in London, but I have found the odd place where I can sit without feeling intimidated.

What do you do with your money? You obviously don't spend it . . .
I put it in the bank – I'm with the Halifax. I'm a desperately humble person – I don't have a yacht you know. I do have a car – a 1961 Consul – but I can't drive it. It's waiting in the garage for the magical day when I learn to drive . . . which of course will never happen because I can't grapple with the Highway Code.

I don't suppose you travel much when you don't have to . . .
No, I don't really go on holidays. I don't like going to other countries to be honest with you . . . I do it *very* rarely.

Have you ever had a tan?

Yes! Yes I *have* had a tan actually. I went to Los Angeles recently and got one there, but it didn't make it back to Britain. It got stopped by customs – you're not actually allowed to come through customs with a tan.

The Smiths are looked upon by some critics as the quintessential British group, whereas others think the whole thing is contrived in the way that the Who's early singles were contrived to give this impression of Swinging Mod London.

I like the idea of the Smiths being thought of as an entirely British group, but it's quite a natural thing. It wasn't an added commodity, never has been. Also, that statement tends to imply that you won't be successful anywhere else in the world, which in our case isn't far from the truth. I do like the idea, though, of being a uniquely British phenomenon. We are *undeniably* British.

Have your attitudes towards sex changed at all? Have you lightened up? You were very uptight about it at one point . . .

Well, I've never really *had* any attitudes towards sex. It's never been my strong point . . . I've not really had much time to cultivate any attitudes. No, it's always been somewhat of a foregone conclusion. I never feel that I give completely satisfactory answers to journalists, which is why they're still asking me, but I'm still mystified by why they want to know. I never wanted to start a new movement, I never wanted to wave a banner for celibate people. I never wanted to go to the House of Commons and lobby, for instance. It's accidental that it actually came out in the first place [the celibate stance], and now it's become a tatty banner. I've been consistently probed on it, and the statement I make is that I've got nothing to do with it. To be honest with you I don't think about it [sex] that often, so I don't see why I should become a spokesman for people who don't do it that often!

How many things have you done which you're ashamed of?

None . . . nothing at all. I say that quite regretfully, because I suppose it's a measure of actually living a semi-exciting life that you've done things that will seriously make you cringe. But not me. Everything I've ever done has been totally legitimate.

When was the last time you felt real passionate love?

Practically never. No, I've never been in that situation.

Really?! Have you never wanted to? Your lyrics imply that you have.

Yes, I have. But in reality it never happens. In order to think, isolation is a necessary evil. I have to be alone. I can't really stand people's company for too long. It's terrible – but I can't really share. Occasionally I feel the need for some physical commitment – which never, I might add, *ever* happens. Everything's so entangled now that I often wonder if it will ever happen. I don't think it will to be honest with you. I mean, not many people reach 28 in my state.

When did you lose your virginity?

I've never been asked this. Actually it was in my early teens, twelve or thirteen. But it was an isolated incident, an accident. After that it was downhill. I've got no pleasant memories from it whatsoever.

Have you ever wished for a more stable, conventional life?
Yes I have, but obviously as you can gather there are several great obstacles that I can't really seem to get past. I can't seem to advance beyond friendship with most people. And for the most part I don't even manage that. I only have one or two friends, whom I've known for years. Generally I don't make friends with people – it's not something I plot, it's not something I insist upon . . . it just naturally happens.

You must be extremely worried now that Johnny Marr has decided to leave the group? Marred for life?
To a certain extent I'm upset and it's quite harrowing, but it's really just something I have to live with. I'm certainly not going to lie down and die, not by any means. Sorry. Most of what I ever felt about the Smiths came from within me anyway, and it can't really be touched by, shall we say, any comings and goings. It was brewing for a long time, and although many people didn't realise it, I certainly did. It was less of a blow really . . . not terribly surprising . . .

But he's half of the creative team of the band!
I know, and it's distressing, but it's not the Smiths' funeral by any means.

You must have thought about going solo, yes?
It's something I'm mulling over. I'm certainly aware of people wanting to bury me . . . now's the chance! No, I have a lot to do and a lot to fight against. But going solo *is* something I'm thinking about.

When people go solo, you expect them to either make a disco record or a religious one . . .
I expect I shall make a combination of the two.

You could make a Freddie Mercury record.
If only I could. I don't think I'm *quite* that talented . . .
   What I'd like to make is a very quiet record, with perhaps just guitars, voice and piano – a very gentle record, very *thoughtful.* But the spirit within me to make extremely brief, loud, raucous songs is just s-l-i-g-h-t-l-y stronger.

You've never learnt music, have you?
I've never learnt music because I've always wanted to retain a fan's response to music. It's a naivety I still have. I've never wanted to become technical about music . . . But lyrics I write all the time. I write all day long – I scribble things down in hundreds of notebooks and I have large boxes full of scraps of paper which I use.

So you don't think there will be any reconciliation with Johnny?

Judging from what he's said in the press since he left, no. I would have been quite happy for it to continue, but . . . As far as I can tell, it seems highly unlikely. It's onward, onward, onward . . .

You've said you don't like playing live. You seem exceedingly awkward on stage . . .
I don't like the travelling and the process you have to go through. I don't like being pulled, push and shoved about . . . I find that very unsettling. In general I like being on stage, but everything leading up to that hour and a half is *very* draining. When I sing on stage I almost slip into some totally separate mode of thinking – not because I'm a different person, but almost as if I become the real me. Many people say that when they're on stage they turn into some kind of different person . . . a kind of act. But that's not the same with me. I think I turn into the real Morrissey on stage, the real me, the real person . . . and when I come off I actually find acting quite useful . . . – *offstage.* Being on stage is like being in a blizzard, like being in some kind of strange tunnel.

That's entertainment!
I don't know whether entertainment comes into it. When you say things like entertainment I think of things like *Saturday Night at the London Palladium* . . . I think it's something more than that. I wouldn't mention the word mission because it sounds a l-i-t-t-l-e b-i-t t-o-o m-u-c-h, but it's definitely something more than entertainment. Seeing groups live really gives the audience great release, and Smiths' affairs tend to be quite expressive gatherings, giving people the chance to step out of their morbid lifestyles.

The typical Smiths fan is always assumed to be a withering adolescent trapped in his bedroom writing angst-ridden poetry ('Writing frightening verse to a bucktoothed girl in Luxembourg'), but your concerts seem to be populated by gangs of beery lads.
Well yes, they're very healthy people. They're not outpatients . . . they can carry themselves quite well physically! This image of a typical Smiths fanatic being a creased and semi-crippled youth is s-l-i-g-h-t-l-y over-stretched . . . it's not really true at all. Smiths concerts are really quite violent things – we even have people breaking their legs and backs. If the audience was a collection of withering prunes those things wouldn't happen. They're overtly expressive happenings. I'm very happy with that . . . I don't want people to sit back, cross their legs and nod off. When I saw David Bowie in 1972 and 1973 there was none of the hysteria that you get these days, even though *Ziggy Stardust* and *Aladdin Sane* were very big. People didn't go mad, which is something I find very hard to comprehend. You'd think that people like Bowie and Bryan Ferry were hellishly worshipped, but I don't remember any of that. I remember Roxy Music concerts where people sat on the floor. But these days that demonstration of mad affection happens to just about everybody. Concerts are wilder, stronger, more desperate that they've ever been before. In those days any hysteria was organised hysteria . . . madness happens as a matter of course these days. Though I must say that the only reason anyone goes to see David Bowie these days is so they can die saying that they saw 'David Bowie – the legend', not because they like his latest records.

Tell me about the new LP, Strangeways Here We Come. *It's got some great moments,*

but it's not exactly a radical departure, is it?
Ha! Ha! Very politely said. You're right, it isn't a radical departure – it's better, but it isn't a radical departure. It's not dramatically enlightening . . .

Do you take much notice of criticism aimed at you and the band?
When it's silly and anti-miserabilist, then it's very boring. But when it comes from intelligent people, I worry . . . I can understand that the Smiths' world doesn't appeal to everybody – I can see that quite clearly, I'm not that narrow minded. But I've never read anything which has made me want to change.

Most of the people who don't like you – they dislike you because they think it's all one big act – a coy role for yourself. I must admit I'm sceptical.
I know. I can't really blame you, but there's very little I can actually do about it, apart from visiting everybody individually in their homes and spending a weekend with them. I can't think of any remedy.

You must be worried about becoming a cliché . . .
Not really, because even though I feel that I'm not about to go off on any new dramatic tangents, I'm always going to be me, however sad that may be. I don't think I could ever deliberately change, even for fear of becoming quite repetitious. And if I don't change, and it all goes downhill, then so be it. I couldn't be a tailormade pop star, not really, not at all.

You must keep yourself to yourself . . .
I have to be alone. I still only have two real friends, and they're both people I've known since I was seventeen. Being in the Smiths and the whole experience has practically changed nothing. I genuinely don't mix. I live a very isolated life. I talk to journalists and I appear in magazines and I make the odd record, but otherwise I live a very unspectacular lifestyle. It's a very peculiar thing to juggle with. I'm an intensely private person, but yet it doesn't get seen that way in interviews because I speak so often and so personally. I think I should back off, disappear and become some kind of stagehand.

What else could you do?
Nothing. I'm entirely talentless . . . it was all a great big accident – I just came out of the wrong lift.

And if it all came to an end tomorrow?
I think I'd slide away to some Devonshire village, somewhere quite dark and green and quiet. The only burning ambition I have left is to write plays . . . but that won't happen for a while. I will do it, but at the moment this thing is wrapped around me like a shroud.

Thank you very much – that's the end.
In more ways than one . . .

i-D, October 1987

WILDE CHILD
—·— BY PAUL MORLEY —·—

The first question, when we finally met, was supremely simple and obvious. As I very grace-fully asked it, I felt a great deal of joy. If genius means a sense of inspiration or of rushes of ideas from apparently supernatural sources, or of inordinate and burning desire to accom-plish any particular end, is it perilously near to the voices heard by the insane, to their deliri-ous tendencies, to their monomanias? The answer was of course very satisfactory.
   'Oh dear . . . Can't we discuss the resurgence of glam rock?'

I remember who and what you used to be. You were like the village idiot, the odd one out, the backward boy.
None of this should have happened, should it?

What did happen?
Whatever it was, it was a mistake.

A mistake for the funny, obsessive loner, Manchester's dreamy alien, to become such an expresser of the feeling of life, and the life of feeling. And so popular!
The *sad* obsessive loner . . . No, obviously it wasn't a mistake, as such. It might even have been fated. But it is difficult to describe how really insular I was. Especially when I was 21, 22, 23 . . . I was entirely on my own. The very idea of me becoming what I have become was unthinkable. I found life unbearable at times. It's very hard when you don't really like people. (*chuckle*) There should be a union formed to protect us . . . I was a very deep, to say the least, teenager . . .

What do you mean by 'deep'?
You really know what deep means. You just want something to put in big bold letters at the top of the interview. Oh, deep for me meant not really accepting anything, whether it was the pop charts or the foundation of life. I think it meant that I was persistently troubled.

Didn't people tell you to snap out of it?
Yes, but that meant very little. I was a particular way, and that was that. I took triv-ial things very seriously, and perhaps I took serious things . . . very seriously as well.

So what did happen? How did you move from being the village idiot to being the gan-gleader?
I started to make records.

Always sartorially himself, but never a big girl's blouse: In the Smiths' heyday, Morrissey mixes and matches stylish strides with an outsize shirt from D. H. Evans.

When we finally meet, Morrissey is as I've always wanted to imagine him – a silly blend of the fairly ordinary and the delightfully ostentatious. For somebody who confesses repeatedly to such chronic inner turmoil, he seems very calm, even in a way delighted with himself. 'Well,' he announces as we shake hands, 'the last time we met we romped naked together at playschool . . .' He might be right. When we meet as adults, the second question that I am destined to ask is damned inevitable.

Is it natural to hate?
Some people are very funny. Some people are athletic. Some people are very hateful . . . It's whatever is in the blood.

I could not feel anything but vulgar admiration for Morrissey. His talent is sufficiently exquisite and perverse for me to consider him a truly great writer. I am not put off even when he is at his most contrived. If Patti Smith's Horses *is my favourite album, then 'This Charming Man' is my favourite single. It's not as if these records have stopped me from being a murderer, or anything like that, but somehow they have found time for me. Morrissey also makes me laugh, as if his life has been him acting out his own violent comedy, unusually amused by the very idea of human happiness. I am very moved by his transformation from utter loser to sly playboy of frustration.*

He came out of a frightened world of small houses, small streets and small lives by turning inward. Patti Smith and T.Rex turned his mind inside out. When the outside world branded him a freak as he slid dangerously on the surface of life, he created his own little worlds. Worlds of withdrawal that he invented so intensely they made up for him a special set of rules, regulations and dreams. Other people became simply voices through a cloud. He was with the people, yet far apart, acutely disappointed with the way they appeared to put up with their squalid predicament.

When he writes songs about his own inadequacy, about a mind under constant pressure from experience, songs that might comically diagnose the English tragedy, I can't help but see his point. He has fiercely resisted the tendency of the modern commercial world to treat people as objects, and, quite possibly by being raised in those streets at that particular time, a time chilled by helplessness, his writing has a sense of evil. Seedy, cheeky, and dignified, his songs have meant a lot to me. As you can see, Morrissey excites all that is sombre and nostalgic and anxious in me.

I am, though, pretty puzzled as to what anybody else sees in his work, so private does it seem to me, so easily interpreted as intolerably cheerless and hunted. At a time when popular music is Carol Decker's mini-skirt and a Pet Shop Boys bass line, the success and adulation of Morrissey, a writer committed to exposing human stupidity, who presents himself, cheaply at times, as being exhausted by life's struggles, is almost truly remarkable. It's as though the ghost of the fourteen-year-old scornfully locked into magical bedroom isolation, feasting in the imagination on the impossible glories of favourite stars, is haunting and mocking the paled, neglected system of pop. Smiling weakly amidst the chattering mastered machinery, the shattering profit motives, floating through the lawyers and accountants, playing at being a smash hit with the charisma of a petty thief, Morrissey as always is the odd man out, moaning directly into the fashions of the time, appearing idiotic and primitive and yet . . . popular music as the fourteen-year-old Morrissey wanted it to be, all the time, all the way. He has willed himself into being.

Apart from whatever else is involved, Morrissey is having a rather sinister last laugh on behalf of those he has loved, those that were spurned, ignored and killed. It's not nearly as drastic or as pompous as it seems. It's merely . . . interesting, to those who might still be interested, to those who always knew. Some people may find the pop charts comfortably, boldly all that they should ever be. For Morrissey, there must always be more. He hates the world so much, it's precious to him. And for Morrissey, the world was pop music.

Do you blame anyone or anything for you being alive?

Not at all. But I wouldn't want to inflict it on anyone else . . . I cannot understand having children. Even if the opportunity arose, I would definitely turn it down. No, I don't blame anyone for bringing me into the world, but I do feel that life is excessively overrated.

Why do you care so much about pop music?

The answer is probably simpler than we both imagine. If you keep yourself quite isolated within it, you tend to hit out against the music industry. If you make lots of friends and get invited to loads of parties, you might not want to think about all the thoughtlessness, you may well enjoy it all and you would tend not to be so overjudgemental. Even now I keep myself isolated, and so I hate what goes on.

What are you caring about?

I think we know why we care. I care because I have always loved passionately popular music. I think even as each day passes and popular music becomes more and more distasteful, its actual history becomes more and more important. I do not like to see it invaded, trampled upon . . . It meant so much to me.

Why, after Patti Smith, Television, Roxy, the Dolls, Joy Division, Eno, Byrne, Morrissey . . . is popular music in such a state? Something went wrong. No one agrees with us!

Yes, something went wrong. But, for me, it was totally important and it affected me physically and mentally. After hearing *Horses* I was never the same again, and I don't say that lightly. It is obviously not normal to think that this sort of music is the important music, the Velvet Underground, etcetera, but it was to me and that is all that can really matter, as such. It doesn't change my mind that people do not agree with me, on the whole. Something horrendous *has* happened. I can't really explain it except to say the obvious – it has been infiltrated by idiots. I do get annoyed because there isn't enough hate in pop, there isn't enough anger. If there are signs of intelligence, they get tired very quickly and give up the fight. They are not properly encouraged. I suppose popular music is now engineered by careless people who never had the imagination to spot or desire the true nature of pop and why it could be so special. The wrong people, as far as I'm concerned, are in control. Lawyers and accountants have become too important. The right stuff is not being encouraged, and the wrong stuff is not being suitably condemned.

Are you just hard to please, a natural critic of life and living?

I have always been intrigued by writers and singers and journalists whose opinions and attitudes seemed to be unpopular but who attained a certain status precisely because of their displeasure with the world. I see nothing wrong with being hard to please. It has its own grace, it's the very least we should expect. I feel that the opinions of the hard to please people are the ones that really count. They are prepared for discovery and change.

Is idealism insanity?
Well, it's a matter of taste, that's for sure . . . I do believe that the quality of life will change because there are people who are very hard to please.

You care in a totally selfish way, or for a great benefit?
I always think it's a positive thing to be selfish. It's not negative at all, it's very useful. People who aren't selfish and don't look after themselves always look dreadful. I always thought that being selfish was the first step to maturity.

Do you think, seriously, that popular music is currently so abandoned and shallow because optimists, who have taken control, write badly?
Dully is actually the word, not badly. They possibly write quite well, but it is essentially repetitive and usual and dull. I think that when you notice the intensity of life you instantly become more . . . exciting. Whether that intensity is truly possible within popular music, well, one would think it is not. But I always thought that it could. And in the end, I do not understand people who are not as serious as me . . .

They probably don't want to get depressed.
Now we know this isn't true . . . They're just as likely to get depressed, and make other people depressed, but they won't admit to it. Being serious is for me the way it has to be. It comes very naturally to me. Making simple dance records was never the point. It would be for me totally futile. I have to make records that transcend the assumed importance of pop.

Is this a ridiculous conceit?
It might be. Another way of looking at it is to say that it's totally brave.

So you're saying that the resolution to do what you do is, under the circumstances, heroic?
Yes. Very heroic. Very solitary. People are always looking at me sideways and saying, 'Well, do you really want to do *that*? Don't you really want to do *that*? . . . Are you really serious?' But also in a sense I do have the ability to laugh at myself, even though amongst the people who consider me overwrought this is also apparently sinful. I have always had to laugh at myself. If I hadn't found my social position when I was a teenager so amusing, I would have strangled myself. The fact I am doing it at all I find incredible.

What is it that you do?
I'm not bad with words.

Are you serious?
I think I see seriousness in everything. Even pop music. People say that it doesn't belong there, that it was never there at all . . . But there we are. Here I am. I think I must be quite unique!

What's so special?
You tell me.

My reasons might be too light-hearted.
I think I became interested in introducing a new language into pop using certain words that I felt would be totally revolutionary, and within the Smiths I thought I achieved that. I'm still quite proud that words like 'coma', 'shoplifter', 'bigmouth', even 'suede-head', are available in pop music. When one considers the realities of the charts, I think it's rare and extraordinary to find any new language at all . . . and perhaps I'm unique because people are so dull. So I stand out. I'm not very good at being dull. You know, all these questions and answers just seem to emphasise how strange I really am. (*chuckle*)

Why did you like to feel strange?
I don't know whether I *liked* being strange in the way that you're implying . . . I felt strange because I was never impressed by the simple things that other people seem to enjoy.

So you fell in love with images.
It wasn't really my fault that images rather than people appealed to me. There were a lot of people about . . . I went to school and briefly to work, I did see people. I lived on a heavily populated council estate. There were people all around. But no one was bothered to penetrate this great wall there was between us. Yes, I was selfish. But I was also, and remain so, the sort of person that not many people want to know. It's hard to believe!

You were forced to construct your own reality?
Yes. This took me a long time. But more importantly, I think that when someone is not at all popular, for whatever reasons, one tends to develop certain forms of survival. A survival which excludes friends, which excludes social activities. That in a sense is how I organised my life. If you cannot impress people simply by being part of the great fat human race, then you really do have to develop other skills. And if you don't impress people by the way you look, then you really *do* have to develop other skills. And if you are now going to ask is everything I did just a way to gain some form of attention, well that's not entirely true. It is in a small way, but that's in the very nature of being alive.

Wanting to be loved?
To be seen, above all else. I wanted to be noticed, and the way I lived and do live has a desperate neurosis about it because of that. All humans need a degree of attention. Some people get it at the right time, when they are thirteen or fourteen, people get loved at the right stages. If this doesn't happen, if the love isn't there, you can quite eas-

ily just fade away. This could have happened to me easily. Several times I was close to
. . . fading away. It doesn't give me great comfort to talk about it. I do not wish to relive
those experiences. But I came close . . . In a sense I always felt that being troubled as
a teenager was par for the course. I wasn't sure that I was dramatically unique. I knew
other people who were at the time desperate and suicidal. They despised life and
detested all other living people. In a way that made me feel a little bit secure. Because
I thought, well, maybe I'm not so intense after all. Of course, I was. I despised practically everything about human life, which does limit one's weekend activities.

What else was there?
Nothing. Books. Television. Records. Overall, it's a vast wasteland.

Has the memory of those years been destroyed?
No, not at all. I remember it all in great detail, I seem to remember it every night and
re-experience the embarrassment of it. It was horror. The entire school experience, a
secondary modern in Stretford called St Mary's. The horror of it cannot be overem-
phasised. Every single day was a human nightmare. In every single way that you could
possibly want to imagine. Worse . . . the total hatred. The fear and anguish of wak-
ing up, of having to get dressed, having to walk down the road, having to walk into
assembly, having to do those lessons . . . I'm sure most people at school are very
depressed. I seemed to be more depressed than anyone else. I noticed it more.

Tell me, have you ever seen a psychiatrist?
Ha . . . not really . . . I have seen one or two psychiatrists. They just sit and nod and
doodle. Perhaps if I was cured, so to speak, I would just walk blindly and amiably into
every given situation, and I don't think that would be me, really. Maybe unhappiness
keeps me going forward.

What annoys you most about yourself?
Practically everything. I miss not being able to stand up straight. I tend to slide into
rooms and sit on the chair behind the door.

Is this all just gross self-pity?
No, not at all. There is the answer to that one. It isn't that simple.

So how, after all this, did the 'great call' come?
The great call . . . that sounds very nice. In a sense, it was always there. But I felt by
the time I reached 21, 22, 23, that it couldn't possibly be there. I couldn't see how it
could be in pop music. I was paralysed for a start. I couldn't move. I couldn't imagine dancing, and I felt that movement was practically the whole point of the absurd
ritual. I could just about imagine singing, but even then I didn't really know what to
do with the microphone and the mike stand. But I had this strange mystical calling.
There's no need to laugh! Once again, because I had such an intense view about taking one's life, I imagined that this must be my calling, suicide, nothing more spectacular or interesting. I felt that people who eventually took their own lives were not

only aware that they would do so in the last hours or weeks or months of their life. They had always been aware of it. They had resigned themselves to suicide many years before they actually did it. In a sense I had, yes.

What stopped you?
I made records. I got the opportunity to make records, and miraculously it all worked.

So has being Morrissey saved your life?
It has been a blessing and a burden. It saved me and pushed me forward into a whole new set of problems.

Problems you seem to quite enjoy.
No I do not! Why do people insist that I scour the world and life searching wilfully for atrocities to punish myself with?

But you always seem to derive pleasure from anxiety.
It was always a very insular pleasure. It was always a matter of walking backwards into one's bedroom and finding the typewriter and perhaps hearing much more in pop music than was really there. The point is, I had always entertained the idea of making records and just as the door seemed to be closing and I was thinking less and less about it happening, I got the chance. Suddenly those avenues were open and I utilised them.

What did you think would happen?
I felt that it would be either totally embraced or universally despised. In a way, both things happened. I often think that people take me either insultingly lightly or uncomfortably, obsessively, neurotically seriously. I was obsessed with fame, and I couldn't see anyone in the past in film or music who resembled me. So it was quite different to see a niche of any sort. So when I started to make records, I thought, well, rather than adopt the usual poses I should just be as natural as I possibly could, which of course wasn't very natural at all. For me to be making records at all was entirely unnatural, so really that was the only way I could be. Unnatural. Which in a sense was my form of rebellion, because rebellion in itself had become quite a tradition, certainly after punk. I didn't want to follow through those established forms of appearance and rebellion. And by the time I was making records, I was 23, an old, thoughtful 23, so I knew there were certain things that I wanted to do. I was very certain. And I do feel very underrated, by and large, considering what I have achieved.

You think you have done something constructive?
Yes, I bloody do! At least, under the circumstances. Ha ha ha . . . why am I laughing? This is very serious. I do think that I have achieved a great deal as a human being.

You're incredibly flattered.
People may fawn and be quite sympathetic, but that doesn't actually mean they understand. People rarely pat you on the back in the way that you really want. I sometimes feel that what I do might come and go without truly being noticed.

This seems pretty ungrateful.
Of course it does. It is very hard to complain when people approve of you . . . but I manage it. When certain people criticise me, I get the point. I can nod and smile when I'm attacked more than when I'm given wonderfully favourable reviews. It's not necessarily useful to a person that people are so keen to give you five star reviews, and who miss the point. There have been people in the past who cannot stand me whose views I find totally interesting. It's not very useful to have someone sat next to you nodding all the time . . . and you purposefully give them a foul idea, and they continue to nod, and you reverse their view of you back on them, and still they nod. But, yes, I think there is more credit due to me. I have done things that if most people had done them it would have narrowed their audience considerably. I have played against traditional audience sympathy. And it did inspire me when I first started that I couldn't think of anyone who was remotely like me.

When did it dawn on you it would work?
Instantly, really . . . because it did happen very quickly, even if we're just talking about the first few Smiths gigs. It was more than I expected. There were lots and lots of people ready to identify with what I was feeling. Hatred! Hating everything, but not being offensively hateful. (*chuckle*) It was like hate from quite gentle people.

Was it easy?
Success is never easy. It could have gone hopelessly wrong for me. It never really gelled until the fourth single.

If it hadn't worked, would you be dead now?
I would certainly be in intensive care.

Do you feel the power of a group leader, at the head of these gentle, hateful people?
Yes, I do . . . I don't feel the need to go out and shake everyone's hands, and get everyone together, but I do know what you mean. I like to think that one can make records and be intensely successful, yet still remain essentially private. That would be very pleasant. Perhaps I do have influence. A lot of young people are very lonely and maybe hearing my records will make them feel less lonely. And there may be many people who are like I was, desperate, incapable, but needing so much to do something. I would like to think a record of mine will make them feel if he can do it, etcetera, then so can I.

That you only appeal to a rash of confused adolescents is just a dried up cliché?
Oh yes. It has expanded way beyond that. I was initially very confused when people wrote that my songs were adolescent. I was 24, 25, so they weren't adolescent, they were something totally new, something that had never been expressed before. It was not adolescent. It was not that easy.

What does your music do to your fans?
Well, they wear heavy overcoats and stare at broken lightbulbs. That's the way it's

always been for me!

What's Morrissey on about today? When we finally meet, Morrissey is holding court in a suite at the lovely, grand Hyde Park Hotel. He is spending some time being interviewed to promote his new solo record, telling a whole zoo of journalists that the real truths are those that can be invented. Journalists sit before him, half in awe, half in dismay, trying to pin him down, pick him out, get him to admit that he's only human, that after all he's really involved like anyone else in the chase for money, disguising his greed with hysterical analysis. And he, with the patience of a saint of course, with a small sigh and a distressed chuckle, will answer.

'Within the framework of pop there is actually room for great individualism. And by writing the songs that I do, I might be able to understand a little more about myself.'

When we finally meet, there is a third question that I just have to ask. I'm not so graceful as I ask this one, and Morrissey sweetly watches me stutter, indulging me for what it's worth. Have you suffered for knowledge's sake?

'But once again, for me, it simply isn't knowledge as such. If it was I would be able to breeze through life smiling. I possess an inexplicable knowledge. In an academic sense I'm hopeless. I really am. I don't have any A-levels. It's a very perverted knowledge. A strange vision.'

He pleasantly smiles as he realises that he is being asked to explain exactly what he means by 'strange vision'.

'Yes, it does have to be explained very carefully, but then I don't understand it myself. I can only explain it by saying that it is there through me being, through me writing, singing and making records.'

And, of course, he is firm and emphatic whenever the journalist starts to worry about his painful preciousness, worry that maybe Morrissey just thinks too much.

'No, I am not being precious. And I don't think it's possible to think too much.'

It's his world, and you can't really touch him. If anyone asks why, if he is so perpetually unhappy, he doesn't just kill himself, the answer is well rehearsed:

'Well, there are things to do . . . like writing the songs on Viva Hate.'

Viva Hate is the first post-Smiths work. Only the pointlessly fussy will wonder if there might or might not be a difference between the group work and the solo songs. As with all Morrissey songs, there are ways to be involved, there is much to investigate. Somehow, it will probably even be controversial. I think it is a record that can easily be loved. Does Morrissey think it is a great work? He is ready to answer.

'It approaches it. I do have very clear sights of what I have to do to, as it were, live up to it all. I think Viva Hate is a lofty piece, but I'm still not inclined to beat the drum too much just yet. I've still yet to touch perfection . . . I'll know it when I do it, and I think it will be totally enchanting to affect other people's lives with a form of perfection. It will be like marriage!'

Morrissey certainly knows how to enjoy himself during an interview. 'I often pass a mirror,' he confides, loving the attention he's getting, 'and I glance into it slightly, and I don't really recognise myself at all. You can look into a mirror and wonder – where have I seen that person before? And then you remember. It was at a neighbour's funeral, and it was the corpse.'

The first single from the album has, the week we meet, entered the charts at number six, boosted by the big EMI backing. Morrissey now perches at the edge of melodramatic superstardom. We might as well take this sort of thing seriously. The next stage will be the most interesting – the final move from the cobblestones of hate to the stars above. Will he make it? The point, the pretence, of Morrissey will be challenged perhaps for the first time. Is he genuinely prepared? He will chuckle at the thought. It seems there is nothing that you can think of that he hasn't thought of already, nothing that he doesn't have an answer for.

What is Morrissey, spoilt, over-defensive, amused, on about today? As he consistently nags and confidently explains, holding on to the real secrets, there is always the hint, just the hint, that he is sniggering all the while. Morrissey has been very carefully worked out, as if it was all planned in the bedroom.

So I suppose you're going to tell me that the phrase 'life is extravagant' means nothing to you?
Yes. I always feel trapped by life. When I heard the title *Stop The World, I Want To Get Off,* I thought – perfect.

Where does the anguish and hate come from?
As with most things, I'm still trying to find out.

Why can you fall in love so easily with images, but not with people?
I'm still trying to find out.

What kind of difficulties do you have with people?
Let's talk about the window cleaner. I'm still in the position that when the window cleaner calls, I have to go in another room than the one he is cleaning. It's very silly. At the time I feel like a bespectacled six-year-old. I always find when the doorbell rings that my automatic response is to hide or run away, to be quiet. They might want you to do something that you don't want to do, want you to go where you don't want to go. It's one of those trivial obsessive fears, like being on an airplane . . . which troubles me enormously. I always feel when I'm on a plane that I have to be racked by physical fear, and if I am I'll arrive safely. I feel if I relax, drink a whiskey, converse, the plane will crash. I have to be in total turmoil or the plane won't make it. That's the way I am and always will be. (*chuckle*) The terrifying thing is, as you get older, it doesn't get any easier. Fears just seem to cement into place.

Do you think that such troubles, and the nature of your sexuality, informs the ways and means of your songs?
What can you possibly mean?

There's a lot of guesswork concerning your sexuality, but it seems very important to your work.
People do try and join up the dots to come up with some kind of answer . . . There may well be no answer. I have to say, and this sounds rehearsed, I've always felt closer to transsexuality than anything else.

What is your ideal sexual experience?

I don't have a vision of it at all. Why do people ask me questions like this?
Because you ask for it. You're the only person who can seriously be asked those questions.
Oh, come now.

Is there any sex in Morrissey?
None whatsoever. Which in itself is quite sexy.

What happened to the sex?
It was never there. Not thoroughly, so to speak . . .

What happened?
Nothing! It goes back to being an incredibly unpopular person. No one asked.

Did you ever ask anybody?
Once or twice. Girls and boys. I sent notes . . . After a while I thought, that is it, that
is the end of the notes. I don't want to go through that anymore. In a particular sense,
I am a virgin. Well, in a very thorough sense, actually. (*chuckle*)

Do you feel you have missed out?
I tend to think so, yes. But so be it. Perhaps if there had been sex, I wouldn't have
written.

Have you had fantasies of fucking?
Yes. But they pass . . .

No sex. No love. What kind of cold person are you?
A horrible one, no doubt. The next answer will again appear in big black bold letters
at the top of the interview. I've always felt above sex and love.

Sounds mighty.
No, it's incredibly light, and you're being sarcastic anyway. In a way, I believe that all
those things like love, sex, sharing a life with somebody, are actually quite vague. Being
only with yourself can be much more intense. I personally have always felt trapped
within the feeling of being constantly disappointed with people. In a way I do feel
things that are conceivably better and more important than sexual situations. I mean,
sex is presumably the final point one reaches, I don't know. It doesn't matter to me. All
the emotions I need to express come from within me. They don't really come from
other people. I seem to feel things far more intensely and precisely than people who
express a ragbag of emotions and survive, just, loads of relationships. I see all situations,
even when I'm not involved and it's nothing to do with me, in a very dramatic way.

You're something of a drama queen?
If you like. That will do.

And incredibly fussy.

Mmmmmmmmmmm . . . (*chuckle*)
Does fame alarm you?
Yes. Sometimes I feel very famous. This week I have entered the charts at number six, and this is a great surprise. And I recognise that very few people have achieved monumental success on a global basis and remained fascinating.

Is this what you want?
Yes and no. In some ways I think to be hugely famous would be scary and meaningless. I saw hints of it when I was in America playing large venues. You feel the power of record companies just waiting to propel you into nonsense states of being.

With the Smiths, that was always a danger, the way the group was being set up as next in line after the Rolling Stones.
Yes, I know what you mean. All that rock thing did confuse me . . . It seemed a preparation for straightforward global success, and in a way I'm quite provincial.

In a way, quite small-minded.
No, that sounds cruel. It's just that the kind of global success that does seem to beckon I resist for the obvious reasons. I just haven't changed enough to accept it. I feel very accomplished with what has happened, in my own way.

How do you resist that particular pressure to succumb to the straightforward?
It's very hard. You get bored hearing yourself say the same old things time and time again. Hearing your voice say no, no, no . . . I got bored saying that. But I do think that I have been very much in control, all things considered.

At times, through being quite childish?
No. Through being protective. It would be very childish to say, well just push me along and wherever I land I'll sing. I have been very careful and very protective.

Is there any way that you consider you take real risks?
I am risking quite a lot. Fame is a risk. I won't be able to change with fame, the same things will always trouble me, and that will intensify by me making strong statements and desiring to be totally human within it all. In a way, you're meant to change with fame, you're meant to adjust. I can't, and I feel quite queasy about that. Being famous, you're not supposed to care about things like the urgency of life, you're not meant to express disappointment that people don't seem to understand the terrible briefness of life. I will not do the kind of things you're meant to do when you're famous. However hard I try, I can't be that obvious.

What's going to happen next?
It doesn't scare me. It confuses me. I can't imagine how I will live if I am not famous. I can't imagine how I would live if I had to start a normally constructed existence. If fame left me, I couldn't imagine living. But I wouldn't ungracefully cling to fame. If it slid away, so be it . . .

What would happen to you?
I haven't a clue. But I do not feel victimised by fame. I always felt that there was a reason for me to be famous, so to speak. I didn't think that my fame would be so superficial that as soon as somebody yawned it was all over. Somebody said that even if my records ceased to sell, I would always have a very high profile. I would like to trust that observation.

Do you ever feel that this whole Morrissey thing is quite silly?
Yes, probably, under a certain light. But then with a certain effort you can make anything in the world seem quite ridiculous.

Do you ever think that the problems of fame are fantasy problems that you tend to overindulge in?
No, they're very real problems. Absolutely real.

So when the tabloids write nonsense, you're truly offended?
It does hurt me, because it isn't true. They compile fictitious quotes.

Don't you take it too personally?
What else can I do? It all makes me out to be a very silly and thoughtless person, and that annoys me, because I am not, and there are enough of them in the world. I'm not thoughtless at all, I think all the time.

But as long as you know you're not silly and thoughtless, then so what?
Well, I accept that . . . but people are reading it, people are thinking it might be true, and I don't like that. I don't get drunk and forget. I just wish that people would represent me as being more fascinating than I actually am instead of so much less. When these fictitious quotes appear, why can't they just be *fabulous*?

It's out of your control.
Yes, and I don't like that. It might ruin all my carefully prepared work!

Now that we've finally met, the last question is supremely simple and obvious. With what you have managed to control, all the odd little details, all the pained expressions, all the pieces of an unlikely glamour, are you flamboyantly setting yourself up for the grand, savage exit – writing yourself into a dramatic, doomed story that the young Morrissey would have totally relished?
I don't know what you could possibly mean! (*chuckle*)

Blitz, April, 1988

PRIVATE DIARY OF A MIDDLE-AGED MAN

—•••— BY SHAUN PHILIPS —•••—

Having seen the Messiah and his Smiths feed the 5,000 with a Mother's Pride and a tin of sardines, no doubt his disciples were a little disappointed when on his own he could only manage to turn the water into house red and not the champagne they were expecting.

When Morrissey released *Viva Hate*, the first album of his solo career, in March, even the Godfather of Gloom shared in the anticlimax.

'Lyrically, it wasn't the best, I'm well aware of that,' he confesses.

'It was a very peculiar time for me, making that record so suddenly, so unexpectedly, and I wanted to try something different.

'Because of the particular status I have, where many people concentrate quite scientifically over every comma, I reached a stage where I wanted to be entirely spontaneous without physically writing the words down and memorising them. Rather, just step into the vocal booth and sing it as it comes. But I don't think I'll try that again . . . back to the typewriter.'

His soul unburdened, Morrissey slips down onto the park's uncut grass and surveys his audience.

To the sound of Friday's angry traffic attacking London's Hyde Park Corner, a thousand beached secretaries go as bare as they dare, oblivious to everything but the carcinogenic summer sun. Morrissey dares to strip down to his roll neck sweater.

It seems an inappropriate spot to prod the protagonist of the dreary seaside resort, the champion of the wet, silent Sunday that comes and stays forever. A dank, impersonal hotel room at the end of a foetid corridor would surely have been more appropriate.

Having just turned 29, Morrissey already feels on 'the tremulous threshold' of 30. His birthday, naturally, passed unhappily.

'I live a very deprived existence. I don't physically go out and get drunk and vomit over policemen or anything like that.'

He nurses just a few grey hairs and an inflamed right eye; the result of an impetuous contact lens. It's causing Morrissey discomfort but does not warrant the risk of a corrective visit to the nearby public convenience. The mere suggestion is greeted with an arched eyebrow.

'I think age personally makes me feel a bit better, because youth for me was revolting and being young and feeling young, I always hated that. I feel a bit better now, as I stumble blindfoldedly into middle age.'

Pop stardom, it seems, need not end in crushing disappointment with the passing of acne. Nor does facetiousness.

Like his heroine, Maggie Thatcher, Morrissey occasionally makes it difficult to distinguish between fact and fiction.

An Englishman abroad: Morrissey performs in New York (with Johnny Marr), every inch the colonial. Who'd have thought he'd exile himself to the US one decade hence?

I mean, did he *really* sing, 'It was a good lay' at the end of 'Suedehead', his first solo single?

'No, "It was a bootleg." I mean, good heavens, in my vocabulary? *Please . . .'*

Honestly?

'Well, have I ever been dishonest?' he laughs. 'Do people *think* it was "a good lay"?' I do.

'And is that quite racy?'

Oh, yes.

'Well, it was actually "a good lay".'

And was there one?

'No, I just thought it might amuse someone living in Hartlepool.'

In matters of grave importance, Morrissey adheres to his idol Oscar Wilde's adage that style, not sincerity, is vital.

However lightly Morrissey chooses to reflect it, his solo career has hardly run smooth. While the consistency of quality ended abruptly after the release in June '85 of *The Queen Is Dead* LP and the excellent 'Panic' and 'Ask' 45s that followed, Morrissey's profile seems to have blossomed.

His popularity owes much to his tongue-in-cheek revolution; one week he'd taunt the *Top of the Pops* audiences with 'Marry Me' slogans, the next he'd mime gunning them down as they danced.

Comparatively, his solo career is far more subdued.

'I think so many people were inspired by the whole Rough Trade ethic of trying to fight, and winning in many cases, which was exciting. And obviously with EMI that doesn't exist.'

It may seem irrelevant that Morrissey no longer buys his underwear at M&S, but it reflects how *everything* about his presentation has changed.

Once, faded film stars adorned his record sleeves, now it's portraits of himself, and he practically looks like a stubbleless George Michael on his latest release, 'Everyday Is Like Sunday'. It's tempting to think his days as the bedsit revolutionary are all but over.

Morrissey, however, still feels like the Che Guevara of pop.

'If you really concentrate on the Top 40 there aren't really that many striking individuals so it is rather easy within that block to be semi-anarchic. But I don't for one second believe that I'm really considered to be entirely trustworthy. I still think that people might suspect me of saying the wrong things or, rather, expect me to say "*the wrong thing*". But I don't feel institutionalised, I don't feel faintly akin to George Michael or his world for that matter. If George Michael had to live my life for five minutes, he'd strangle himself with the nearest piece of cord.'

But one could think Morrissey's revolution had gone underground with his solo single releases, as neither has met with such hostile reactions as certain Smiths releases. 'Handsome Devil' (the B-side of 'Hand In Glove') was thought by some to allude to child abuse; 'Panic' was a racist attack; and 'Girlfriend In A Coma' was gross bad taste. But *Viva Hate* treads a far more precarious line.

Yet Morrissey refutes allegations that he courts controversy.

'There is no controversy on *Viva Hate*, as far as I can see, apart, perhaps, from the title. But I've never been deliberately controversial. It just so happens that because of the climate and the standards of writing in pop music today that if one has any self-judgement about the things you write then you're bound to be considered not controversial but at least . . . I've forgotten the word . . . *Tesco's!*'

While accusations of racism were spurious for 'Panic', revolving around Morrissey's reasons for wanting to 'Hang the DJ', tactless lyricism on the album's 'Bengali In Platforms' leaves it open to a racist interpretation.

'Bob Geldof In Platforms you nearly said,' quips Morrissey, treating the issue with far more contempt than it deserves.

Was it intended to have a double edge?

'No, it still doesn't, not at all. There are many people who are so obsessed with racism that one can't mention the word Bengali; it instantly becomes a racist song, even if you're saying, Bengali, marry me. But I still can't see any silent racism there.'

Not even with the line, 'Life is hard enough when you belong here'?

'Well, it is, isn't it?'

True, but that implies that Bengalis don't belong here, which isn't a very global view of the world.

'In a sense it's true. And I think that's almost true for anybody. If you went to Yugoslavia tomorrow, you'd probably feel that you didn't belong there.'

Morrissey, however, makes no such disclaimers for the album's last track, 'Margaret On The Guillotine'.

Originally the working title of *The Queen Is Dead* album, the lyrics in this shortened form were put in cold storage because they 'didn't fit any music that was presented at the time'. But there is little doubt about the singer's impressions of the Iron Lady.

'The kind people/Have a wonderful dream/Margaret on the guillotine . . .'

'I follow her career,' Morrissey explains. 'Obviously, I find the entire Thatcher syndrome very stressful and evil and all those other words. But I think there's very little that people can do about it. The most perfect example, I suppose, is Clause 28. I think that absolutely embodies Thatcher's very nature and her quite natural hatred.'

The time when Oscar Wilde is banned is nigh?

'I think so, possibly. But protesting to me is pointless because people suffer this delusion that the very issue of Clause 28 is actually anything to do with the British people. They have no say in the matter. I think that's been the story throughout Thatcher's reign, so I don't see the point of wandering around Marble Arch in a pink T-shirt, carrying books by Andrea Dworkin.'

(Andrea Dworkin is a feminist writer who had, among other things, rather a lot to say about the sexist nature of *The Bible* and how that affected society.)

And isn't committing your feelings to records as pointless?

'Not really, because it's there forever.'

But if the world won't listen now, it seems highly unlikely it will listen in the future. And if George Orwell's prophecies in *Nineteen Eighty Four* were ever to materialise, the Ministry of Information would delete your record anyway.

'In a sense, that almost gives people qualification to write more and stronger. I do believe if we lived in a harmonious environment, everybody would be excessively overweight and they would all listen to records by Vince Hill, even you.'

Anyone with a rudimentary knowledge of Bob Geldof's career will know that, even with a free world advert, going solo can be a disaster.

And as the Smiths fizzled out with their lacklustre last album, *Strangeways, Here We Come*, from which two further singles, 'I Started Something I Couldn't Finish' and 'Last Night I Dreamt That Somebody Loved Me', failed to make any great impression on the charts, Morrissey feared that his first solo release, 'Suedehead', 'would gasp in the higher 30s and disintegrate'.

He hadn't even wanted to release the song as a single but was 'carried along on a wave of general enthusiasm'.

The song was not as good as prime Smiths, but it was a beautifully reflective tune, showing that ex-Smiths co-producer Stephen Street could step into Marr's previous role as composer, and that Vini Reilly (guitar), Andrew Paresi (drums) and a six piece string section could adequately cope with the departure of Marr, Rourke, and Joyce.

Backed by two equally inspiring numbers, 'I Know Very Well How I Got My Name' and 'Hairdresser On Fire', the record rewarded the confidence of Morrissey's colleagues by getting into the Top Five while no Smiths single had ever got higher than number ten.

'I thought this was the time for people to destroy me,' Morrissey reminisces. 'I think it's remarkable that the records [both the single and the following album] were successful without a solitary television appearance or tours etcetera.'

One such 'etcetera' was a planned Peel session for Radio One, which although recorded was never released.

'It was really awful, horrible,' says Morrissey, reflecting on the treatment he received from the technicians at the Maida Vale studios.

'They're quite accustomed to treat everyone like they were some insignificant, unsigned group from Poole. And that's how I felt on that day. I felt as though I'd never seen a record let alone made one. So I found them a bit rude and I couldn't sing because I was so annoyed and angry. I think John Walters made a reference to it, saying I just didn't want it aired because I didn't think it was good enough but that really wasn't the case. It certainly wasn't good enough but the reasons behind it were the situation at Maida Vale. I suppose a lot of new, naïve, untested groups go through that situation and they have no choice and they're happy to do it. And in a sense it is quite a good opportunity but it really is a put up or shut up situation.'

Will you be doing any more sessions?

'Not as long as I've two legs . . . which possibly means I might be doing a session next week!'

And that is just as likely as the rumour that Morrissey would be appearing live at the ICA. Touring is not high on his agenda.

'In a sense I don't feel instantly inclined to attempt anything. It was perfect, and the Smiths did play a lot. I was slightly satiated at the time that it ended, but it's nice to be able to step back but not disappear entirely.'

So have you made any plans?

'None whatsoever.'

In fact, Morrissey's only live preparations have been for the forthcoming live Smiths album on Rough Trade. He titled it ('*Rank* as in J. Arthur'), chose the tracks (the listing was approved by Johnny Marr) and designed the sleeve 'with the excellent assistance of Jo Slee and Caryn Gough'.

But it's not necessarily the last time you'll hear Morrissey sing a Smiths song. Were he to perform again in the future, he is adamant that he would sing songs from the Smiths' repertoire.

'I was there when those songs were recorded; I wrote the words. Just because the group ended didn't mean that suddenly all those feelings dissolve. It's still very much a part of me in 1988.'

That Stephen Street would compose the music in Morrissey's post-Smiths career came as a surprise to many but, in retrospect, the singer had little alternative. Morrissey's own musical accomplishments begin and end with a one-fingered piano recital on 'Death Of A Disco Dancer' on the last Smiths LP.

'It was the first time the group played it together and we just switched the tape on and didn't take it terribly seriously. And I just fell onto a piano and began to bang away. We kept the tape because it had some unnameable appeal.'

And people kept the piano away from you after that?

'People kept away from me after that!'

Unable to compose for himself and go completely solo, Morrissey's only other option was a demo tape provided by Street.

'At the time there were no other people presenting things and I happened to like what Stephen had done. It happened very quickly. I mean, this time a year ago the last Smiths album was nowhere near being released. It has been a very hectic year. I know it's quite tempting to think I'm coasting to some degree and I'm not playing live and all those usual things, but I haven't stopped at all.'

Is the partnership open ended?

'It's entirely open, it's not the *new* Smiths or anything like that. There's no existing group.'

And you're happy with it?

'Er, yes.'

Has anybody approached you with another offer?

'Er, no, not at all.'

Would you consider anybody?

'Well, I wouldn't object to being approached, put it that way.'

Is there anybody at the back of your mind, who you sit at home thinking . . .

'George Michael . . . no. Andrew Ridgeley . . . Fairground Attraction!'

What about the rumours of a Marr reunion?

'Are there rumours? I haven't heard anything about him or of him since a year ago. The last time the Smiths were together was May 21, 1962, or whenever it was, which was a year ago. So since then I haven't heard a dickie bird, as they say.'

In fact, the only other person from his past who has expressed any interest in Morrissey's post-Smiths compositions is Sandie Shaw. Her association with Morrissey first came to light in April '84, when she had her first hit in fifteen years with a cover of the Smiths' first single, 'Hand In Glove'.

Shaw's latest acquisition will appear on her forthcoming album. 'Yes, it's called "Please

Help The Cause Against Loneliness" and it was originally written for *Viva Hate*. There wasn't enough space and it was frozen. Sandie picked it up and put it in the microwave.'

There may not be a queue of musicians begging to work with Morrissey, but there's little doubt that his work with the Smiths is highly valued by his peers.

Ex-Smiths bassist Andy Rourke regularly performs an onstage duet of 'The Hand That Rocks The Cradle' (from the Smiths' eponymously titled debut album) with Sinead O'Connor (ex-Smiths drummer Mike Joyce is also in her band) and many other artists have expressed an interest in covering Smiths songs.

Most surprisingly, perhaps, is the story that Dave Stewart of Eurythmics intends to cover 'Last Night I Dreamt That Somebody Loved Me'.

'Is that true?' asks Morrissey, somewhat startled.

'I get sent several tapes from people who are considering them and I get really disappointed when they're not released.'

Johnny Marr once said his ambition was to see someone get a Smiths cover version to number one.

'Oh yes, it would be wonderful, regardless of what position it received, but that would be great.'

You wouldn't be jealous?

'I'm not really a jealous person. I mean, I liked the Dream Academy version of *that* old Smiths song ['Please Please Please Let Me Get What I Want']. Everyone despised it and it got to number 81, which is nearly a hit.'

Two planned covers which excite Morrissey are Nottingham's Hope Augustus' release of 'There Is A Light That Never Goes Out' on WEA, and Kirsty MacColl's proposed 'You Just Haven't Earned It Yet, Baby' for the B-side of her next single.

MacColl, whose most recent success was a duet with Shane MacGowan on the Pogues' Christmas hit 'Fairytale Of New York', has worked with Morrissey before, performing backing vocals on the Smiths' 'Ask' and 'Golden Lights'.

But this enthusiasm pales next to his desire to work with, or even meet, Shirley Bassey.

'I went to see her last night, I thought she was excellent. I'd love to meet her, I'd love to touch the end of her dress.'

Clearly, Morrissey envies Shirley Bassey's stature.

'It's the kind of position I, not aspire to, but like the idea of. I don't think people consider me to be a superstar, or a world superstar, or a rock star or anything like that. I think I'm just considered to be a British phenomenon . . . as well as a sex symbol.'

So would you like to do . . .

'A nude centrefold?'

The theme tune to a Bond movie?

'No, what on earth for? Because *she* did it? Oh, I see.'

No, because Duran Duran did it.

'Yes, I would actually. I liked "Diamonds Are Forever", "Goldfinger", things like that.'

Sheena Easton did one as well.

'Could you name it though? "For Your . . . Legs Only"!?'

So you're *not* a big Sheena Easton fan?

'Not at the minute.'

You'll be taking the Shirley Bassey route to stardom then?

'Good heavens, that means I'd have to stay alive for another 22 years. Could you imagine that, it's a ghastly thought, all those Christmas *Morecambe and Wise Shows* . . . No, I'm alright actually, because they're already dead.'

Morrissey's solo career may not have been stunning to date, but at least he didn't simply try to emulate the Smiths. Instead, he had the *audacity* to be different and employ various styles.

The resulting *Viva Hate* album was disappointing but it had perfect moments, including the new single 'Everyday Is Like Sunday' – a perfect rebuff to the Cliff Richard 'Summer Holiday' hit syndrome with its drizzly chorus 'Everyday Is Like Sunday/Everyday is silent and grey.'

But it's really the B-side that holds the secrets to Morrissey's future.

'Will Never Marry', 'Sister I'm A Poet', and, particularly, 'Disappointed' indicate a turning point in his new career, a return to eloquence, satire, contempt and wit. Morrissey's trade marks before he forsook them for the elegant tranquility of *Viva Hate*.

Recorded two months ago, they also see the return of his old writing style – the first songs hot off the typewriter.

'They were the first three songs that I actually set down and pandered across. Which is probably quite awful to admit, but I had reached the stage where I no longer wanted to be intense. I wanted it to be straightforward and almost, in another way, I wanted everything else to take over. But that didn't really happen in the way people viewed the record. So many people who bought *Viva Hate* and bought Smiths records actually lived with the lyric sheet for days before they would play the record. So I think that's a unique position, but it's one that momentarily began to suffocate me slightly.'

What also makes the B-sides so important is a change in Street's music. They are much rounder and dare to employ devices one might associate with Johnny Marr.

Morrissey refutes the idea that Street held back on these more punchy numbers for fear of having his head nailed to the floor by critics for being too derivative of Marr. He considers the new compositions to be 'a progression from *Viva Hate*' and 'quite magical'.

He also denies that the change of mood had anything to do with his own influence, or that it was a conscious decision by Street 'to do something more aggressive'. But it has given Morrissey new confidence.

'Yes, I feel a bit happier with a pulverised manic sound.'

Ironically, 'Disappointed' sums up the new mood perfectly. Vini Reilly's reverberating guitar echoing Marr's 'How Soon Is Now?' style and accentuating Morrissey's kick in the eye to all those who would have seen him burn, hearing aid and all.

'This is the last song I will ever sing/No, I've changed my mind again/Goodnight and thank you . . .'

So typical of Morrissey. Just when you thought it was safe to put him on the chopping block, when you believed the omnipotent to be impotent, the bigmouth strikes again.

Sounds, 18 June, 1988

PLAYBOY OF THE WESTERN WORLD
—··— BY ELEANOR LEVY —··—

Morrissey puts his hand to his stomach, scrunches up his eyes in mock pain and – as genteely as such things can be – burps.

'Oh, excuse me,' he apologises.

A green bottle of Perrier water stands guiltily on the table between us, its former contents going down as well with the Morrissey digestive system as much of the great man's more inspired verbal moments have gone down with the musical establishment.

The Morrissey of 1989 is a very different figure from the one who first waved a bunch of gladioli around a Manchester concert hall. The pink and white striped shirt is crisp (and tucked in), the jeans are spotless, the shoes and hair gleam with newly accumulated prosperity. But as the ultimately tasteless mineral water is put to one side and the Mozz pours a comforting cup of quickly ordered tea, it's good to see that fine old traditions will always win out in the end.

The Smiths may be no more, Morrissey may well have, in his own words, 'recently become extremely wealthy', but the funny, infuriating, brilliant, arrogant yet self-deprecating Morrissey we've always known refuses to go away.

With the release of his finest solo offering to date in 'The Last Of The Famous International Playboys', it's comforting to know that in the supermarket shopping list of pop, the brand name Morrissey is still as dependable as ever.

QUESTION TIME

Why does 'The Last Of The Famous International Playboys' mention the Kray twins? It seems strange that you should feature such obviously southern 'heroes' in a song?

Yes well, they are known in the north, you know. We do have television now, although there's a slight shadow on the commercials.

What was it about them that fascinated you?

The level of notoriety that surrounded them – the level of fame they gained from being unreachably notorious. When you reach that stage, you are admired.

And it doesn't matter what you've done?

Well, no. The worse the merrier. There's a certain sense of glamour attached to being a notorious media figure . . . as I obviously know from experience!

Some people have such an immense physical and clinical need for fame and attention they'll do almost anything. Of course, if the law was such that we paid no attention whatsoever to mass murderers or great train robbers these people would be less inclined to put themselves out. Unfortunately, do a dirty deed and, hey presto . . . *News at Ten.*

Do you find it riveting?
Do I? No, I don't but the media seem to; they seem to quite enjoy it and they seem to enjoy it more if the attack's been upon women, particularly young women.

The sleeve of the single shows you at six years old – up a tree. Have you changed much since then?
Well, I have a new sweater.

What were your hopes and expectations at that age?
I didn't have any, I knew it was too late. That's why I was climbing that tree.

HISTORY TREE
Do you crave a number one single?
Well, I'll survive without one. It's really the only thing left that I haven't achieved. But it isn't crucial. So many fools get to number one it's hard to consider the position to be totally holy. But it would be quite nice.

There's been a long running debate in Record Mirror's *Letters page between fans of the Smiths and followers of . . .*
Stock, Face-ache and Waterbed. Yes, I did see it.

It seems you are seen as one end of the musical spectrum and they at the other.
Well, I tended to agree with the readers who didn't support Stock, Face-ache and Waterbed, who I obviously scratch my head at.
     It's comforting, though, for the Smiths to be considered as part of British pop history already.

Is it enough?
Not entirely, not entirely enough.

What would be enough?
That's a very loaded question. What *is* enough? I think – and this may sound odd – it will be on the day when I have powerful, serious contemporaries and it looks as though I'm finally being usurped, which some people think has already happened, although I don't. It's about time somebody else came along. Somebody should have replaced the Smiths; somebody should have replaced me.

People are desperately looking for someone.
Yes, but can you replace Stan Laurel? Can you replace Judy Garland? Can you replace Shirley Bassey? Can you replace Mrs Mangel? The list goes on . . .
     I don't say I'd like to be replaced, but it's important for the evolution of pop music that there are constantly changing voices. But they're nowhere to be seen; they're not coming and they couldn't possibly be further away than they are today.

PLAY TIME

Is it true you're a closet Manchester United fan?
It's a much guarded secret but yes, I do like football. To watch and follow, I don't spectate. I don't have the scarf, I don't have the hat . . .

It's a very easy way to escape mentally – it's light entertainment. I can just put on the television, watch a game of football, get the cans out and drift.

Have you ever dreamt of scoring the winning goal at Wembley?
Well, I suppose, in a sense I have. I can certainly get irate if somebody takes the wrong turning. Bryan Robson is impressive. And he lives quite near me. And there *are* sightings . . .

What do you think of Paul Gascoigne?
Well, he could do with a hair cut.

At least he's not Chris Waddle.
Well, there's only one Chris Waddle . . .

SHOW TIME

What was it like playing live again when you appeared in Wolverhampton in December?
It was nice. I did enjoy it. It was nice to be fondled.

Was it good to be back on stage?
No, it was just nice to be fondled.

I was a bit wobbly. I thought that as I was walking on stage I'd change direction, but I didn't. It was great to be back in the natural habitat.

How did it feel with Andy Rourke, Mike Joyce and Craig Gannon backing you?
Very tearful. There was a radiant feeling on stage. You knew where everybody was and who they were, which was astonishingly good. It was a really comfortable feeling. No, comfortable sounds like an old cardigan . . . but it was nice.

In an interview last year you said you hadn't heard from them since the Smiths split. You seemed bitter and hurt . . .
Well, I did feel a little upset but that has passed now.

How did you get back in touch?
Quite craftily. I asked somebody else to phone Mike, Andy and Craig to see if they'd be interested. If I'd have done it and they'd said no it would have been like a hammer blow.

So are the Smiths dead?
Well, they don't exist anymore. Did you know that? Well, the Smiths don't exist so, I suppose, in a round about way, that does mean they're dead. How can they be alive?

Rockin' with the crew: After his early solo period, Morrissey put together a regular band whose harder-edged style drew on influences from rockabilly to T.Rex.

You seem to be saying you'd still like to be the Smiths . . .
Well, I thought of the name and I thought it got better as time went by – the bigger the Smiths became, the funnier the name was.

So yes, when Johnny left I wanted to continue with the name but contractually it would have to have been agreed by both of us, and he did not agree.

Have you had any contact with Johnny since the split?
I haven't seen him since we were in the studio doing a song called 'I Keep Mine Hidden'. So that's 22 months ago.

Do you miss him?
Um . . . (*long pause*) . . . look, you can see the Pennines from this window . . .

CARTOON TIME
Would you say your eyebrows are your most recognisable feature?
Oh, they're almost Denis Healey proportions, really.

They don't curl up at the ends, though.
They don't. They're very well-behaved. They do exactly what I tell them to do.

When people draw cartoons of you, they pick up on two things – your eyebrows and your chin.
Well, the chin . . . The chin usually takes up half the page. And that Desperate Dan stubble! I mean, I might have five o'clock shadow but I never have stubble.

But yes, my chin is definitely centre stage. It makes me very self-conscious of this great big piece of furniture stuck on the lower half of my mouth. I'm not Bruce Forsyth by any means, though.

Who would play you in a biopic of your life?
Who would play me? What a great question. Who could possibly do it? Who do you think?

Perhaps Matt Dillon could look like you if he tried.
But he's American! Do you think he could? Physically, I suppose . . . with Sir John Gielgud's voice . . . or Dandy Nichols' . . . Is Clive Dunn still alive? That's the question.

TEA TIME

If you could give your name to an inanimate object that would forever bear the tag 'Morrissey', like Lord Sandwich did for two slices of bread or the Duke of Wellington for the boot, what would it be?
It would have to be something tasteful. I've seen my picture in a great deal of hairdressers. It would be nice to be noted for a particularly identifiable style. No, that's too easy. Tea, perhaps. Yes, that would be nice. Morrissey tea.

Finally, if someone from the past was told that in the 1980s there'd be this bloke called Morrissey who went on the telly with a hearing aid, a bunch of flowers, an old man's cardi, flapping his arms about . . . and would get in the top ten, they'd think a) you were mad and b) that it would be impossible – wouldn't they?
Well, it is for anybody else. If *you* were to put on an old man's cardigan, as you call it, and a hearing aid, you probably *wouldn't* get in the top ten. It's a gigantic fluke of nature, that's all I can say . . . and let's leave it at that!

Record Mirror, 11 February 1989

THE SOFT TOUCH

BY MAT SNOW

For a man who, in his time, has sprouted a bush from his back pocket, sheathed his torso in capacious ladies' blousewear from Evans Outsize, strung great ropes of bright plastic beads round his neck and, indeed, sported a conspicuously large, outmoded and quite unnecessary hearing-aid, the icon they call Morrissey seems ever so slightly rattled when asked about his latest contribution to the world of fashion and personal grooming.

'Aah, the question is so basic it's hard to answer: why did you shave your armpits ? I find it very fascinating. I did it for a long time, all through the Smiths' career and I still do it occasionally. I can't remember how it began. I don't think there's any great mystical reason. It's very natural,' laughs the eccentric Mancunian hitmaker uneasily. 'Surely you do the same?'

Can't say I do.

'Then you don't know what you're missing, haha!'

And what is your motive?

'Just extreme physical beauty, obviously. Surely you realise that?' he squirms, fiddling with his shoelace. 'This is the first time anybody's asked and I'm very embarrassed. It's not to make a point, or even taking oneself too seriously and trying to project a fascinating pop image. It's just a curious whim. I'm surprised it should be of any faint interest . . . It has a strangely serene quality, a smoothness to it.'

Then is it the sensation of shaving you like?

'No, hate it. But I never go a day without shaving. I had to shave when I was thirteen. That's reasonably young, isn't it? And I do not have a five o'clock but a two o'clock shadow.'

'But no, I've never shaved my legs . . .'

In February 1988, Morrissey's single 'Suedehead' became the first release on EMI's HMV label since Joyce Grenfell's 'I Wouldn't Go Back To The World I Never Knew', twenty years before. It was followed that March by his first solo LP, *Viva Hate*, and a cameo role in the *Brookside* spin-off *South*.

Since then, sightings of the man called Mozzer have been few and far between. The one live excursion was a free show held just before Christmas last year in the Wolverhampton Civic Hall where the only condition of entry was that you wore a T-shirt emblazoned with the Morrissey mug: 1,700 got in, but 2,000 were turned away amid scenes of mild pandemonium. As for records, the non-LP singles 'Interesting Drug' and 'The Last Of The Famous International Playboys' have been seized on by fans as bulletins of where Morrissey's head is currently at. While he has maintained, these past eighteen months, an uncharacteristic near-silence, rumours have flourished.

What is known is that after an acrimonious split with his musical collaborator

Stephen Street, Morrissey is now recording with Clive Langer and Alan Winstanley, best known for their productions of Madness and Elvis Costello's *Punch The Clock* LP. The first fruits of this new partnership are the new single, 'Ouija Board, Ouija Board', and the flip, a cover of 'East West', originally by those sixties pop sensations from Manchester, Herman's Hermits. Having oscillated between London and Manchester since the Smiths' first flush of national success in late '83, Morrissey is back in his hometown, for the time being at least, back among his roots.

Does 'Ouija Board, Ouija Board' denote an interest in the occult?
I've always had an interest in the occult, but not an inexhaustible interest, just a passing interest. I had an experience in 1984. I lived in a rented flat for a while and there was definitely a presence, and a friend of mine who is a medium came to the flat, and I didn't tell her that I'd had vibrations. When she came in she immediately went into a semi-trance, walked around every corner of the flat and stood outside the bathroom door and said, It's here. It's coincidental that each time I'd stepped outside the bathroom, even though I'd always keep the heating on really high, I'd felt a great chill.

I found out that somebody had died in the flat – the usual story – but I didn't feel any hostility. It was calming, really, in the simple sense that I didn't feel any danger or horror. It was the kind of feeling you get when a real human being walks into the room.

I've tried it on occasion, with friends, to make contact, as it were, but nothing has really ever happened; the pressure on the glass has always come from the same index finger. I try to instil a degree of humour in the record. I know it isn't terribly apparent, but I find it amusing.

The song is primarily me, once again for the 8,000th time, losing faith in the human race and almost turning to the other side of life for communion and friendship.

Have you ever turned to religion?
At no time. I am a seriously lapsed Catholic. It was at the usual time, ten, eleven, twelve, after being forced to go to church and never understanding why and never enjoying it, seeing so many negative things, and realising it somehow wasn't for me. I can only have faith in things I see. I could never be converted to Buddhism.

The new single is your first collaboration with Langer and Winstanley. Why them?
I was a serious Madness fan years ago, and that's how I knew of them. It was largely their sense of perverse fun I quite liked. I never considered the records to be standard pop fare. I quite liked the peculiarity. People say music hall, which I suppose is quite true.

Rumour has it your first ever collaborator was Billy Duffy, now guitarist with the Cult.
Yes, it was for two weeks in 1979. I met him and we wrote some songs and joined the rhythm section of what had been the Nosebleeds, of which Vini Reilly had briefly been guitarist. But yes, Billy Duffy was the first person I wrote songs with, and in fact he pushed Johnny Marr in my direction, which was very decent of him. But he made very negative comments about the Smiths some years ago, and I find it hard to forgive him.

Rumour also has it that you drive a white Golf GTi.

I do possess one but it's mostly driven by other people. I can drive but I don't have a licence – I've never taken the test. But rather than hiring cars at every opportunity, it's just become easier for me to hire a person who can drive, which is how I move around.

Do you have a personal staff?
No, I don't have a manager. I don't have anybody who works for me at all. But occasionally I have a friend who I'll pay for a certain period when I have to do something, and he'll drive.

Is it a full-time job being Morrissey professionally?
Yes, it is, because if I'm not in the process of making an actual record, there are many other things that have to be done. I have to see lawyers a great deal; there's always ongoing court cases that I have to deal with. Currently in dispute is a case with Mike Joyce, the Smiths' drummer, and a case with Craig Gannon, who worked with the Smiths for a while. Both are claiming, as usual, percentages and so forth. Mike Joyce is demanding 25 per cent of everything the Smiths ever earned. To talk about it now would be slightly unpleasant. But in a small way it's always happened. There's always a tour manager who pops up demanding more, there's always somebody who claims to have been your manager and who is claiming more. I think it's just par for the course. All the Smiths companies are defunct, but I'm being sued as an individual, as a former director. Every day of my life I have letters from lawyers, whether it's mine or somebody else's. It's extremely depressing, but to be seen to be complaining about it is, I think, to the general public, unnecessary. I don't think they want to know about this. Certain people would look at my life now and say, How could you possibly complain compared to what you once were? In a way that's true, but it still doesn't make it any easier to deal with the constant barrage of offensive letters. But I can't remember a period in my career when there wasn't something ongoing, somebody who had managed to get legal aid and had decided to chase you for every penny you have, and that seems to be happening more and more.

Your time and energy must be severely taxed.
I don't know how I get the fortitude to deal with that kind of thing, and as a consequence, in the public sense, over the last couple of years my activities have slowed down somewhat. I've had to put so much energy into other areas. With the Smiths I had a great need to oversee as much as physically and mentally possible, and that's how my life has continued. I dislike it a great deal and wish I could find a body of people who I could work with, who were my friends but were also very strong and could deal with certain things and be with me all the time. It would make it easier to do more. But I can't find those people, which you might find slightly absurd. You either end up with the manager who wants 99 per cent of what you earn and can only see you in terms of earning and working as much as possible, which I totally despise, or you do as I do, which is deal directly with a lawyer and an accountant.

Was covering a Herman's Hermits tune by way of reaffirming your roots in sixties Manchester?

Yes, it was, and also a way of saying goodbye to certain things, a certain period in my life. Perhaps not directly a sixties obsession, because I think all that's fading away and the world of the single is fading away, which was obviously the world of Herman's Hermits.

Were the songs 'Suffer Little Children' and 'The Last Of The Famous International Playboys', concerning respectively the Moors Murders and the Kray Twins, about the working out of childhood memories?
In a sense, yes. A lot of people are very intolerant of any sixties obsession. It just does- n't seem to wash anymore with people; they're tired of the 1960s, they're exhausted at the whole Beatles myth and so forth. Personally, I find the story of Madness more interesting than the story of the Beatles. But I never for a second intended the Moors Murders to be, if you like, part of my history. And I never wanted the whole sixties thing to be part of my history. But it has become that, and I feel I have to move away from that. And I want to, also. 'East West' was just closing the door and saying good- bye. But that doesn't mean I'm now moving forward to 1974. With the passing of time, I, like most people, can see the sixties and seventies much more clearly. At the time they were meaningless, because the present is always meaningless. Looking back fascinates me, how things change and how, in some ways, things don't change. When I think back to the period of Silver Convention and music like that, I feel very much that is how the chart is now.

Do you listen to chart radio?
No, I never listen to the radio, but pop music is absolutely the soundtrack to my life. I can hear 'Pretty Flamingo' and it reminds me of a particular time. One way or another I get to hear most things in the Top 40, though to be honest I don't know who most of the people are. But one somehow eventually stumbles across these records; one hears them on television in other programmes, which is strictly a late eighties phenomenon. Obviously, in the seventies you never heard pop music at all.

So you're still a pop fan?
Very much so. I've bought a lot of things recently just to listen to and then throw them away. I'm still a big record fan. I really enjoyed the Black Box single. It's odd for me because it's not my world at all and there's no reason on earth why I should enjoy that record, but when I first saw them on *Top of the Pops* I thought it was pretty extreme. She also looked brilliant, and I still love the record after nine weeks.

And the revelation that it is not, in fact, her voice?
I'm more interested in the rumours that she has been male. I'm hoping that it's true because it makes it more interesting. If you look at her from a certain angle, you could possibly see her playing for Wigan.

Yet when 'Reel Around The Fountain' was released in '83 and the tabloids mistaken- ly accused it of being a celebration of paedophilia, presumably readers took a similar prurient interest?

I find transsexuality very interesting but, yes, it's probably the same feeling. At the time I was feeling very browbeaten. It's quite different when you're on the receiving end of what set out to be smears. Sometimes I can read pretty revealing stories about certain people which are supposed to be damaging, but they just increase the admiration I have for them. But I'd rather not name anybody.

Do you feel your fans who queued in Wolverhampton in midwinter and got soaked, cold, manhandled by police and still *didn't get in might have felt a little cheesed off with you?*
I didn't meet anybody who was. They didn't have to come if they didn't want to; they must have been aware of a certain element of risk. It isn't my fault if at the final minute someone came from the back with huge muscles and removed them. It's symptomatic, I think, of life in general.

Was the show an effort on your part to recreate the hysteria surrounding your own idols of the sixties and seventies?
Believe it or not, that always happened with the Smiths anyway. Even abroad it was very expressive and extreme and even violent. But I thought a free concert was a very good gesture. I couldn't think of anyone who'd done it in recent years. I was and still am in a situation where I could sit down with some very heavy money moguls and organise huge tours with highly inflated ticket prices. I don't do that because it's against my nature. So I thought above all people would see a free concert as a very welcome gesture, regardless of who got their sandals stolen or dropped their crisps in a puddle. In the hall that night there was a great aura of love and gentleness, and all the people who came on stage treated me in a very gentle way. I wasn't kicked or punched or dragged, although they were very emotionally charged. I came away with no bruises.

Do you thus feel an affinity between your fans and acid house ravers?
Yes, but I think that with the Smiths and my audience there was never a drug element at all. 'Interesting Drug' is about any drug, legal or illegal. We have to face the very simple fact that drugs can help people in many ways. Even with acid house parties and constant police invasions, it almost seems to me that whenever people in working class situations try to enjoy themselves or escape from what is forced upon them, they are stopped. It's almost as if this current government want people to be sheepish and depressed and not seen, and whenever they attempt to break out of that bubble, they are hit on the head.

Don't you think the powers-that-be are 'cracking down' on acid parties principally because the noise and traffic causes a public nuisance?
I think that's also true, but I think it's more than that – a slightly disturbing element of keeping people in their place, which is the basic law where drugs are concerned: people can't have drugs because it makes them see or want to do more than they should. But I have no experience of acid parties; I have never been to one.

Has your audience changed over the years?

I've noticed dramatic additions and I've noticed that a lot of the crusty old faithfuls have strayed somewhat, away from music. Even initially there were older types and younger types. But now I meet so many people who never saw the Smiths because they're fifteen years of age and so to them they're simply a legend. I'm astonished by the variation in types of people who stop me on the street. It can be very fresh-faced young fans, and it can be very serious people who are . . . heh, heh . . . shall we say middle-aged? In the prime of their lives, ha ha! Quite largely they're very normal people which is very entertaining. Quite often if you only read the normal media blurbs on me you'd assume I could only appeal to people who'd either suffered a recent loss or paint themselves black from head to foot, ha ha!

When you were a teenager, were you a fan of Buffy Saint-Marie and the New York Dolls at the same time?

Yes! Which really made me what I am today. If I was simply a hard-edged Stooges, Dolls buff as there were quite a few of in the late seventies, I'd probably be in the Alarm playing bass. I'm not because I can also appreciate people like Buffy Saint-Marie. I'm a little bit of each now, but not totally a great deal of either. But even today I get very excited by Buffy Saint-Marie. I thought she had a great voice and great passion. In 1964 she was singing about drugs in a very exciting way: 'My mother, my father, said whiskey's a curse, but the fate of their baby's a million times worse . . .' This was 1964: The Beatles were singing 'She loves you, yeah yeah.' It didn't catch on and I can't imagine why. A very underrated artist; there's millions of them.

Do you like artists because *they're underrated?*

If I like them and they're slighted, the only instinct I have is to assemble a placard. Certainly, if people die and their deaths are overlooked, I feel I have to do something about it, I have to speak for them. Even with the recent death of Bette Davis, which I thought was typically slighted by the entire media, as if nobody cared. Here was this absolute, total legend, possibly the very last one, and I have the impression that if Joanna Lumley had died it would have gained more space, which foxes me. I'm generally attracted to people who are mildly despised and Bette Davis was. I bought all the newspapers the day after her death, expecting huge, blinding banner headlines. But it was simply 'The Bitch Is Dead', on page fifteen, which I found astonishing. I just assume it's a new generation of journalists who don't really know and don't really care. Perhaps it's too long ago. I think that people do forget. Bette Davis was a very formidable spirit who risked going against audience sympathy to get what she wanted, risked narrowing her audience to convey how she really felt. Which is quite largely how I feel about my career. I'd rather walk away than do anything unnatural. I appreciate that spirit because it's very, very rare – and extremely rare in dear old pop music, if it exists at all.

What about Madonna, whom once you dismissed?

I do have a slightly altered view of Madonna. I can see how her career could be considered very determined, a person who absolutely pleases herself, which is quite good.

She doesn't give interviews, which is very impressive, and she works a great deal. I can see she has remained true to herself over the last five years. She will go down in pop history as a legend.

It is often held that the pop star's most common motivation is the desire to leapfrog an adolescent lack of self-esteem. Your story too?
With me it was being overlooked. Also, an intensified shyness yet a desperation to do it, like someone who really wants to sing but prays that nobody asks. Very confused. Revenge initially was a strong element for me. In a meek way I tried for many years to do something quite useful and visible, and nobody ever wanted to help me or take my calls, whether it be trying to break into music journalism or trying to form a group. I remember once, a long time ago, somebody at the *NME* slamming the phone down when I called, and that seemed to be the last straw in a bucket of many, many straws. Yet to say now that that might be the basis of one's career seems childish. It obviously isn't; I do enjoy every aspect of what I do.

The fame?
There are so many mountainous myths surrounding recording, performing, and being on television, and these myths don't seem to collapse. People do assume that if you're engaged in this whirlwind that you're surrounded by friends, enormously rich, the world is at your fingertips, you have enormous ease and the pick of the crowd, which has never ever been true in my case, nor in the performers I personally know. I could phone up certain people who are, if you like, famous every Monday night at eight o'clock and they're sitting at home. And they're quite frustrated and they want to go out and meet people and make friends, and it's very hard. Yet they sell enormous amounts of records.

It becomes impossible because of the public's method of approach. It takes a very long time to make friends with people, and if you're walking down the road and suddenly there's somebody talking to you who you don't know and have never met, yet they know you and they know what they want to say and they want an instant reaction, it's very, very difficult. Personally, I just begin to clam up. I think sometimes people become confused by a lack of response, but it's an alarmingly unnatural situation.

Even though you may go out with the aim of meeting people and having a good time, it isn't that easy when that other person conceivably knows everything intimately or professionally about you, and you know nothing about that person. And that person seems to have very strong views on you and your life. That person is a great deal up on you. The situation is very unbalanced. Sometimes I feel that the only friends performers can have are other performers, but then there's that strange jealousy, that strange air of competition that creeps in. I've never felt it because I've always been happy with my status; it's very respectable and useful. I've never wanted to be part of the global pop aristocracy. I've never wanted to play Wembley.

Does it bother you that the likes of Sting, whose music you don't care for, can use his status to draw attention to a cause you also endorse?
It's encouraging, but he also draws attention to the fact that he's bored stiff – bored

with his career, bored with making music, he's bored with rain forests. Sometimes it can be useful, but now causes within music are so common that I think the record has to be incredibly good to prove that the political cause is useful. Unfortunately, look at *Spirit Of The Forest* which had enormous publicity yet sold twelve copies.

Do you worry that a record might flop?

I don't, because people tell me that there's no way it can, because I seem to have a very loyal audience who are waiting for the day of release. I suppose, like most things, it must end eventually. I think when there is a visible dip I wouldn't continue. We only realise something's of value if people want it, and if they begin not to want it, then why persist? I don't think longevity is a particularly good thing. Some artists are extremely powerful within a short space. But I don't see the point with certain artists just staying around and applauding themselves for the fact that they're still standing and this is their hundredth single. So what?

Perhaps they don't realise their work is now substandard. Would you?

Yes, I think I would because I have a reasonably serious audience, who think very deeply about the things I do. They criticise me a great deal, and most of the time they're wrong. Sometimes they're right. But because they're so staunchly loyal, if they deserted me in a large number, I think it would be more than coincidental. Obviously I must have come out of the wrong lift somewhere on the way.

Q, December 1989

LYRICAL KING
—— •─── BY STEVEN DALY ───• ——

A fire crackles in the hearth, a fax machine purrs in the distance, and a handful of Italian fashion mags nestle in the rack as Morrissey reclines on his favourite chaise longue, contemplating life without the Smiths.

'I didn't have any high expectations of my solo career. There are lots of lead singers in groups who attempt solo careers and it never happens. Mick Jagger couldn't sell a solo record to save his life, so why should it happen to me?

'I think a lot of people were very, very surprised that I've continued to sell records. The general opinion was that once Johnny Marr unplugged that umbilical cord I would just kind of deflate like a paddling pool.'

There's little smugness in this softly spoken statement, but perhaps there should be. Since the dissolution of that prolific partnership, Morrissey has remained, as ever, just 'Morrissey', while it is guitarist Johnny Marr, hotly tipped as a long-term talent, who bears the markdown tag 'ex-Smith' as he languishes among minor rock royalty, a Jeff Beck for the nineties, eighteenth in line to the Traveling Wilburys' throne.

By the final Smiths album, *Strangeways, Here We Come*, there were strong hints that Marr had stripmined his record collection once too often, that Morrissey might profitably seek fresh settings for his finely tuned couplets and overwrought emotions. These he found, from the stentorian strings of 'Everyday Is Like Sunday' to the baroque bathos of the current single, 'Our Frank', the best of his post-Smiths work. Morrissey is a man still at the top of his game.

Considering the prodigious output of the Smiths, though, these have been an alarmingly peaceful couple of years for Steven Morrissey. The period since *Viva Hate* has been marked only by the sporadic release of what the singer has called 'funny little singles' (recently assembled on the *Bona Drag* compilation). To the new studio album, *Kill Uncle*, we must therefore apply, must we not, the prickly term 'comeback'?

'Well, I haven't been anywhere, but I suppose some people will view it as a new beginning.'

How would you, I ask, define the progression from *Viva Hate*?

'I think it's a much better record, particularly in terms of lyrics. Beyond that I can't really say much because it is still basically my voice, and I only have one voice. And it is still what's considered to be a very traditional musical line-up.'

Do you ever feel constricted by such orthodoxy?

'No I don't. I absolutely don't. I don't really have anything to do with the music industry. I don't possess instruments and amplifiers, I don't have a studio tucked away in the basement. Pushing musical barriers doesn't interest me at all, I just have a particular instinct that I follow. Which is less to do with music than it's to do with other things like the voice and words. I do absolutely understand the construction of the

113

song, but as far as creating a new form of music that has never been heard before . . .'

That kind of thing is best left to bands such as Nelson and Wilson Phillips. I was thinking, though, in terms of different approaches to production.

'Well, the Smiths were never terribly well-produced, terribly polished – it doesn't mean the records were bad of course, because they weren't – but when I listen to a lot of the Smiths' discography I wince slightly and decry the fact that we were often forced to do things under somewhat threadbare conditions.'

Surely after racking up a few hit albums you could have demanded a modicum of luxury?

'Not really, because we were terribly eager and polite, and therefore you just wake up and do it. You realise later that things could have been slightly better, that if someone had made a significant phone call you could have been reasonably pampered.'

Which, presumably, you are these days.

'Yeah, definitely reasonably pampered.'

Getting one's due, as it were.

'Well it's about time,' he concludes with a trace of indignation.

Though Morrissey's tendency to draw from a comfortable pool of musical references can occasionally be infuriating, he is of course one of the lyrical miracles of our time, someone who can legitimately claim to have expanded the poetic vocabulary of the popular song, dragging it into the heretofore-unexamined realm of hairdressers on fire and girlfriends in comas. Not to mention the sackload of other ticklish taboo subjects he's tackled.

'I don't know what makes them taboos – I don't recall anybody appearing on television and saying, "If you happen to be thinking of writing a song tonight, don't forget that you must not . . ." I've never come across any written guidelines, but obviously we know the society we live in, and we know what gets people's backs up. And anything vaguely real tends to ruffle people's feathers.'

So these subjects attract you?

'No, not at all,' he says innocently, then titters. 'It's just the world I live in, the state of mind I tend to have.'

Well, songs like 'Bengali In Platforms', and the new one, 'Asian Rut', tend to arouse suspicion. It's highly unusual to write about Britain's Asian community.

'I disagree. There are a lot of Asian people, so why is it unusual?'

I was merely curious. It *is* an unusual subject, one that certainly wouldn't crop up in, say, a Prefab Sprout song.

'But surely that tells you more about Paddy McAloon [Prefab Sprout's singer/songwriter] than about me. I'm actually a fan of his; I criticised him recently and slightly regretted it, even though I believed what I said. I thought the first record that he made was reasonably priceless.'

Are there any other of your peers worthy of your attention?

'Yes, there are a few. I was terribly fond of Paul Weller.'

From her guest shot on Morrissey's too wacko-for-most single 'November Spawned A Monster' we can assume that quirky Canadian canary Mary Margaret O'Hara can join this stellar company. What brought them together?

'A great gust of wind,' proclaims Morrissey with a flourish. 'I was very attracted by her eccentricity, so I though she'd work quite well; and as it turned out she was quite perfect. I find it fascinating that someone can vocalise without using specific words.'

Like Liz Fraser and the Cocteau Twins, right?

'They make me vomit on sight,' he declares, sobering up instantly. 'I think there's a right way and a wrong way, and I think the Cocteau Twins have always applauded themselves for doing it the wrong way. They're outstandingly unappealing on every human level; they look awful, their interviews are awful, and their records are just utter stupidity.'

Jeepers, I cry. I seem to have touched a nerve.

'It's the way you're sitting.'

'I've calmed down slightly since the Smiths,' Morrissey contends. 'I'm not as desperately eager as I once was, and I'm very happy about that. I think it makes me a slightly more adjusted human being.'

As we gaze out on the well-manicured garden of Morrissey Mansions, situated on the outskirts of Manchester, I wonder if this newfound contentment might not endanger his creative impulse.

'No, because I still make the crucial error of believing that records I make are my life. But these days I want to be slightly more methodical. I do realise that I have an audience and that they would possibly like me to be on television a lot more than I am, but I can only orchestrate things in a natural way. There's nothing show business about me, nothing at all. Sometimes I'm astonished that I manage to do as much as I do when I consider how detached I am. You don't seem very convinced . . .'

Well, the detached part certainly rings true: One can't help hearing stories about Morrissey breaking off friendships and doing so 'big-style'.

'I'm a terribly glamorous person, you know, I like to do everything big-style. But when I fall out with people there are usually certain contractual things involved.'

Does this carry over into your personal life?

'Usually not, no. Though I don't suffer fools gladly. I feel that if someone lets me down or crosses me, if I phone and they don't reply, well that's it, the drawbridge goes up.'

Where do you seek outside stimulus? I see the odd theatrical biography scattered around.

'Oh yes, I'm terribly clichéd,' he grins bashfully. 'It's books and videos . . . and lawsuits.

'I think I probably do all the things people expect me to do. It's all very private and very quiet, I don't see that many people. I do have some friends. I'm not as overbearingly intense as everybody thinks.

'The life I lead is reasonably routine. I have no notions of travel. I see holiday advertisements on the television, and I don't know what they are. I never, ever go on holiday. Though I'd quite like to lie on a beach in the sun which I don't think I've ever done, being one of the old British Brigade.'

Surely, I probe, the accumulated wealth of the Smiths' years combined with today's major-label moolah must significantly alter the outlook of the man who mined this former *petit bourgeois* poverty for so many *verité* nuggets?

'I don't have an exotic lifestyle. I know that people think that if one is vaguely famous then you belong to this celebrity community, but I need hardly say that I have not filled in that application form. Well I did, but it was rejected.'

One thing that certainly doesn't exercise the Morrissey mind these days is inventing pissy quotes for journalists. A handful of less-than-favourable notices in the British pop papers has resulted in a virtual embargo on interviews, depriving Morrissey's apostles of his once-regular epigrammatic epistles.

'The last few times I've been interviewed there has been enormous conviviality between me and the journalist, yet what emerges in print is generally unpleasant because of recent trends.'

Recent trends?

'I think sympathy for me in England has disappeared slightly,' he explains. 'I think there is a general rule that you have your time, and then it has to be somebody else. And I don't think it matters what your standard of work is – you can make bad records when the wind is in your favour, as it were, and you will always be warmly reviewed, then you can make records at another time and nobody cares.'

Surely it was Morrissey who set the tenor of his relationship with the press by his willingness to, at the slightest prompting, let loose with splenetic quips directed at the transient talents of the day. Could it be, I venture, that his role as the portable curmudgeon has backfired on him?

'Not really, because if you say, "I'm not interested," or, "I have no thoughts on . . ." they just assume that you're slipping slightly and that you're not as in tune as you should be. I don't feel obliged to keep up, and I'm not embarrassed if I don't know. I don't care to be abreast of trends and times.'

Before the present press clampdown, a regular fixture of the Morrissey interview would be a call to insurrection, a plea for the younger generation to take up arms and establish its very own hegemony, an aesthetic coup like the one he and his fellow punk rockers once plotted. Well what do you know, with groups like the Happy Mondays, the Stone Roses, and their perpetually blooming progeny, it looks like he's got the revolution he ordered, with its source, ironically enough, in his beloved hometown of Manchester. Or has he?

'I feel numb with disappointment,' Morrissey says with customary understatement. 'I honestly believe that the records aren't good enough. Though it's very hard to judge when so much hype surrounds the situation. It's almost as if there came a certain time when the music press, which is where it all started, decided that this must happen in order to give the papers themselves extended life, because things were very dull at the time.'

While I take deep issue with his chronology, I concur with Morrissey's assessment of the smothering attention paid to marginal talents who, faced with the obligatory backlash, will rapidly find themselves back behind the counter of the local 7-Eleven. But is he confident that the young Smiths would have survived such premature acclaim?

'Yes, because a lot of these newer groups don't release records very often, and I don't think have many songs. I find that a lot of their songs are stretched out and fleshed out, which was obviously never the case with the Smiths.

'I think if it's a question of individualism then nobody can stop you. But if you don't have that individualism then it won't happen. So I must be honest and, without being particularly rude to anybody or wishing to sound totally damning of the situation, I'm not aware of any individualism in Manchester at the moment.'

With such ignominious developments on his own doorstep, one would hardly blame Morrissey for simply taking the only way out left to an English gentleman. Yes, touring America.

Despite his reversal of fortune in the UK, his star continues to rise stateside, where fans nurture dim memories of the Smiths' last triumphant tour in 1986. ('Let's just say someone lost a leg,' Morrissey says cryptically of the jaunt's premature end.) The 'most poignant' of his fan mail these days bears an American postmark, while he describes last year's on-air appearance at Los Angeles radio station KROQ as 'very, very emotional'.

Morrissey appears poised to make significant impact to the world's biggest record-buying market, but he remains rather less than gung-ho at the prospect.

'I totally, absolutely wanted to be a British pop artist, which is what I became. I just wanted British success because I don't travel very well, I tend to have terrible spasms in airports; I can't really pack a suitcase, and I don't leave England very often. So the idea of running around the world in a pair of Lycra bicycle shorts is not very appealing.'

Presumably, though, this has to be faced at some point during your solo career?

'Well yes, it will be. But without the Lycra shorts.'

Intimate apparel aside, does the thought of all that hard slog put you off?

'No, no, it doesn't put me off, I'd like to do it. It's just that keeping a personal grip on the situation is very daunting.'

Does that mean there's a reluctance to go all the way in America?

'Hmm, all the way . . . I'll definitely get as far as Connecticut. I don't feel that if I tour America I'll instantly become one of the world's biggest recording artists – I don't think I ever will because of the way I am as a person. I could never have huge, suffocating mass appeal because, to begin with, I'm too intelligent.'

Even if you say so yourself . . .

'No, that's the opinion of others! I think that if and when I go to America it will be quite successful, but I don't think I'd ever make a very good American rock star. At all cost, however I'm displayed, it must be me and how I am. Once again, it must be strictly on my own terms.'

Alas, Morrissey professes to be nowhere near finding that elusive 'body of people' with whom he could confidently undertake a tour.

'It's very difficult because I don't socialise and it wouldn't occur to me to advertise. So when you don't socialise and you don't advertise' – he trails off laughing – 'you're reasonably limited.

'I have very strict guidelines, very strict rules of basic taste in human beings as well as in music, which narrows life somewhat. Either the situation is right or, as in most cases, it's wrong.

'I get a lot of approaches from people who want to manage me, but they seem to always spell my name wrong or say something wrong. I'm not interested in a money mogul or anybody who wants to ram me down the public's throat. I have never been rammed down anybody's throat, and I think that's why the audience has remained very loyal. They appreciate the fact that it was a very honest success.'

But who are these 'loyal' supporters who have buoyed Morrissey's fortunes even amid the direct predictions of artistic bankruptcy and commercial decline?

'I'm not sure, I can't tell. I prefer not to think that they're all of a particular breed. I don't think that's true. In fact I'm very surprised at the style of certain people who are interested in me.'

Of course there is, I note, the stereotypical view of the typical Morrissey fan.

'Yes, yes, the hysteric depressive who rarely leaves the closet under the stairs.'

But you find otherwise?

'No.'

Sorry? I thought you just said –

'Yes, I do.'

So they're normal people then?

'I'm hesitant to use the word *normal*, but since you've used it I will.'

Everyday folks . . .

'Everyday folks with everyday tales of everyday sadness.'

We both howl with laughter at this.

Does Morrissey think that he is as important in the lives of his followers as the New York Dolls and Patti Smith were to him back in the day?

'I think I'm more important because to begin with I sell more records than they ever did, and by the tone of letters and conversations a lot of them know me more intimately than they know their own friends. Well, they believe they know me more intimately, though in fact they don't really.'

Do you find it all a bit disconcerting?

'It's a very awkward situation. I get very embarrassed and self-conscious because I feel that if I were to sneeze when I met one of them it would be described halfway around America.'

He must by now accept that for many of these obsessive fans, sex is an intense part of his appeal. Does his oft-stated unavailability serve to heighten this?

'I don't think it increases it, I think it's part of it. The confessional aspect is part of it; being very, very open about innermost feelings is, I think, quite unusual. I simply don't believe it when somebody tells me that physically I am what they've always wanted. If they don't know me personally, which is usually the case, then it becomes very abstract. I certainly never, ever feel, even in my most self-opinionated moment, that I am a sex symbol. But to some people I am.'

You often say that the energy that others expend on love and sex, you put into your work . . .

'That's very, very true because I think human beings are only capable of concentrating on one thing . . . mostly. I think you either go one way or the other.'

Given Morrissey's cerebral bent and his well-known aversion to dance music, did it irk him to see former confederate Johnny Marr working with the New Order/Pet Shop Boys aggregate Electronic?

'I stayed awake for three nights worrying,' he remarks tartly. 'No, I don't think anything at all crossed my mind. I don't monitor Johnny's movements. I don't know anything about his life other than what people tell me. I thought the record Electronic released was totally useless.'

'Getting Away With It'?

'Yes, very apt title.'

This is more like it. You don't have much time for the Pet Shop Boys then?

'No, not at all.'

Some see you as kindred spirits, I prod.

'I get very angry with artists who have it easy,' says Morrissey gravely, 'who don't really put that much into what they do, who fall into favour with people who expect nothing of them.'

But for all you know, Neil Tennant may be stretching to the utmost of his abilitis.

'I didn't mention Neil Tennant – I was talking about Engelbert Humperdink.'

Another well-worn Morrissey theme is that pop, as we knew it, has ceased to exist, that for one reason or another the form has been systematically drained of every drop of vitality.

'I still believe that, and as time goes by I believe it more strongly; I do see an enormous amount of mental decay. I think it's over, I really do.'

Cause of death, Quincy?

'I think possibly the realisation that the albums and the concerts which have become important are those which cost a lot of money and are a lot of trouble to produce. I think that's because so many artists are managed by accountants now. Music isn't as special in 1991 as it was in the years when you could watch punk unfolding. Because punk was something that was happening for the very, very first time; there is very little that occurs now in music that is really happening for the first time.'

Thus, Morrissey explains, the recurring fascination with the cultural fertile period of his early youth.

'You look back at the films and music of that time and you just hear a certain appealing naïveté, an innocence that no longer exists. Now we all know far too much for our own good. Back then it didn't matter if you didn't become a millionaire, it didn't matter if you didn't eke out some fantastic career for yourself. It was just good enough to exist, and to have a bit of fun.

'I think the world has speeded up in every way, and that people in 1991 are heavily burdened with this enormous pressure to be perfect, to be enormously interesting and successful. I think that's unfortunate and it makes people very unhappy.'

Continuing on this dolorous note, Morrissey laments the passing of another much-eulogised commodity – Englishness.

'England is not England in any real sense of the world, it has been internationalised, and that's screechingly evident wherever you look around the country. The English people are not strong enough to defend their sense of history. Patriotism doesn't really matter anymore. So I think England has died.'

Last year he found his Anglocentric sentiments echoed in the unlikeliest of places: 'The only time I thought Mrs. Thatcher made a sensible statement in her entire career was her defence of sterling. She was laughed out of Parliament.'

He refers to Thatcher's stand against the prospect of a single European currency, which Morrissey thinks 'has to happen. If we meet in two years, you and I will be speaking French.'

So what was Morrissey's reaction when the Iron Lady was finally hauled off to the scrap yard?

'Well, not the reaction that people may expect me to have. I thought the way she was quite literally publicly beheaded was outrageous. I found it astonishingly un-English and very strange.'

Momentito – have we all been misinterpreting 'Margaret On The Guillotine' all these years?

'Her policies, I thought, were the work of the Devil. I thought she was purely, intentionally evil,' Morrissey grins. 'But it's impossible to deny that she was a phenomenon, and you couldn't help but overdiscuss her. The blunder wasn't that she was decapitated, but that she hasn't effectively been replaced. I think that John Major is in nobody's mind a Prime Minister; he seems to have no human presence at all.'

To my shame I repeat a current rumour concerning the sex life of the apparently personality-free Major.

'Well, that's the first interesting thing I've heard about him. Now he deserves to be Prime Minister.'

There follows an ill-advised attempt on my part to pursue a line of questioning about northern English culture – not in relation to the current Manchester scene, but as it pertains to Morrissey's work, to his iconography.

'What, like James Dean and Joe D'Allesandro?'

No, obviously I . . . knew . . .

'Well, I don't consider myself part of a line of great northern comedians, if that's what you mean.'

Oh, I don't know –

'I think that has to be the last word.'

As I don my galoshes for the trek back toward central Manchester, I ask whether Morrissey has yet had a chance to see *The Krays*, the celluloid biography of the twin London gangsters referenced in the exquisite 'The Last Of The Famous International Playboys'. He hasn't, but remains curious as to its content. It transpires that Morrissey was himself name-checked by Reggie Kray in his recently published book. He plucks the tome from his enviable library and indicates the relevant passage:

'There was even a hit single about us, Morrissey's "The Last Of The Famous International Playboys" in January 1989. I liked the tune, but the lyrics in their entirety were lacking a little. They came quite close . . .'

'Just my luck,' sighs Morrissey. 'I can't get away from critics.'

Spin, April 1991

MORRISSEY COMES OUT!
(FOR A DRINK)
———•—— BY STUART MACONIE ——•———

From the look of things, reports of his death have been greatly exaggerated. He sits casually on a barstool, sipping large glasses of Pils and smiling.

He's an unmistakable figure, even though there are certain unusual accoutrements: the beer, the magenta nail varnish, the T-shirt, with its garish illustration of legs ending in half-mast jeans and fearsome sixteen-hole 'Docs', and bearing the legend 'Skins: Alive And Kicking'. In fact, I don't think I'd be surprised if he pulled a Woodbine from behind his ear.

He sits at the centre of a boisterous, wisecracking group. It could be any bunch of Saturday night barroom revellers. But it is not. 'So this is what they mean by an entourage,' he jokes, indicating the group around him with a sweep of his hand; the journalist, the press officer, the personal assistants and, at his right hand, the band – four young bucks in quiffs, tattoos and drainpipes, enjoying the beer and the atmosphere, looking for all the world like figures from one of those films that he built an iconography around; *Saturday Night and Sunday Morning, A Taste of Honey, The Leather Boys*.

He looks at home. Indeed, were it not for the way the conversation naturally, nervously gravitates towards him, the way the eyes flit to him more readily, the extra weight his words carry, Morrissey could almost be 'one of the lads'.

A spring evening in Berlin. A night off for Morrissey, the most interesting bloke in showbusiness and the man that you have to have an opinion about. Let me assure you that nothing, not even the Manic Street Preachers' latest shirt stencil, is as guaranteed to set the *NME* ablaze with hyperbole, insult, slander, accusation and threat as this man. To some he's a mystifying dandy with ideas above his station, to others an off-the-rails god now flaunting his feet of clay. But, to a few, he's an enormous, capricious talent who's come through a hail of slings and arrows of outrageous fortune with the stoic optimism of Captain Mainwaring, and remains one of pop music's greatest treasures.

Did I say a few? I make no bones about belonging to the latter camp. The cross that Morrissey has to bear is, of course, that he happened to be part of the most important and original British pop group since punk, a group who altered a generation's ideas about what pop records could be, what they could mean to you and where they could stand in your life. (There's a great joke to be made here about Ed Banger and the Nosebleeds but I just can't bring myself to crack it.)

Smiths fans are, of course, relentlessly sneered at by the professional rock lobby. When the white boys discovered dance music in 1986 (where had they been all their lives?) Smiths fans came to embody the dreaded 'indie kid'; the anaemic, provincial wallflower of the born-again raver's imagination. Prejudice like this had dogged the Smiths every step since 'Panic' (ludicrously accused of 'racism') and hounds Morrissey to this day.

He knows it's over, but friend and foe alike will not let it lie. Enemies use his glorious past as a stick to beat him with and well-meaning allies pen gushing, pedantic, idiotic tributes to the letters page of the *NME* each week. We should all be wary of re-writing history. Only a fool rates 'Ouija Board, Ouija Board' higher than 'This Charming Man' but, equally, only a twerp doesn't realise that 'Suedehead' or 'Driving Your Girlfriend Home' or the forthcoming single 'Pregnant For The Last Time' are more than a match for 'Never Had No One Ever' or 'Death Of A Disco Dancer'.

And, without becoming embroiled in an ungracious slanging match, Johnny Marr may have significantly upped his average with Electronic, but Moz's post-Smiths work still leaves that of his erstwhile colleagues standing. Two shining talents were left orphaned by the Morrissey/Marr divorce, not one.

But onwards, to Berlin. Morrissey's outrageously successful continental tour is drawing to a close after ecstatic receptions in Dublin, Paris, the Netherlands and Cologne. Ahead lie three major Scottish dates and, beyond, an eight-week tour of the United States culminating in an appearance at Madison Square Gardens. His star is still very much in the ascendant across the Atlantic, as evidenced by the fact that tickets for the show at the LA Forum, a 15,000-seater in Los Angeles, sold out in fourteen minutes.

Add to this the fact that the first tracks with this new band, 'Pregnant For The Last Time', 'My Love Life' and an inspired reading of Bradford's 'Skinstorm', all fly in the face of those who pronounce him dead, and we perhaps understand why those around him claim not to have seen him in such a terrific mood for years. Morrissey never asked to be a solo artist and he never attempted to hide his grief at the death of the Smiths. But he is looking forward with good humour and apparent relish and you would have to be peevish in the extreme, not to say stupid, to deny him that.

As dusk falls in Berlin, we settle down to speak in a hotel room several floors above the city. What follows is a sizeable proportion of our conversation presented practically verbatim on the grounds that you'd prefer to listen to him than me.

So, how is life 'on the road' treating you?
Well, I'm as healthy or as sick as I look. If it was a profession, for heaven's sake, I'd find it depressing. But, as it is, there's something magisterial about sweeping through Europe like this. Although if somebody had the temerity to describe me as a 'rock star' I'd spit straight in their eye. But, yes, it does appeal to me in a strange way.

It's those strange fractured moments that make it all worthwhile. Yesterday, someone hit me on the head with a bicycle. I was having my picture taken, on the floor naturally, eyes heavenward. And they hit me with their bicycle so I had to decide whether to throw it into the Rhine or whatever it's called or pretend to be a gentleman, which I'm quite good at. So now I finally understand the plight of the so-called football 'hooligan'. And I'd like to help them in any way I can (*laughs*).

Why have you decided to tour now?
Well, I could have rushed at it like a bull at a gate two years ago but it wouldn't have been right. It wouldn't have gelled with the musicians I was working with. And the Smithology was still clinging like wet seaweed around my ankles so I couldn't really move . . . but suddenly it was gone. And I met some musicians who, well, *made me see the light* and made me very happy about what I'm doing. So here I am . . . in Denmark!

'Saw the light' sounds terribly dramatic.
You must remember that I was hideously dogged by all the widowed Smiths nonsense. And I became angry. For years I had to compound to journalists and the public, the genius, or the greatness, of the Smiths. I was bruised from that struggle. But with the untimely death, it seemed everyone wanted to discuss, in enormous detail, the ins and outs of the Smiths. And I became infuriated. It's the dreaded nostalgia. Not cherishing something 'til it's gone. Which is why, before you can get a word in edgeways, these days I'd be happier to talk about me – today and tomorrow – if that's possible.

If you mean you don't want to talk about the Smiths, I'm sure it's possible.
At the moment, I look on the Smiths as a dead cat that must be buried in a shoebox at the bottom of the garden. And that is not to spit upon anyone who might walk in here wearing a Smiths T-shirt. I would never do that. But my past is almost denying me a future. The irony is that, in days of old, I was always accused of being steeped in the past – in Will Hay and the New York Dolls. But now I want to talk about today and the writers want to talk about the past. A curious reversal. So, as for the Smiths, I have my tin hat on . . . and I'm bringing down the blackout.

Fair enough. So what's it like to go onstage and know that the audience are simply aching to touch you?
Oh, well (*laughs*) the way you put it! It's drastically simple. At the risk of sounding more pompous than I am, I was always more loved than admired. I think musicians are admired. But I was always loved and I felt it. And I prefer that. I mean, Eric Clapton is admired. But who could love him? His own mother, perhaps.

Without getting too scientific, the audience reflects the artist. Greasy heavy metal maniacs attract greasy heavy metal maniacs. But if, like me, you try and do something with a certain amount of passion or vocation or love, then the people attracted are like that. They understand me.

Do your fans represent a constituency?
Yes, they do. They are a reasonably separate group within the pop audience. I can't recall a following quite like them. If you look at most pop audiences, you can trace their notions back. But if you look at the people who like me, they are a strange and unique phenomenon . . . apart from the ones who've gone off me, of course!

But can you understand what drives them to invade the stage and touch the hem of your garment?
When I'm being cold and analytical I think it's simply because it's permissible in the

pop arena. If I was in Marks & Spencer and I met half a dozen of these people they'd be very polite. It's to do with the arena and the atmosphere that permits expression. You can't behave like that in the streets, which is sad. Such thunderous emotion is waiting to get out, and dim lights and loud music can bring it out.

But when I'm being less self-critical, I think they really do think a great deal of me. And, curiously, since we left Dublin, in Paris and Holland and Belgium and now here, it's got more extreme. I can't say why, since their English isn't very good and I speak nothing else. But since I'm not promoted anywhere to any degree except America, I'm comforted that it must be by word of mouth. They're a private and extraordinary club.

Everyone tells me you're in great spirits these days.
I've been pinching myself so much that my legs are brown. I'm frighteningly happy. Everything I've worked for these past 24 months has come right, and the core of that is the four individuals I'm working with, whom I hope you won't overlook. They are central to everything I do and they are, though you won't believe me – well, you might in five years – they are the best musicians I've had the joy of working with.

I can already hear people gasping at that remark.
They will gasp, but with relief I hope. Surely they're glad that my library ticket has been extended. They are simply the best, and the last week of concerts have been the best I've ever experienced. I don't take drugs, I don't drink alcohol except when I'm forced to, which is twice a day, so please accept this statement as shatteringly clear. I do hope people will not constantly want to write about the Smiths and the 'good old days'; the days when we got bad reviews and we didn't play very well sometimes. These musicians are better – and the harmony of the set-up . . . well, let's just say it's all very precious to me. And I hope people realise that now instead of in the year 2001. I don't want people to wait 'til I'm hit by a milkfloat to realise what a great group this is.

Do you think it's true that you've used the interview situation in a better way than your peers – for example, to carry on a dialogue with your fans?
Not necessarily. I'm perfectly aware that this conversation is not just between me and you. (*pause*) There is someone listening at the keyhole, and we both know who it is! But, truthfully, I always get waterlogged by the false intimacy of the interview. It's a bit like appearing on television. It's not that I'd say anything untrue. But you know how artificial interviews are.

Think about your job interview with the *NME* . . . no, don't. I'm sure it's too sordid!

But, by common consensus, you are the world's best interview.
Oh, you're too kind and I'll bet you a pound you won't print that. But, being self-critical, I come to the conclusion that that's because everyone else is such a walloping buffoon! Given the competition, it's easy to shine . . . or at least gleam in a reasonably buffed manner. The rock press currently is having to create personalities out of a dull herd of new groups and artists. I'm not fooled.

Is it fair to say that you had a love affair with the British music press that went sour?
Well, that has happened but it doesn't have to continue in that way. It went sour in
about September '89 when I simply became bored with answering the same few questions over and over. Also, the tide had turned and I was beginning to get sand kicked
in my face. I think there's a credo in the media – you have a five-year run and then
they think surely they're rich and happy enough to continue without the triviality of
our affections. I think people just get bored with the same old faces and that certainly happened to me. And despite what people say, I accepted that. After talking nineteen to the dozen for so long it was fascinating to sit back and watch others at play
and see who emerged. Nobody did. You're kidding yourself if think the Manic Street
Preachers mean anything to anybody.

Are you contemptuous of journalists now?
No. In fact when I was very tiny I had great ambitions to do the very thing you're
doing now, but luckily I found something with a bit more . . . scope. Admit it, it must
be the height of tediosity having to write excitedly about all those groups you can't
stand! This will seem an unreadably bloated remark but, as time goes by, my individuality is affirmed by those writers who can't stand my guts. They are constantly hand-
ing me backhanded compliments. There are certain journalists who profess to think
I'm useless and they cannot fill in an application form for a driving licence without
mentioning my name. I must mean more to them than their own mothers. And in
their endless, poetic hatred of me, they have made me important. To the point where
it doesn't matter whether 'Sing Your Life' enters the Top 30 or not, or whether my
record sales in England decrease or not.

How do you view your supposed 'decline'?
(*laughs*) Well, a piece on my 'decline' makes the covers of all the glossy magazines. Of
course, if I was truly in decline no-one would write a word about me because they'd
be too busy writing about other groups. I assume you're putting the word 'decline' in
inverted commas, and this 'decline', apparently, is more important than any other
group or artist in the world. And anyway, one way or the other, pieces about me,
whether they praise or damn, are never tedious. They're always a good read.

*But you yourself have referred to the 'funny little singles' you've put out of late. Isn't
that very disparaging?*
No, not necessarily. I do think they're quite funny. But it's definitely Reevesian
humour. I know Vic Reeves and I see a lot of myself in him. If he'd been born 30 years
previously his mother and auntie would have locked him away in a very dark room.
It's a form of madness. And we're very lucky to be able to convey it in some entertaining, socially acceptable way. It's termed eccentricity rather than madness. And
there are millions like me out there – dreadful thought – who want to sing and write
and climb over the wall. But they never will. I'm afraid the hole in the net is only big
enough for one or two. So, though my lips will freeze when I say it, I suppose I'm one
of the lucky ones (*laughs*).

And what makes you so special?
Well . . . it's because everyone else is so deadly dull, I suppose. Need I go on? If you examine my position, and I know you have, you'll see that Morrissey's position in British pop is completely central but completely problematic.

Are you a different person from the young man who sang 'Hand In Glove'?
Yes, I am. I am much more self-reliant. I have, shall we say, been through a great deal. I put an enormous emotional investment into the Smiths and something . . . well, something went slightly wrong, in a manner of speaking (*chuckles*). I think my solo situations and achievements have been outrageously undervalued, whilst that of certain other ex-Smiths have been outrageously over-valued. I think there's been less sympathy for me because I survived. I came through and retained a very sizeable and appreciative following. If I'd become some pathetic, knock-kneed soul who, in 1987, had ended up having to sign on in the dark bowels of south Manchester, I'd have been put on an unreachable pedestal. As someone called Oscar Wilde once said, your friends will sympathise – and you can complete the sentence I'm sure – with everything but your success. They'll gladly bemoan the fact that you used to be an international singing star but should you get up and go on . . .

Do you feel that people have been disloyal to you?
I absolutely do. I know a lot of people live by the music press and when they read that Morrissey is a heap of rubble in the corner, they absolutely believe it and they withdraw their support. A lot of the Smiths audience did that and deserted me. But a significant proportion stayed and I'm very grateful for that. I have been approached by people in Happy Mondays T-shirts and hair trailing the ground who've said to me, 'We're unhappy like this. We hate the Happy Mondays. We don't want to do this. But nothing has happened since you. We wish you would dust off your battle dress.' Even David Bowie, of all people, said to me, 'You have to jump back and attack.' And I thought, 'Why?' But recently it has occurred to me why.

Well, why?
(*emphatically*) Because everything is so bloody boring. I'm sick of picking up the *NME* and not recognising the people on the cover. But then you know I'm old fashioned. You know I believe in talent. You know I have standards and I won't lower them to put up with the merely trendy. I'm not frightened of people just because of their supposed hipness. I absolutely believe in talent and I don't think it's an embarrassing Eric Morley word to use.

And you don't see much of it about . . . ?
You know yourself that those Manchester groups can't be much cop, or their contemporaries for that matter, because of the way Radio One has picked up on them so enthusiastically. If they were faintly dangerous, then the fat, bearded establishment would not have embraced them. Pop censorship is in operation, here and in America, and I am on the receiving end of it. I saw an American programme the other day which listed the artists who should be censored and right next to Ozzy Osbourne was

the sleeve of *Kill Uncle*. I know I'm blacklisted, but I take it as an honour, because all groups who've had anything to say have been censored. All the great British writers were exiled, though I wouldn't have the gall to put myself in that company.

Are you unreservedly proud of your solo records or do you think, 'well, that was quite good but **that** *wasn't'?*
Yes, but I've always done that. What amazes me is the number of people who say my solo records aren't as good as the Smiths. It's a logic they don't apply to the recordings of any other ex-Smith. So what they're in effect saying is, 'Morrissey, we consider you to have been the Smiths.' When I consider the whole shebang that surrounds me, it seems the whole world thinks I was the Smiths.

And is that a reasonable assumption to make?
Yes, I think it is.

Are you saying that the indefinable something that made the Smiths more special than all other groups, well, that something was you?
If that's what you're saying then I would agree with you. But I won't go into the whys and wherefores of the Smiths because it really would be refreshing to bury that dead cat I mentioned earlier.

Do you think you've been influential? Have you really, as I read recently, 'expanded the vocabulary of the pop song'?
Oh yes. Well, I can hear my influence in certain modern successful groups but, before you ask, I won't say which ones because it's perfectly fair. I've been heavily influenced by other artists. It's fascinating and completely permissible to dig into other people's notions. In fact, it's vital for creative life.

But how about the sound of today's pop chart? Isn't it the complete antithesis to what you stand for?
Oh, you're totally right. The joke is that during the Smiths' lifespan no independent music was played on daytime radio. And it seemed that that changed on the very day of the Smiths' amputation. Suddenly independent music was on daytime radio. I recently heard a daytime sessions from the High broadcast with a message to the effect that this group had met in the lobby earlier that day and, inspecting my position on EMI, I realised that I'm still in the wrong place at the wrong time.

So, yes, I'm rueful about the success of all the new herd . . . except James. I've been a good friend of Tim and Martine (*James' manager*) for many years and I know their struggles. Their success is the first that's been truly deserved of all the new Manchester groups, although when I heard they were doing *Wogan* I almost dropped the teapot, appalled. But I thought it was very successful, actually.

But your kind of pop, is it dead?
Yes. About 120 years ago, when *The South Bank Show* produced an 'effort' about the Smiths, I uttered something inaudible about 'the death of pop' and everyone said,

'Oh, you're just saying that, let the rest of us have a chance.' But I do believe it is dead and gone. Since that point between the first Summer of Love and 1983 nothing has happened. There's nothing new, no one making an authentically original contribution.

British pop has succumbed to an American influence, and not a positive one, but the basest, dullest, thickest ones. I find that criminally sad. I don't want a Top Ten crammed with Manfred Mann and Twinkle and Dave Dee, Dozy, Beaky, Mick & Titch, whatever people might think, because that would be unhealthy. But if I watch *Top of the Pops* or, dare I splutter it, MTV, I have to turn away very quickly. It's like watching a road accident.

But I live in hope. It isn't my 'chosen way of making a living' as you put it. It's a vocation, at worst a sickness. And there was a point when I thought I'd simply disappear into the Forest of Dean . . . no, not that forest, another one! But now I realise that I will go on and on until EMI have to take me into a field and shoot me. But I don't want to belong to the pop bubble. And it doesn't want me. The industry doesn't want to touch me with a barge-pole.

Why is that?
Because I've got a terrible voice, of course.

Moz fact Number Three. 'He's got a terrible voice,' 'he's miserable,' etc. I'm sure some people would accuse you of being miserable if you made an out-and-out comedy record.
Oh but I have, Stuart! Didn't you hear 'November Spawned A Monster'?

Earlier in your career . . .
Is that what I've had? A career? You make it sound like I went down to the Job Centre and asked if they had any vacancies for 'dire troublemaker'.

In the days of the Smiths – and beyond – you made some explicitly political remarks and records; about the Royals and Thatcher, etc. Are you still 'political'?
Well, I rarely watch TV. I never read a newspaper. I feel separate from the political world. I just find it harder and harder to care. Occasionally I will hear truly sensible voices such as Clare Short or Tony Benn and, of course, these are the ones who are scorned and gagged. So I despair of politics and, interestingly, the 'murder' of Margaret Thatcher was the last point of my interest. I'm not interested in John Major. The Gulf War I didn't care about or want to know about. So I'm certainly less political than I was.

Songs of yours such as 'Asian Rut' and 'Bengali In Platforms' have prompted some of your critics to label you racist.
Well, of course, these are the same people who baulk at the idea of me writing about someone confined to a wheelchair. You mustn't do it. You can't mention 'Asian' or 'Bengali' regardless of what follows lyrically, regardless of what you're trying to say about the situation. I'm incapable of racism, even though I wear this T-shirt and even though I'm delighted that an increasing number of my audience are skinheads in nail

varnish. And I'm not trying to be funny, that really is the perfect audience for me. But I am incapable of racism, and the people who say I'm racist are basically just the people who can't stand the sight of my physical frame. I don't think we should flatter them with our attention.

Could we go back? Your perfect audience is skinheads in nail varnish?
Yes, it's mushrooming and it's very heartening. As you're perfectly aware, the audience for all those groups from that little island of Manchester all dress in completely American style which befuddles me. So the sight of streams of skinheads in nail varnish . . . it somehow represents the Britain I love. Wouldn't it be awful to find yourself 'followed', as it were, by people you didn't want? You must find this yourself . . .

How do skinheads represent the Britain you love?
Well, correct me if I'm wrong, but I thought the skinhead was an entirely British invention. If I was ever asked for an autograph by someone wearing those awful Cure baseball boots, I'd take it as a sign from Hell that the curtain was coming down. It would be Hell's hottest hob.

Do you pine for a mythical Britain?
Perhaps. It's certainly gone now. England doesn't only not rule the waves, it's actually sunk below them. And all that remains is debris. But in amongst the debris shine slits of positivity.

If you aren't a racist are you a patriot?
Yes I am. I find travelling very hard. I miss England. But the last few interviews I've given have centred around (and not at my instigation) the decline of the Ealing studios and Alistair Sim. It gives the impression that I do nothing from morning 'til night but think about the once proud Empire, which I never do. It's another ghost that needs exorcising, rather like the one that says my fans are all pathetically devoted Virginia Woolfs who can't dance.

But you can't deny their devotion. Why do they feel this way?
Because they know I've never been a slag. Never been, in simple language, a whore. I've never chased the money. Which in this dastardly business is something. When you close your hotel room door on EMI Belgium, you're something of a troublemaker. Even EMI in England . . . they promoted *Viva Hate* very well but now they don't know what to do. I am not promoted in any sense of the word. Good heavens, EMI could not get one of my records played on the radio in England if the future of the company depended on it. I feel the same in '91 as I did in '83 – that whatever I've achieved I've earned it. The only things that have been handed to me are invoices and lawsuits.

I suppose what will happen is that my singles will stop making the British Top 40. Records are hits because the record company decides they'll be hits. EMF are the perfect example of this. But my situation is precarious. I wouldn't say I expect to be dropped but I could be in the archives before this interview is over. In America, Sire could not be more enthusiastic. Consequently, they seem to want me there. My records are selling as well as they ever did during my time with the Housemartins (*much laughter*) . . .

What was the last record you got excited about?
Err . . . 'Rockin' In The Cemetery' by Ronnie Dawson. It's the first track on the tape we come on to.

Ah, rockabilly. Your supposed new love!
Well, I have vague recollections of songs like 'Vicar In A Tutu', 'Shakespear's Sister' and 'Rusholme Ruffians' I recall talking in early interviews about Elvis. People always overstate the case. If I mention one rockabilly artist, it doesn't follow that I'm running around in drainpipes and a huge DA. I simply find a lot of rockabilly exciting in a way that modern pop songs aren't.

How would you like posterity to remember you?
If it doesn't sound too much like Malcolm Muggeridge, I'd like people to say that I wrote with blood, not ink. Did that sound like Malcolm Muggeridge? Alan Bennett? My reputation goes before me and I can only follow. And it isn't particularly contrived. I never went to a theatrical agent. And no matter what people say, I've won. In a strange sense, the battle is over. It was over when *Viva Hate* went in at Number One. Everything else has been a fantastic, ongoing bonus.

When Oliver Stone does get round to the movie, will you be flattered?
Yes, I will. And I quite like your idea of Dirk Bogarde playing me. Well, after all, Dandy Nichols is dead.

And what of the other, shall we say, central figures in your drama?
But there are no others. But if you insist, I'm sure certain members of New Order would fit the bill!

Do you love your enemies?
I sympathise. And then I arrange to have their heads kicked in. I do have friends in high places. Tower Hamlets, for instance . . .

But when you want to live, how do you start, where do you go, who do you need to know? When the best tunesmith and the best singer/lyricist of a generation meet, sparks inevitably fly. The dissolution of the Smiths left both Morrissey and Marr unexpectedly single, and both have drifted, at times uncomfortably, from partner to partner.

Morrissey's solo outings have involved a shifting array of backstage personnel; Stephen Street, Vini Reilly, Andy Rourke, Langer and Winstanley, Mark Bedford and latterly Mark Nevin. This lack of a stable collaborator, the search for a 'steady', has been the source of some mirth within the music press. And haughty suspicion never ran so high as when Morrissey announced that his new band were a gang of North London rockabilly rebels, including ex-Polecat Baz Boorer.

Moz's keenness for 'th'lads', as he half-ironically refers to them, to be taken seriously is manifest. As our interview concludes at around 11pm, we arrange to repair to the hotel bar, but first he politely but firmly repeats his request that I have a word with his band. We meet over a few drinks and immediately, however tough your carapace of cynicism, you're infected with their ingenuous enthusiasm.

The switch from the capital's pub circuit to delirious hordes in continental stadia has been rapid; a transition that's left them bemusedly grateful. Boorer is something of a minor legend in the rockabilly world, the others – guitarist Alan, bass player Gaz and drummer Spencer – are as far removed from 'indie kids' as it's possible to be. They grew up blissfully unaware of the Cure, Bauhaus and the Sisters of Mercy or, less blissfully, the Fall, Joy Division, Aztec Camera or indeed . . .

'We were never Smiths fans,' says Alan cheerily, 'and I think this is one of the reasons that we've got on so well with Moz. The fact that he was in the Smiths doesn't really mean a lot to us. I think he's glad about that, because it means we take him for what he is, which is a good bloke, rather than because of his past. He was keen to have a band, a real band, rather than a bunch of session men behind him. And as a band, we get on very well.'

For drummer Spencer, teenage years involved 'the Who, the Kinks, Jimi Hendrix and running riot with the mods and skins down Carnaby Street.'

For Gaz, it was 'punk, ska and fifties rock 'n' roll'. They're all vaguely aware that the Smiths and Morrissey meant something inordinately special to large numbers of people, but beyond that, as Gaz points out, 'I love the stuff we play on stage. But I'd never really been exposed to Morrissey's stuff before. If someone had sat me down with his stuff I might have got into him earlier, of course.'

Spencer never heard the Smiths, but he was dimly aware of the name. 'It was the sort of music that, if it came on the radio, I'd turn it off.' Alan is similarly neutral about the Smiths but feels that *Bona Drag* is an excellent record. 'I'm a big fan of his recent stuff.'

They bumped into Morrissey via a 'rockin' club in Kentish Town', and the English rockabilly sub-cultural style clearly being attractive to Moz, were subsequently asked to appear in videos for 'Our Frank' and 'Sing Your Life'. Session work followed and, ultimately, Morrissey's decision to use them as his permanent band. The sound is gutsy, organic and guitar-based, obviously a sound Morrissey loves. Spencer shows me his blistered hands and reminds me, surreally, that 'balls-out is my only speed.'

Boz is something of an old hand at this. Having done studio work with Morrissey before Christmas, he had heard rumours of a tour but thought no more about it until receiving a frantic summons from his wife whilst he was watching some old blues veteran in Burnley.

'I just took leave of absence from the demo studios where I work and here I am! At first, we all took it one day at a time, but now it looks as if the band might have a future.'

Working with everyone from Sinead to Deep House has, he claims, made him pretty adaptable, but he's full of praise for the younger lads: 'Considering they've only played rockin' music before, they've adapted very well.'

All of them are understandably delighted at the frenzied audience reaction to date.

'A multiple orgasm,' as Spencer puts it. And they're not in the slightest nonplussed by the audience's obvious intense concentration on Morrissey himself. 'He's the main man,' Gaz says. 'It's his show and I'm just glad to be part of it.'

The 'main man' arrives and takes his place at the bar, scotching any expectations that he'd be tucked up by ten with a Horlicks, some pressed flowers and *The People's Friend*. Instead, we get a genial drinker, wryly caught up in the jokes and backslapping bonhomie. He is painfully amused when I tell him that the new Nolans single is a disastrous, Tina Turner-style clomp through 'Panic'.

'There's always been talk of cover versions, the Eurythmics and several others, and I've always been very excited but they've come to nought. I do know that Chrissie Hynde is doing "Everyday Is Like Sunday". I've heard a demo version and, well, my cheeks are moist.'

Caught up in the *esprit de corps*, I attempt to charge a frighteningly substantial drinks round to my room. Oh, how our Teutonic hostess laughed when we remembered that I was staying in a different hotel. After this our orders came with glacial speed and stern-jawed disapproval, and it occurred to us to sample other aspects of Berlin nightlife.

Berlin's decadence must be well-hidden these days, we muse, as we cruise the streets hellbent for kicks. Moz and support act Phranc act the goat in the street in a heartening manner, playfighting, wrestling, and generally sparring affectionately. Someone spies flashing 'disco style' lights at the top of an office block but, with no working lifts and no visible staircase, we can only stand and imagine the debauchery overhead.

Someone spots a man with a quiff who is instantly and, in my view, erroneously seized upon as something of a style authority and nightlife connoisseur. I am right. He directs us to some dreadful hole where the only fun is watching Moz queue up with the *herren und frau* to have his hand stamped. Inside, stout-looking youths play pool badly whilst some patently demented girls shuffle listlessly to an old Donna Summer B-side. This is the last time I remember seeing the band. I sincerely hope they've since turned up.

Outside, Phranc remembers that there is supposedly a great club next door to David Bowie's old house. Tragically, no-one can remember where this is, but knowing German precision, it's probably on 'Davidbowiesoldhousestrasse'.

When the pizzeria turns its nose up at us, common sense tells us to call it a night. Several questions remain unanswered; about the future, about nail varnish and about why the Germans put those paper doilies on the stems of beer glasses, but Morrissey's current ebullience is undoubted, to fan and cynic alike. When he is taken into that field and shot, Popstrasse will be an infinitely less interesting place to be.

New Musical Express, 18 May 1991

OOH I SAY!

—·••·— BY ADRIAN DEEVOY —·••·—

'Monsieur Morrissey?' puzzles the well-preserved concierge. 'Eez a pop group, non?' Upstairs in his room on the third floor of this cloyingly plush Parisian hotel, Monsieur Morrissey, pop group, has just taken delivery of the finished artwork for his new long player, *Your Arsenal*. Its cover is a live photograph of the singer, tongue out, shirt asunder (stomach scar courtesy Davyhulme Hospital), suggestively waggling his microphone at fly-height.

Morrissey studies the sleeve intently, then holds it at arm's length and squints inscrutably – or could it be myopically? – at its cover star.

'What do you think?' he asks eventually.

Can we use the word 'homo-erotic'?

'Is that how it appeals to you?' he enquires, arching an amused eyebrow. 'You're the first person who's said that and it's nice that somebody has.' He frowns pensively, 'But what are you really asking me?'

Well, you were once the thinnest man in pop and suddenly you developed this muscular physique. What did you do?

'I did nothing,' he shrugs coyly. 'It just suddenly and miraculously happened. I didn't go out and do a course of cybergenetics. It was just nature, for once, being reasonably generous.'

Judging by the title, you're still a student of innuendo.

'I'm sure I don't know what you're talking about.'

Your Arsenal, indeed.

'Surely you're not going to ask me what it means?' he says sniffily, then concedes. 'In a small way, there's something about innuendo that's entertaining. I like to think it's sometimes done fairly cleverly. It's by no means stupid.'

And is widespread sexual arousal the sole aim of the album cover?

'Really,' he sighs, summoning a typically Morrithetic punchline. 'What would be the *point*?'

Morrissey is *en France* and on form. He's now been a solo artist for fractionally longer than he was a Smith. Sometimes, he says, it feels like all he's done for the last ten years is write, record and perform songs. But in doing this he has become one of Britain's most lauded songwriters and surely our finest lyricist.

His past life – which has served as a seemingly bottomless well of inspiration (although he would theatrically claim it was more like desperation) for his songs – has recently been subjected to a thorough rummage for an unendorsed biography-of-sorts, the grandly titled *Morrissey & Marr The Severed Alliance: The Definitive Story of The Smiths*. Prior to its publication, Morrissey issued a characteristically two-bus-stops-from-reason pronouncement demanding the immediate death of the book's author, Johnny Rogan, in a motorway pile-up.

Today, as the sun shines upon the city by the Seine, Morrissey is in a forgiving mood. Just as long as Rogan dies slowly and painfully, he smiles, he'll be happy.

It's been a long time since you've granted an interview.
Give the public what they want. That's what I always say.

Do you think this new record will broaden your appeal?
I'd put a pound on it.

You seem to have a very shrewd sense of who your market is.
Well 'market' is a horrible word. You make me sound like Pete Beale.

But you're aware of your size?
Not the exact dimensions (*laughs*).

Do you feel over-protected? You're very hard to get hold of.
Well I do live in Primrose Hill. The bus service is atrocious. I'm a very personal and protective person. I've got no notions of being a rock star, I don't go shopping for yachts with a minder. No, that's simply me. That's my personality.

To fend people off?
Not to fend people off, but I'm not in a desperate hurry to attend any parties, shall we say . . . I don't get any invitations but that's by the by.

Morrissey & Marr: The Severed Alliance. *Have you read it?*
Well a friend of mine had a copy and I squinted at it across the room for three days and then curiosity drove me to the index. Just to see who'd blabbed.

Were you shocked?
Certain things shocked me. It's promoted as the definitive story of the Smiths. Of course, the only definitive story of the Smiths is my story, if ever that's told. It seems like he – Johnny Rogan – has interviewed anybody who basically bears a grudge against me. Any of the people who've been close to me over the past decade he has not got near. So I saw more reviews and I felt very sad because they were saying, At last! Here is the truth! The level of information that this person has unearthed! Basically, it's 75 percent blatant lies. The rest is reasonably factual.

I made a statement when the book was published which said, Anybody who buys this book wants their head tested. As far as I can tell, according to sales figures, a lot of people need their heads tested. A lot of people have bought it and, of course, a lot of people will believe it. But I hope, more so, that he dies in a hotel fire.

Presumably you were approached to participate in the book?
Well of course Johnny Rogan has been explaining to the press that he had a conver-sation with me. I've never met him and no conversation has ever taken place. One night the phone rang and he said, This is J . . . and I put the phone down. He wrote

me a series of letters over a three-year period, all of which I scarcely opened.

Did he approach your mother? The book isn't too flattering about her.
Yes, he did. But she didn't speak to him. He didn't speak to any of my family. He spoke to people on the periphery of the whole thing and he spoke to Johnny Marr. Later, after the interview had taken place, I spoke to Johnny Marr about it and he regretted having done the interview enormously.

Did your mother read it?
No. Suffice to say, if she had such things as a bargepole . . .

The book was similar, in a curious way, to the Princess Diana biography.
Oh, that was just the covers. They're virtually interchangeable.

Lyrically, you seem less neurotically self-conscious on **Your Arsenal.** *Is that due to changes within the author?*
I don't know, I'll go and ask him. But yes. I didn't want to use a lyric sheet. I wanted to make as physical a record as I possibly could instead of constantly being curled up in a little ball at the foot of the bed.

How do you go about making a more physical record?
You just unbutton the buttons on your shirt and . . . (*laughs*) Well, if you don't know now you'll never know.

Are you more at ease with yourself?
Yes. I am actually half way towards being 66. I can't be categorised as being especially young. Time has passed and I'm not really the person I once was. I think I've changed in certain ways. Perhaps the world I live in isn't as narrow as it once was. You'll notice I said 'perhaps'. I'm not entirely convinced (*laughs*).

You've always been obsessed by the onward march of time, haven't you?
Enormously. All of us are working against the clock in our own way. I tend to . . . have a cheese butty and sit back and relax. Everything eventuates. Time will pass. The day will arrive when you and I are not on this earth. I think people who have a sense of time and therefore urgency are quite fascinating people.

How has your attitude towards death changed? You've been accused of being flippant about the past.
More than that, I've been accused of paying too much attention to death generally. I've belaboured slightly on the subject, but what's wrong with that? It's a pretty serious matter. Especially when you're lying under the wheels of a double decker bus.

Once again, as with 'Bengali In Platforms' and 'Asian Rut', you have flirted with racism on the new song 'The National Front Disco'.
Well I like to feel, in some small way, that I'm not actually restricted in anything I

wish to write about. Of course, within the exciting world of pop music, the reality is that we are restricted. Whether you choose to write about wheelchair-bound people, 'November Spawned A Monster', or the subject of racism, 'The National Front Disco', the context of the song is often overlooked. People look at the title and shudder and say, Whatever is in that song shouldn't exist because the subject, to millions of people, is so awful.

Do you think people are innately racist?
Yes. I don't want to sound horrible or pessimistic but I don't really think, for instance, black people and white people will ever really get on or like each other. I don't really think they ever will. The French will never like the English. The English will never like the French. That tunnel will collapse.

The song 'We'll Let You Know' seems to sympathise with football hooligans. Is this the case?
Well they have such great taste in footwear (*laughs*). I understand the level of patriotism, the level of frustration and the level of jubilance. I understand the overall character. I understand their aggression and I understand why it must be released.

Are you suggesting you've had firsthand experience of this?
I'm not a football hooligan, if that's the question. You might be surprised by that. But I understand the character. I just do. I've got a computer at home for such things.

Is this not just Morrissey picking up on another controversial theme?
It's hard to believe but no, it isn't. I can't fully explain. When I see reports on the television about hooliganism in Sweden or Denmark or somewhere, I'm actually amused. Is that a horrible thing to say?

It could be construed as such.
As long as people don't die, I am amused.

You're still mourning the death of Englishness on this record.
Well aren't I always? That's just me. It's a part of my overall psyche. It's not unique to this record. I suppose a few years ago I would have spoken more morosely about this great, dying tradition. Well, now it has died. This is the debris, now.

What exactly do you think has died?
Basic identity.

Do we need a war to re-establish our identity?
I think we already have one. I don't want to be European. I want England to remain an island. I think part of the greatness of the past has been the fact that England has been an island. I don't want the tunnel. I don't want sterling to disappear. I don't want British newscasters to talk in American accents. I don't want continental television. But that doesn't mean that I'm some great twit who lives in a hut and eats straw. I'm

not a thing from another age (*laughs*). I'm actually quite modern in some respects. But there's no hope of anyone marching around Westminster with . . . well you complete the sentence.

As a long-term fan of pop music, what do you think about its current state?
It has actually died. Pop music has ended.

Do you no longer watch Top of the Pops?
It's astonishing to even think it, but I don't. It's astonishing simply because (*strikes breast passionately*) I *love* music and I *love* pop music. And now *nothing* will induce me to watch *Top of the Pops*. My feeling is that *Top of the Pops* finished in 1985. I don't feel that it actually exists anymore. Similarly with radio and the Top 40. That shouldn't and mustn't imply that I have ceased to be interested in music, because I haven't. As I become older I have a keener interest in music. I think a wealth of truly excellent music has been made and a lot of music is there to be discovered which was never popular, never made the Top 40. I feel actually quite happy knowing that I will spend the remainder of my life listening to music and investigating things that I missed.

There's a theory that enough music has been made.
That's right. Because as an art form – and I've truly never seen it as anything else, even the trash element – it has done its bit.

Did dance music do for pop music?
Yes, it really did. And I don't just say that because I *hate* dance music.

Is there not an argument that simply says you're getting old?
No, I don't accept that. I don't mean to sound silly but part of me was always old, and I'm actually intelligent enough to take that into account. It's more than that. It's real, factual deterioration.

One would think that you'd have sorted out your love life by now.
I expected to, but I haven't.

Have you come close?
Not at all. Not at all. I know that there's an understandable overall feeling that once you pass 21, certain things will fall into place, but by some curious twist of fate I remained on the path I was always on, which has . . . really surprised me.

Do you understand that people find this hard to believe?
Well, no one more than me! I often feel that this is the way it must be. It's not entirely up to you whether you have a relationship with another person. It's either a two-way thing or the other person decides that it will happen. And they don't.

Do you get desperate?
I think I passed the point of desperation, quite seriously, about seventeen years ago. I

slipped into resignation. I'm a human being, I live on earth. I go out, I meet a lot of people but nothing ever, ever, *ever* happens. More than that I cannot do other than appear on national television in a red suit saying, I am said to have a sense of humour, I enjoy Bacharach/David and I like going for long walks.

It's actually . . . quite a serious matter. It's something I can't deny has caused me decades of anxiety. People always assume that I'm covered in dust, sat in a corner reading *Hard Times*. Admittedly in the early days of the Smiths that was something I fostered slightly. But as you know, within the dizzy world of pop music everything is always enlarged beyond its natural proportion. All I seem to hear these days is that I'm 'working with a young rockabilly band'. They're not *young* and they're not *rockabilly*, but everything gets expanded until it becomes a cliché. So part of me has become a cliché also. An unlovable cliché!

But you seem an affable, warm person . . .
I am!! Two exclamation marks. Ask anybody! I think I'm just one of those people that God marked on the forehead saying you're meant to do something else. You're not meant to have a happy, fulfilling physical relationship.

Your relationship with Michael Stipe seemed very promising at one stage.
Promising?! What did you think we were going to do? Become a Millican and Nesbitt? But, yes. The temperament is the same, the sense of rationale is the same.

Do you think you'll 'make music' with him?
(*laughs, raises eyebrows*) I can't think of any reason why! No, the whole joy about the friendship is that music doesn't ever come into it. We don't ever talk about REM or whatever it is I do. There are other things to discuss.

How did you actually meet?
Well he wrote to me for a long time and I wondered why. I was initially sceptical. I can't remember why. Then I decided that I would like to meet him, so we met and I was surprised that it was so easy and . . . compatible. It's very nice and, who knows, we may even get a cover on *Hello!*

Michael and Morrissey invite us into their lovely home!
We can but dream.

Do you have any thoughts on Vic Reeves's creation, Morrissey the Consumer Monkey?
I saw it for a split second and instantly loathed its creator. It was meant to be hurtful. I've met Vic Reeves a few times and it hasn't gone too well. He is a person who cannot close his mouth for three seconds because he feels he'll disintegrate into a bowl of dust. He has to keep going on and on and on. Completely loathsome. Bob Mortimer, I liked. I think he should make a hasty exit from that duo. Can you smell the venom?

It's like Tony Wilson making this statement saying that I am a woman trapped inside a man's body. He's a *pig* trapped inside a man's body. If one has to be one or the other I know which I'd prefer.

He called you 'a cunt'.
Well, he has to be the biggest pop star in Manchester and he must trample on anybody who threatens his position. He always has surrounded himself with people who can barely talk and who are no threat to his 'personality'. The day that somebody shoves him in the boot of a car and drives his body to Saddleworth Moor and leaves it there, is the day that Manchester music will be revived.

Have you severed your connections with Manchester?
Not in my mind. Physically I've been forced to. I had to leave because 24 hours a day people would be at the door, at the gate, banging on the windows, and it became intolerable, so I had to move away. I couldn't think how else I could deal with it.

There's the most vicious sense of competition in Manchester, as well. So many jealous, vile creatures. This is what the song 'We Hate It When Our Friends Become Successful' is about. In Manchester, you are accepted as long as you are scrambling and on your knees. But if you have any success or are independent or a free spirit, they hate your guts.

Let's go back in time to 1983 and the Smiths.
Why stop there? Let's go back to 1749.

When you look back on the Smiths now, does it make you proud?
A lot of it I don't actually like. I don't like the visuals, to be honest. I don't like any television footage or videos. I don't like what I see within me. I don't like what I see in the other three also. That's not supposed to sound rude. There's a couple of songs I don't like. In fact, I didn't really like them at the time. Like 'What Difference Does It Make', I thought was absolutely awful the day after the record was pressed. I don't look back and think we were perfection in everything we did and everything we said. But I do think that just over half the output, to me, is really . . . beautiful. Is that a silly word?

Billy Bragg said that it must be hard being Morrissey, this fabulously witty, Wildean character, 24 hours a day.
Oh, I clock off. I clock off and brew up. It must be very hard to be Billy Bragg, but I won't say why! Actually, I retract that, I'm a big fan of his.

But the implication is that Morrissey is a slightly contrived character.
Well I don't slip into a suit and practice a certain tone of voice, no. There's no *persona* as such. It's just what you see across this table.

Full time?
Unfortunately, yes. Now how would you feel? Talk about trapped!

Why do you think you provoke such extreme reactions? Some people really hate you.
Because I have a specific identity. I have a very clear idea what I want to say lyrically and the approach I have is just far too direct for most people. A song like 'Interesting

Drug' spoke about drug culture, and I think the pop establishment can deal with pop drug culture in its present form because it doesn't convey anything. It's very vague and wispy and (*lolls tongue out and rolls eyes*) uuuuung, unngh. But if you say, Interesting drug/the one that you took/God, it really *helped* you. That line was just far too direct.

Have you taken Ecstasy?

Yes I have. I've taken it a couple of times. The first time I took it was the most astonishing moment of my life. Because – and I don't want to sound truly pathetic – I looked in the mirror and saw somebody very, very attractive. Now, of course, this was the delusion of the drug, and it wears off. But it was astonishing for that hour, or for however long it was, to look into the mirror and really, really like what came back at me. Now even though I had that wonderful experience, and it was a solitary experience – there was nobody else present – I'm not actually interested in drugs of any kind. I'm not prudish, I don't mind if other people take them, but it's not for me. I just don't have the interest.

As someone who is periodically celibate, what do you do with the urge you must get to have sex?

Well, it'll sound unbelievable but until I was 28 (*whispers*) I never had the urge. I don't mind saying that but I can understand that it will look ridiculous in print. I never did. Maybe I was too preoccupied with something else.

So what happened when you were 28?

I just suddenly changed. I can't explain why but things are different for me now. I do actually understand that people have physical relationships. And I understand why they need them.

Other than that, do you have anything to declare?

Only my jeans.

'Awright, Moz! Wanna beer?' It's hardly the way you would expect Britain's only Olympic-standard shrinking violet to be addressed. And as guitarist Boz Boorer prepares to order a round in unpolished Franglais, how does his employer respond? 'No ta, you Brylcreemed brute, but I'd love a cup of Red Label and a fondant fancy'?

No, he doesn't. Standing on the pavement, with his quiff dramatically silhouetted against the neon-lit Moulin Rouge, Morrissey nods thirstily and heads towards the bar.

Boz and Morrissey are Marc Bolan fanatics for whom no Boppin' Elf minutiae is too minute ('Did you know he wore size five women's shoes?'). Earlier, Morrissey was hopelessly defending 'Certain People I Know', a track from *Your Arsenal* which is all but a cover version of 'Ride A White Swan'.

'I don't know if you know anything about Marc Bolan,' he says haughtily, 'but he took a lot of inspiration from rock'n'roll. If, for example, you listen to early Carl Perkins you'll probably hear,' and this is where his argument began to falter, 'Marc Bolan playing "Ride A White Swan" in the background . . . although I doubt it.'

Morrissey suggests we take a taxi to Pigalle to have his photograph taken outside the explicitly-illustrated sex shops. The 'one-handed' literature and outsized rubber appendages, he enthuses (fully aware of how thoroughly un-Morrissey the setting is), will provide a stimulatingly sleazy backdrop.

Throughout the session, he maintains a sitcom vicarish innocence, putting it on hold occasionally to scrutinise an especially gymnastic video cover or savour a fruitily punsome magazine title.

And it is here, in the condom of Paris, that we leave Monsieur Morrissey to saunter between the live lesbian sex shows (Sex-o!) and the 'specialist' hardcore backrooms (Porno Shop!). Saying his *au revoir*s he extends his hand, and, as you reach out to shake, he withdraws it and – in the hilarious music hall tradition – thumbs his nose. How very *tres*.

'When you reach this age,' he sighs, 'you have to accept that you are what you are, whatever that may be. Because of the position I have in life people tend to always treat me in exactly the same manner.' He exhales dejectedly. 'Nobody ever grabs hold of me and says, Let's go down to the red light district, there's something I want to show you.'

Q, September 1992

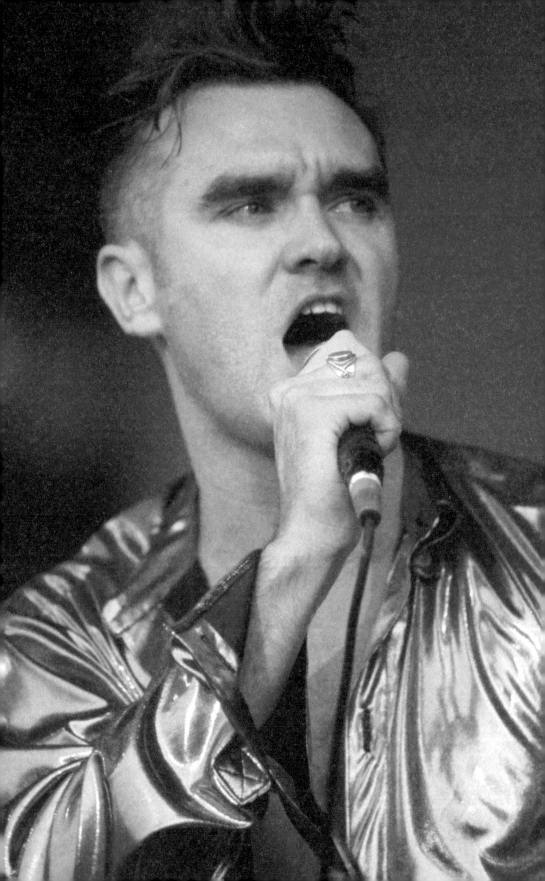

HAND IN GLOVE
———◆— BY ANDREW HARRISON ———◆—

'Ladies and gentlemen . . . Hello? Ladies and gentlemen, on behalf of the staff and members of the York Hall Gymnasium I would like to thank each and every one of you for coming here tonight for what promises to be a fine evening's boxing entertainment. Later on we have British flyweight champion Francis Ampofo, middleweight challenger Derek Edge and reigning British super-middleweight champion John 'Cornelius' Carr for you, but first . . .' And the spotlight swings from the ring to a seat two rows back where a figure in a dark brown jacket and check shirt squints and hides his eyes.

' . . . I'd like you to welcome a very special guest this evening. Not just a great patron of the fight game, not just a friend to the East End community and to this gymnasium in particular . . .'

The crowd turns and the figure rises, wreathed in cigarette smoke. They see that he is of medium height and good-looking, with thick eyebrows, sharp razored sideburns and a boxer's jaw. His hair has a distinguished fleck of grey at the sides and he is wearing a two-inch button that reads 'FAMOUS WHEN DEAD'.

' . . . But perhaps the greatest popular singing artist that this country has produced since the days of Lennon and McCartney. Always original, relentlessly controversial and defiantly out of step with the critics, he's nevertheless conquered America without once bending his knee. We're honoured to have him here with us on the eve of the release of his fourth and best solo album, *Vauxhall And I*. Ladies and gentlemen, please be upstanding for our very special guest Mr. Steven Patrick Morrissey . . .'

He would, of course, have run a mile if that had happened, and you really wouldn't blame him. There aren't many private pleasures to be had when you occupy the rare position in the British mental landscape that Morrissey does, but a boxing match on a Friday night ought to be one of them. Even so, a couple of the doormen at the York Hall near Bethnal Green were intrigued when he arrived for the *Select* pictures, wondering, 'Didn't he used to be in the Smiths or something?'

And what is it all about anyway, this well-known sensitive soul taking an active interest in young lads smacking seven colours of blood, snot and cranial fluid out of one another? What would the pacifist Moz of old have thought?

'It is actually something I have been set on for quite a long time,' he'd said later. 'I'm by no means a boxing expert, but I've followed it long enough to hold a decent conversation about it.

'For me it's the sense of glamour that's attractive, the romance – which of course is enormous, as anyone who's attended bouts would know – but mainly it's the

'*Fame, fame, fatal fame*': Morrissey faces down a hostile crowd at his 1992 'Madstock' support slot; the prelude to ostracism in the UK/conquering the USA.

aggression that interests me. It has me instantly leaving my seat and heading for the ropes to join in.

'And it does give me a heightened sense of satisfaction, because in my life obviously there is absolutely no aggression at all. There is very little physical expression at all apart from standing on a stage and singing. Otherwise the body is firmly under control. It's a vessel, but it's docked with a very heavy anchor . . .'

The following Sunday, the day before *Vauxhall And I* comes out, I'm due to meet Morrissey at the Hook End Manor residential studio outside Reading, where he and the band are recording two B-sides for the next single to come off the album, 'Hold On To Your Friends'. A huge complex of converted farmhouse buildings and stables hidden in a labyrinth of badly-signposted country lanes, Hook End is something of a retreat for Morrissey, albeit one with a mixed history – he recorded both the doomed *Kill Uncle* as well as the triumphant *Your Arsenal* here.

It's a bad day at Hook End. The reason, as ever: the press. Morrissey's personal assistant-cum-chief of staff Jake – a stocky ex-boxer at the twenties-thirties crossroads, with a skinhead crop, a white Fred Perry-style shirt and hard blue eyes – is furious about a 'stitch-up' of Morrissey by Julie Burchill in that morning's *Sunday Times*. He had had to go on a ten-mile run that morning 'to work off the aggression', he says, and he makes it clear that Burchill should count herself lucky she's not a man, otherwise . . .

Jake's loyalty to Morrissey couldn't be fiercer. As he leads me to the studio's sitting-room, he tells me how frustrated he is that nothing he's ever read about Morrissey ever communicates what a great bloke as well as a talent Moz is, that he doesn't deserve the things that are written about him. And that if this piece is a similar stitch-up to the Burchill story, I'd better watch my back.

It's a big lounge and on one of three couches there's a turntable with a handwritten notice reading 'DO NOT PLAY THIS WHILE MOZ IS ASLEEP AS HE IS OLD AND NEEDS HIS KIP' – 'I wrote that, but don't read it,' Jake grins as he leaves.

Alain Whyte, guitarist, backing vocalist and writer of the music on *Vauxhall*'s more reflective songs, brings a tray with tea and two chocolate fingers and puts it on the coffee-table next to an audio-book, *Alfie Lends A Hand* read by Thora Hird. He's tall and seemingly shy, his quiff is more precarious than Morrissey's and he wears the denim uniform – he looks like Mark Lamarr's little brother. When I comment that *Vauxhall* is a wholly fantastic record, he's almost embarrassed, and replies to the effect that absolutely everything Morrissey has ever done has been fantastic, like it's the first time anyone's complimented him at all. A bizarre notion considering that he wrote almost all of the blistering *Your Arsenal* too.

Then he's gone, and Morrissey's here.

It's been said before that Morrissey has charisma, but never quite how much he has. It's like a forcefield coming into the room, a personal magnetism of quite epic proportions, and if one thing's for sure it's that – despite all the I'm unloveable protestations – he knows it. Whatever the charm that seeps off the vinyl or the rapacious allure he gives off onstage, face-to-face Moz is something totally different. In a moment I understand why Jake and Alain are so utterly committed to him. Never mind MacPhisto, we should have dressed Simon from *Brookside* up in a denim jacket, a quiff, a 1 oz pendant and a Union Jack.

He looks well, very well, and furthermore he's doing what pop stars aren't supposed to do: looking better as he gets older. The rumours that he's been working out and now looks like one of the Gladiators are not true, but it's hard to see how the wan skinnymalink in those early Smiths pictures has metamorphosed into this Gregory Peck character here. (Tea, Morrissey? Don't mind if I do.)

In fact, what with the boxing and the chunky pendants and the tattoos on the record sleeves (it's Jake on the back of 'The More You Ignore Me', although the 'MOZ' is fake), people might suspect that Morrissey is developing a laddish side.

'No, it's not true! I don't by any means want to turn into a 52-year-old *lad*,' he says, spitting the word out as he settles back on the couch. 'And I can't imagine that that is a very attractive thing to be, but equally I am no longer strapped to the Women's Studies section of Waterstones on Kensington High Street night and day, as many people still seem to believe. The world that I live in is quite broad. For instance, I go to the football whenever I can and whenever seems decent. And whenever I can get in for free.'

Do you follow any side in particular?

'Not avidly. There's no side that's close to perfection, there's no side that deserves unanimous blind adoration from my point of view.' Not even the fantastic . . .

'Tranmere? No, not even Manchester United. But whenever our dear old friend Morrissey [*John Morrissey, Tranmere Rover super-sub and provider of many comedy headlines in the* Liverpool Echo] comes on to the pitch and I hear the chant of "Morrissey!" I leap from the settee and hit my head on the ceiling. I'm sure he hopes we're not related, otherwise he'll remain Number Twelve forever.'

Ah, here we go . . . Morrissey in self-deprecation mode. No one else in pop has quite the same absolute no-contest self-belief coupled with a desire to knock himself at every turn. It's more complex than false modesty – nobody believes in Morrissey as much as Morrissey does – but at the same time it's perplexing.

Morrissey, do you hide behind all these quips and witty badinage?

'I don't consider it wit, to be honest,' he replies. 'I think I'm quite dull, really. I see myself rather like an old discarded dishrag. I don't deny that, you know, stand me next to Primal Scream and I'll eat the lot of them alive – and I know you worship the very hair that they stand on – but next to someone like that there is no competition. Intellectually there is no competition at all in pop music any longer! Everybody is so boring! *Relentlessly* boring! Even those who are considered not to be, bore me stiff. And I can forgive people of anything except dullness.'

Hold on, are we into a rant now . . . ?

'It is easy pickings in pop now,' Morrissey declares. 'The job is anybody's in 1994 – hence the ascendancy of Suede despite the obvious fact that they did not do their apprenticeships. If you have the stamina and the gumption and the mettle, pop music is there for anyone right now. And I hope someone comes forward very soon.'

You've been banging the gong for Echobelly

'Echobelly's new single ['Insomniac'] is, in a truly sane world, an indisputable Top

Five record. It is astonishing and in my eyes they are an astonishing band. They are naturally, simply, very good, they play very well and their songs are very attractive, which is sadly very rare . . .'

Hang on, Suede have some quite good songs . . .

'Yes, Suede have got some *quite* good songs but Echobelly have some *great* songs. We have very low standards these days. If you study the music press over the past six years you see acres and acres of critical errors made by absurd journalists. Hosts of horses that were heavily backed but broke their legs before the starting gun. The new Smiths! They all faltered and failed and fell before the summer ended.

'All the rock writers who make those outlandish, superlative whatnots – they never have to stand up and say, Yes, we were actually *wrong* about the Wheelchair Muggers From North Manchester or whomever. They never have to apologise.'

Oh dear – the press again.

It's been hard work being a Morrissey fan for most of the 1990s – if not for the cre-ative doldrums of *Kill Uncle* then for the, ah, 'controversies' surrounding *Your Arsenal*, of which more later. Whatever, *Vauxhall And I* ('It's a reference to a certain person I know who was *born and braised* in Vauxhall,' he says) is a five-star payoff, featuring some of the best songs he's written together with that rarest thing in a Morrissey record, a tiny sense of optimism.

Though songs like 'Now My Heart Is Full' are sprinkled with characters from *Brighton Rock*, the record is far from the ritualistic excavation of his past that was serving Morrissey less and less well as inspiration. It's also an acutely beautiful record.

'Well I am an *extremely* beautiful person,' he shrugs. 'And I'm not just searching for a joke there. Yes, it *is* a beautiful record and I set out that it should be so. I thought it was time to put lots of things away in their boxes and their cupboards, and allow age to take its natural toll, for better or worse.'

It has been described as the beginning of Morrissey's Mature Period.

'Which is of course a grave insult. To mature at the tender age of 34 is like Doris Day being the world's oldest living virgin. It's nothing to boast about in the steam baths at York Hall. But I think I was certainly really tired of the past. "Now My Heart Is Full" has a sense of jubilant exhaustion with looking over one's shoulder all the time and draining one's reference points. I mean, even I – *even I* – went a little bit too far with *A Taste of Honey*.

'I have perhaps overtapped my sources and now all that is over, basically. I have a vast record and video and tape collection, but I look at it now in a different light. It's no longer something I feel I need to be embroiled in night and day. I have realised that the past is actually over, and it is a great relief to me. It's like being told that you've been cured of chronic tuberculosis or housewife's knee or something.'

Yet you've never been seen as a person who looks forward to the future with a sense of anticipation.

'Well, I always tried to *form* the future – which I know sounds far too intellectu-al for a pop magazine – but I don't any more. I feel free to do absolutely nothing at all, and it is exhilarating. In the past I always felt an enormous sense of self-responsibility and of permanent self . . . *actualising*. Which has gone. I have realised that it really doesn't matter any more.'

With the result that the old scathing Morrissey is developing a sense of mercy. There's a song on *Vauxhall*, the pop at empty-headed beach culture called 'The Lazy Sunbathers', that fits right into the Moz canon of hate-songs with 'Ordinary Boys' and 'Rusholme Ruffians', yet for the first time it sounds like there's a little affection in your voice.

'Mnnnn . . . Not really, it just sounds that way. As you know, I have a very soft voice . . .'

But are you developing a soft spot for the people you used to lampoon and mock?

'No, no, quite the opposite. I'll always be in the blue corner.'

Vauxhall also does one thing which you've never really done before in your solo career, which is point a little at the Smiths – particularly 'Hold On To Your Friends'. Why is that? Are you more comfortable with the Smiths' legacy now?

'No, there's no intention there at all. There is this worldwide assumption that since the demise of the Smiths I have done relatively little, yet if you study the Smiths discography and my discography it almost matches now. Sometimes I do get tired of going back to the Smiths, because it is not as if I have sat around in a rocking chair since *Strangeways, Here We Come* faded away. I *have* actually kept moving.

'In any case it's very hard for me to say because there has never been another part of my life at all. From "Hand In Glove" to "Hold On To Your Friends", it simply *is* my life (*he spreads his hands*). Which is why I resent the Smiths being put forward as somehow being other people. The Smiths were just as much me as *Vauxhall And I* is. Johnny has not been there recently, shall we say, but otherwise everything has always been the same.'

In last month's *Q*, you described Andy Rourke and Mike Joyce rather cruelly as Rick and Bruce. How could you say that about your old muckers?

'The original Rick and Bruce I actually loved! The Jam are one of my favourite groups of all time. But why can't I say that? I can say what I like.'

But they were such great guys! The bassline on 'Barbarism Begins At Home', the drum intro to 'The Queen Is Dead . . . they were so loyal and, and . . .

'But they didn't drag *you* through court, did they? Let's see what you feel about them once they do. I can arrange it!'

Alright. It's now known that the supposed acrimony between you and Johnny Marr is no longer a going concern. When were you last in touch?

'Yes, all that is completely over. I spoke to him yesterday and we'll be meeting in a few nights' time just to chew the fat and complain to one another . . .'

Last autumn he told us, after much pestering, that if you two ever did anything again it would be as Morrissey and Marr, not the Smiths. Would you write with him again?

'Of course, yes, but immediately I don't see the point and neither does he. So, why? Obviously I would consider it. I would love to hear his music again. And sometimes I do feel sad that he gives it to certain people who can't write lyrics terribly well . . . ha ha!'

You mean Barney Sumner? Come on, why can't everybody make an Italian disco record or two at some time in their lives?

'I fail to see why they have to . . .'

You seem to be a lot happier than the Morrissey we've come to expect – the caricature of relentless miserabilism – yet *Vauxhall And I* is quite an introspective, melancholy album even by your own sober standards. It has a tone of resignation.

'Yes, but no surprise, surely. I am not trying to manufacture some dramatic new twist in the proceedings. I would never claim that I am not fraught with immovable depression day in day out – which I am. But once you've made so many records, certain changes do take place in any case. Don't they? Otherwise you just fade away. Which I never have, despite certain enormous military efforts on behalf of certain magazines, I never have. The magazines that want to shoot me at dawn are still on their knees saying, *Please would you, we beg you, please please . . .*'

The press, the press, the perfidious press. Like a spinning compass needle that inevitably settles pointing northwards, Morrissey's conversation is always drawn to journalists and the evils they've perpetrated against him. Be it Johnny Rogan's book *The Severed Alliance* and its attendant fatwa, or the music weeklies' periodic fits of the right-on vapours against him, Morrissey can neither forgive nor forget.

Surely the latter was inevitable considering he'd never said much about his increasing fascination with skinhead culture and imagery, or about the songs in question – 'Asian Rut', 'Bengali In Platforms' and 'The National Front Disco'?

'Well, every time I do I get bottled. You can't really talk about those things in this country. For instance, there was a spate of television programmes at the end of last year about the BNP and it was very noticeable to me how the National Front are never *ever ever* given a clear voice or platform. They never are. Which baffles me.'

Some would say, Good thing too.

'But the reason why "The National Front Disco" was pounced upon was really because – if I may say so – it was actually a very good song. And if the song had been utter crap, no one would have cared. I was stopped by many many journalists who obviously raised the topic in an accusatory way, and I would say to them, *Please, now*, list the lines in the song which you feel are racist and dangerous and hateful. And they couldn't. Nobody ever ever could, and that irked me. Even though, simply in the voice on all of those songs, on "Asian Rut" or "Bengali In Platforms" or "The National Front Disco", one can plainly hear that here is no hate at all.

'But you soon realise that they are just out for you, and that it doesn't matter what you say or do. You can dress up as the Pope and they'll still be out for you. A short while later, on the front of *Select*, there was our friend from Suede and behind him was the Union Jack – and of course there was not a squeak from anywhere that he had become a club-wielding racist. It has really got nothing to do with racism, it is to do with *me*. It really is – or *was*, hopefully – a mere witch-hunt.'

What do you say to the argument that it's right that the National Front and the BNP should be denied access to the news media if they pursue their political goals through violence, and that you're being irresponsible?

'Well, I think that if the National Front were to hate anyone, it would be me. I would be top of the list. But I think it opens the debate. If the BNP were afforded

television time or unbiased space in newspapers, it would seem less of a threat and
it would ease the situation. They are gagged so much that they take revenge in the
most frightening way by hurting and killing people. But part of that is simply their
anger at being ignored in what is supposed to be a democratic society.'

Letters to the usual address, please.

Pop's relentless tedium, former colleagues' treachery, the press . . . this afternoon has
dredged up rather too much for Morrissey. When he came in he seemed, well, as
bouncy as he gets. Not now, though.

'I'm sorry,' he smiles. 'But when you sit for an hour or two saying, Me, I, Me, I,
Me, I, you turn into something rather shrivelled and ugly. I mean me, not you.'

Have you ever been in analysis, Morrissey?

'I have, yes, many a time, and left in extreme disgust. I find the billing unre-
warding, certainly. But I have been steeped in personal depression for so long that I
feel there is nothing any doctor or psychoanalyst can say to me. I know all about
depression and the weakening of the human spirit and struggle, and there is no one
who can tell me anything about it, and there is nobody who can help me.'

He stands up and crosses to the big stereo system in the corner of the room, picking up an album on the way and placing it on the deck. He's momentarily flum-
moxed by the controls on the turntable, which, oddly enough, is that dance-culture
icon the Technics AL1200 Vari-speed ('Maybe I ought to listen to more *techno*,' he
glowers, only half in fun) but finally fathoms it.

'I'll play you a song. This is my youth in one piece of music. Don't talk while
it's on.'

The song is 'Innocent And Vain' by Nico, from an LP called *The End* – one vast
grampus-wheeze of harmonium with Nico's ice-cold tomb-voice creaking away
inside an arrangement that is the very pinnacle of painful listening. Towards the end
it collapses into a montage of sourceless shrieking and random echo reminiscent of
the Aphex Twin at his most science-fictiony. Every empty-head who's ever dismissed
the Morrissey catalogue – with its wit and playfulness and deadpan humour – as
depressing, ought to be forced to listen to this torture and reflect that *this* is what is
going on in Morrissey's head.

And throughout Morrissey sits on the corner of the couch, head bowed, eyes
closed, arms folded, and fists driven into his armpits. He's just made possibly his
greatest LP and he looks like he's in hell.

It works out fine in the end. The following week Morrissey is all but mobbed to
death at HMV Shop signings in London and Manchester (and he plays Nico on the
in-store sound system at both). *Vauxhall* goes in at number one, the first Morrissey
LP to do so since *Viva Hate*. The *Sunday Times* piece proves to be a harmless bit of
farce in which Moz visits Castle Burchill and Julie B is horrible to him because he
didn't make an appointment. What does he have to worry about anyway?

Before I left Hook End, I asked him about last year's rumours that he'd finally
come to the end of his tether, that *Vauxhall* would be Morrissey's last stand. Had he
contemplated giving it all up? Could he, physically?

'Yes, I could, definitely,' he'd replied brightly. 'That is the great new feeling I have. *Vauxhall And I* affords me that feeling and no other record has. Never. It has always been a mission 'til death, but now I just no longer feel *obliged* to anyone.

'I now feel I *could* live and be Dirk Bogarde. I could live in a mansion flat in Chelsea and see nobody, which would be a perfect life. I could be 76. He sent me a card the other day . . .'

Who, *Dirk Bogarde?* Are you sure?

'Yes, and I almost cried with joy when it arrived. I thought, Put it this way, *Mozzer*, you have a card from Dirk Bogarde here (*and he slapped the settee*). You have Alan Bennett sitting in your kitchen having tea. You have David Bowie having sung one of your songs quite beautifully. What else are you looking for? What right do I have to be sour-faced and complaining, queuing up at Waitrose in Holloway being annoyed because somebody in front of me has got a leg of lamb? What more could there be?'

Select, May 1994

DO YOU F★@KIN' WANT SOME?

—————— BY STUART MACONIE ——————

'I'm not the man you think I am,' he tells the girl but, of course, he is and she knows it. The look on her face is something to behold. She stops two blokes for directions to a Camden pub and one of them turns out to be, you know, *him*. The quiff. The most famous jawline in pop. The works. 'No, really, I'm a roofer from Balham,' he offers evasively. But she is not to be dissuaded, and her persistence is rewarded when she walks away clutching a scrap of student notepad on which is daubed in child-like hand: 'Morrissey'.

He lives in a fashionably squalid postal district of London, though there is nothing squalid about his habitude; well-appointed, airy, the huge, brash, matt black TV might fox Loyd Grossman but the gold discs and the blow-up of the 'Boxers' sleeve would give the game away to Eamonn Holmes or Eve Pollard or even one of the stupider cast members of *The Bill*. But the thick, humid evening air forces us outside on to a patch of communal grass. And at least one American backpacker will be forever grateful.

Southpaw Grammar is Morrissey's new album, his first for RCA and, let's not be coy, it rocks. The opening track, 'The Teachers Are Afraid Of The Pupils', may be the best thing he has done since the collapse of his former group. Dark, dramatic and a reversal of the caustic sentiments of 'The Headmaster Ritual' whereby Morrissey takes pity on a bullied and hunted pedagogue. There are ominous strings and, sensationally, chordage of a volume, amplitude and bulk that would put Pearl Jam or Nirvana to shame. Elsewhere, he takes swings at journalists who dabble in the low-life and boy racers who 'have the whole world in their hand as they stand at the urinal'. There is even, implausibly, the second song in the history of rock to bear the title 'Dagenham Dave'. To say that Mozzer's new single is better than its Stranglers namesake is to damn this great tune with faint praise. As always he is effusive, witty and wicked about everything from Liz Hurley to the Jesus and Mary Chain, from Paul Weller to those deluded unfortunates who think leggings are a good idea . . .

Why did you leave EMI?
Well, why indeed, seven years, seven albums . . . Terribly nice people. I've very good friends there but it seemed the thing to do. I realised that I was in the building so often that I was surprised they didn't give me a janitor's bucket. 'Here comes dear old Mogsy; let's give him a few Angelic Upstarts eight by tens and he'll be happy.' But there was nowhere else to go with EMI. It was enough time to know whether I was going to rule the planet or not. And I expect I won't.

So moving on is part of a campaign for world domination?
Not in the least. Can you imagine anything so boring as world domination. What would you do in your spare time?

Why RCA? Elvis Presley?
Well, partly, I can't deny that. But it sounds good, doesn't it, RCA? Modern record labels don't sound good. Morrissey and RCA sounds good, don't you agree?

***Southpaw Grammar** has got an eleven-minute track, a ten-minute one. Have you gone progressive rock?*
Oh, definitely, I'd love to continue where Van Der Graaf Generator left off. No, we just didn't know how to stop the tape. There's no great point. I mean, they're still pop songs, aren't they? Enough said. As musicians, they've improved enormously from when we began and we've become a group and it shows. It's not a matter of me saying, 'You get on with it while I go and ski somewhere.' We're just getting better. That simple; that complicated.

Another boxing allusion, I see.
Southpaw Grammar is the school of hard knocks. It's coming up the hard way and taking your bruises with you.

So you see yourself as a graduate of the school of hard knocks?
Well, it's not been easy. Put it that way. Whether we're talking about life or the dear old music industry. But of course, that drags us into extremely depressing territory. I don't know a great deal about boxing. I released a single called 'Boxers' and everyone assumes I'm some authority and I'm not. I'm not an expert on the manly art or the sweet science as it's called. I just enjoy the violent aspect of it. I think it's quite glamorous. I long for my chance to join in. No, no, I don't think I'm ready to spring into the ring.

Axl Rose once wrote a song . . .
Nobody's interested.

. . . called 'Get In The Ring', in which he invited his detractors to sort it out pugilistically. Does that appeal to you?
No. I've got better things to do . . . like planting bulbs.

People will say it's pure affectation, like the current bourgeois football fad.
Well, some people will always say something. I'm not an expert. I'm just a face in the crowd who enjoys it for maybe a misguided aspect. But I do enjoy the unpleasantness. And the working-class aspect, which I don't need to mention, do I?

Been to many bouts?
As many as I can get to. Some of which are extremely boring. But some are very interesting. There are lots of unusual characters. And, of course, our Prince friend [*Hamed Naseem*] is top of the list. I long to see him trip over the ropes, which of course he won't.

What are the advantages of being rich?

None really. Which is why I find it sad to meet people who are totally geared toward finance. I know for a fact that it's quite meaningless. Of course, it's easy for me to say that as I lounge here. But it's true. You may be a billionaire, but if you contract cancer, you may as well live in a bedsit in Birmingham.

'Reader Meet Author' seems to be about people who 'slum it'.
I've come across it many times. It's a fascinating phenomenon. Especially amongst music journalists who pretend to understand all aspects of life however degrading. It amuses me that these people are middle class and I know a few and their preoccupation is in meddling with the destitute and desperate as a hobby. Middle-class writers are fascinated by those who struggle. They find it righteous and amusing.

Is 'low life' the right term for what you write about?
No, it's my life actually. It's not affected in the least. Working-class culture isn't particularly going anywhere. On the song you mention, I sing, 'The year 2000 won't change anyone here' and that's true. It won't change their lives. They won't be catapulted into space age culture and mobile fax machines. The poor remain poor. Someone has to work in Woolworth's.

And it could have been you.
No. I haven't got the legs.

Do you enjoy provoking people?
Not in the least. I've never tried . . . have I?

The Union Jack business was pretty provocative.
I didn't invent the Union Jack, you do realise that don't you? I didn't knock it up on a spinning wheel in the front room. I can't account for people's reactions. Some people adore it; others are embarrassed by it. I don't get it. I don't understand the fascist implications of it. I think it happened because it was time to get old Mozzer. Nothing more sophisticated that that.

How do you feel about Eric Cantona?
I feel very excited by him as long as he doesn't say anything. He certainly made the world of football slightly less boring this year. I approved because it was very entertaining and I found the witnesses in the crowd very suspect. When I saw it on television, I howled. I watched every version of the news. He also happens to be a great player. The negative publicity doesn't matter . . . as don't the Crystal Palace fans. I think he set a good example. I found it very encouraging and glamorous and exciting. And it wasn't violence as much as self-defence. He is a human being and the abuse hurled at him was incredibly personal and disturbing. How could he have lived with himself if he had not reacted? Everyone secretly agrees with him anyway.

What of Hugh Grant?
I couldn't care less, but if forced I'd say it makes him more interesting than he actu-

ally is. People who are insufferably respectable are just not interesting. It'll work in his favour. He should do it more often. If I was Elizabeth Hurley *and he hadn't done anything*, I wouldn't stand by him. He's so overrated. All he seems to have is an English accent. I don't believe incidents like Hugh Grant's and Cantona's are moments of insanity. Those seem like moments of sanity. Perhaps it's the rest of their lives that are insane. People are terribly stifled and apart and not in touch with how they feel.

This sounds like the Oprah Winfrey show.
I haven't been on there recently but I know what you mean. But if people took the plunge, they'd find that they wouldn't be rejected and life wouldn't deteriorate, but people are terribly frightened. Within pop music people are frightened of not being accepted. I've never felt that but I know others do.

But if people were healthier emotionally, surely artists like yourself would be out of a job.
But haven't we had enough art? How much art do we need? It results in analysing vomit. There are better things to do.

Do you get recognised in the back of taxis?
I get recognised in the front of taxis as well! But I've learned my lesson. My celebrity doesn't cause many problems because I don't do anything extreme. There are constant nudges and winks and nods as I walk around. But that's survivable. But at the level of Cliff Richard or Michael Jackson life would be unbearable. Money can't compensate for that lack of freedom. I'm happy with the level of fame I have. Fame really isn't as useful or attractive as it once was. If you are famous now, you have to pay for your fame and answer for your existence. And anything you do, however innocent, can be made to seem devious. The only interest we have is in revealing famous people as something unsavoury. I know that some people who are famous are terrible, relentless slags but most of them aren't. That's why I never buy newspapers. I have no interest in seeing people destroyed whether I like them or not. I don't want to know about Hugh Grant. I don't want to know about Tommy Steele even.

Were you happier as a teenager?
No, I was never happy then. Not for one day. But I think I've probably touched upon that in the past. I've mentioned it somewhere! I never thought it was possible to get this old. I thought when you reached 35, you were shipped off to Anglesey. But I don't want to go back. There's nothing happy there for me. I'm getting happier as I get older but that's sheer perseverance. I've just stuck with it. I never enjoyed life in my twenties, not one minute of it. It was a test of endurance that I'm surprised I survived. Professionally, of course, I was doing very well but personally it couldn't have been worse or more difficult for me if I'd been living in a mud hut in Leeds.

Have you ever had a religious impulse?
No, I haven't in all honesty. I would like to but I haven't. There must be consolations and comforts because millions of people can't be wrong but I think I'm just a doomed realist.

'Incidentally, do you f*@ckin' want some?': This burlier, beerier model developed throughout the 1990s, worlds apart from the perceived wimpishness of the Smiths era.

What do you think of Oasis?

I've always liked them. I think they're very amusing and very Mancunian and the best Manchester group since . . . (*shrugs smilingly*). But I do wish the singer wasn't so put out. 'Do I *really* have to sing this next verse?' He could always go back to being a painter and decorator in Burnage. I read a comment supposedly by me in *Club International* where I called them boring electricians, words which have never left my lips. So they've slagged me off, of course, they have to, but I like them. Noel's very funny. Very runt of the litter. You can tell that he'd run off with the fillings in his grandmother's teeth but that doesn't mean he doesn't love her.

Would you pass Norman Tebbit's cricket test?

Yes, I would. Anything Norman Tebbit has anything to do with must be a bad idea but if someone else were to word it differently I'd probably support it.

If you were forced to leave England at the point of a gun, where would you go?
Jersey, Guernsey, anywhere with a decent postal service.

Not Los Angeles?
No. I need grit and struggle and Los Angeles is terribly nice but people once they get there cease to be real. Constant and repetitive fulfilment is not good for the human spirit. We all need rain and good old depression. Life can't be all beer and skittles.

What do you think of Martin Rossiter from Gene? He sounds uncannily like you.
Well again, you'll fall over but I wasn't aware of Gene until someone handed me a tape of their album and said, 'Have you ever seen *Stars in Their Eyes?*' And I said, 'I'm not aware of it,' and they said, 'Well you are going to be now.' I thought it was a good record. It didn't so much remind me of the Smiths as (*coyly*) well . . . me. When people sing like me, and thankfully very few do, people think it's like the Smiths but the musicians in Gene are not like the Smiths. Let's face it, when we begin, we all take from the people who influence us until we find our own ground. I don't want to be cynical, old and crusty. Why should I criticise Gene? I don't feel inclined to. But neither do I feel that I should race toward them waving the gladioli saying, 'Now it's your turn.'

Where do you go for your holidays?
I don't go on holiday. Not since they shut down Butlin's at Bognor. No, I just hang around the East End in a long black cape.

You once said to me that your ideal audience was skinheads in nail varnish. Is that still true?
I'm sure there was a certain flippancy to that remark. I wasn't banging a mallet on the table.

But there's many a true word spoken in jest.
Not by me. No, I really did get tired of being considered the flat-footed wallflower, which still haunts me a bit. And yet I listen to other people's music and it never strikes me as anything like as hard or confrontational as mine. But I'm still considered this weakling.

Ever fancied Prozac?
I know little about Prozac. I've tried it of course. We all have. But it just didn't work for me. So there's no appeal in something that doesn't work.

Did you take any interest in the Tory leadership election?
Yes, I did. I was very excited by John Redwood. And very depressed when he failed. But it's all inconsequential because Major is doomed and it doesn't matter how many Eurovision Song Contests he wins and how much he polished his spectacles. His life has got doom sealed around it and rightly so because he's astonishingly weak. Redwood was

amusing and in political life that's extraordinary. He seemed amused by what was going on and he had a spark of life, which is incredibly rare. People like that don't succeed in politics, which is so drab now. Bad politicians are elected by good people who don't vote. At the final hurdle it will be Tony Blair and Michael Portillo. And I think Michael Portillo will probably do it because the press like him. And that's all that counts. Kinnock, who was a great orator and politician, was destroyed by the press not by the people of England. The press like Michael Portillo so it shall be him. John Major is weak and I don't think we should feel sorry for him. Do you find you have several hours to kill in the day in which to feel sorry for John Major? There are people starving to death in Preston you know.

Where do you buy your clothes?
I buy them second-hand from Camden market; I have an extraordinary capacity for disguise. I dress up as a train driver. I never buy anything new. They do make good new clothes but I think of the West End and Comme Des Garcons and I don't really fancy it. You walk in the door and you're besieged by glamorous assistants and that's no good. It's very intimidating.

Would you like to be like Van Morrison or Neil Young, an elder statesman of rock?
Not particularly, because the celebration of those people is that they are still alive and they go on and on about how healthy they are as if it's a miracle. That's not for me. I don't want to stick around longer than necessary. 'So why are *you* still here?' I can hear millions of people saying. The Rolling Stones are an industry and nothing more. I've met Keith and Mick and they were very, very nice. The only useless thing is the music. Do people listen? Part of me thinks that the notion of pop and rock being for young people is very true.

You favour a compulsory retirement age then?
Yes, I do. It should be whatever age I'm not. I said in 1988 I thought pop music was over and I still believe that. Very few of the newer groups have anything original to offer. I quite like Supergrass. But the trouble with new young groups is that the press always ruin it. You always want to seem ahead of the game.

Do you still watch Top of the Pops?
No. What's the point? I've seen it by accident and it seems always to be the same dance song, and I've always believed that dance music should not be allowed to infiltrate the pop chart. It should be separate like it was in America in the seventies as was country, etc. It makes it impossible to listen to the radio or watch *The Chart Show*. It's always dance stroke rap stroke whatever.

Jungle?
Jungle! I don't know what it is.

It's someone shouting incomprehensibly over mechanical rhythms.
But I thought that was the Jesus and Mary Chain.

What do you think of the Criminal Justice Bill? Do you think people in leggings have

a right to live wherever they choose?
I don't think people in leggings have a right to live. I don't think people should hold raves because I don't like rave music. I suggested the Criminal Justice Bill, so I'm glad that it's been taken up.

Ever bought a Lottery ticket?
Absolutely never. When anybody mentions the Lottery I feel quite ill. It's one of the worst things ever to happen to England. It makes people savage and tedious. Do something useful instead. And I absolutely loathe Anthea Turner. If she gave me a cheque for twenty million I'd hand it back. She's awful to watch. That fixed smile, that fraudulent jollity. She's on breakfast television and even if she were telling you that a planeload of children had died in the worst Air India crash ever, she would still keep smiling. How has she got a job? Her happiness actually makes me depressed.

Ever been to a karaoke evening?
Yes, at the Little Driver in Bow and it was shocking.

Why?
You know why. I like simple pleasures and uncomplicated people but that takes the biscuit. I can't understand why anybody would want to do it. There are easier ways to embarrass yourself.

I see Paul Weller's back.
Back? Where's he been? I haven't noticed. He was encouraging at one time because he was one artist who surpassed his heroes. The Jam will be very special forever. I think people are saying thank you for the Jam. And for younger groups like Blur obviously it struck a chord. Weller performed 'Woodcutter's Son' on *Later* and immediately after, Supergrass came in with 'We are young . . .' and I thought, 'There's a gigantic message hanging in the air there for you, Uncle Paul.'

What did Kurt Cobain's suicide mean to you?
I felt sad and I felt envious. He had the courage to do it. I admire people who self-destruct and that's not a new comment for me. They are taking control. They're refusing to continue with unhappiness, which shows tremendous self-will. It must be very frightening to sit down and look at your watch and think, 'In 30 minutes I will not be here.' Thinking, 'I'm going to go on that strange journey.' Modern life is very pressurising. We're all on the verge of hysteria. There are people around who'll shoot your head off because you forgot to indicate.

Could you survive in prison?
Only as a stand-up comedian. No, prison would probably be the making of me. It would be the beginning of life. Freedom doesn't always mean freedom. I'd probably prosper. We all need a bit of restriction.

Have you ever been to a Yates's Wine Lodge?

Yes, there was one in Manchester in the old days full of drunken men in overcoats with sick on their lapels. I like pubs; they're one of the last bastions of Englishness. I like quiet old men's pubs. I mean, I like the pubs to be quiet not the old men.

Ever been in trouble with the police?
Never. Well, that's a lie. I was visited a long time ago about a song I once did.

So the 'Margaret On The Guillotine' story is true?
Of course. Yes, ridiculous grounds. But they don't need grounds, they've got a funny little hat and a truncheon. They recorded a conversation for an hour and searched the house for a guillotine. Curiously, they actually found one. They thought I was public enemy number 72. And at the end of the grilling they actually asked me to sign various things for ailing nieces, which I thought was a bit perverted.

Riots are back. Do you approve?
Yes, I do. (*laughs*) No, I don't. The seventies persist, don't they? I saw some Chopper bicycles outside a pub the other day, which I thought was extreme. I've only ever found violence attractive from a distance, which is a bit pathetic, I know, but I suppose if you're in the thick of it, it's a bit unsettling. Incidentally, do you fuckin' want some?

Do I take it you're a fan of Quentin Tarantino?
Is he *Pulp Fiction*? I haven't seen that. I'm not ready for John Revolting yet. I have bigger fish to fry.

Are you a member of anything?
The Skinhead Benevolent Fund. No, I don't mix. I don't make friends ever. I don't see the point.

But you have friends, so you must have made them at some point.
Don't complicate things. We have as many friends as we have personalities. Do you know who said that? Emerson. Keith Emerson.

Do you work out?
No, not at all. I don't do anything. I'd never feel confident in a gym. I wheel a trolley around Waitrose.

Do you ever stand in front of the urinal and think you've got the whole world in your hands?
I don't need to walk towards the urinal, I already know. And you should know better than to ask.

That's an enigmatic answer.
Well, we do our best.

Q, September 1995

THE KING OF BEDSIT ANGST GROWS UP

BY WILL SELF

It's a well-known fact about Morrissey that his record contracts stipulate various wacky, star-like things. One of them is the presence of certain, very particular kinds of snack food during any interview. So it is that the first thing that meets my eye when I enter the penthouse boardroom of RCA records is a table; laid out on it are plates of crisps (plain, or so I've read) and some KitKats; to one side are bottles of pop.

At the outset, Morrissey is drinking a cup of coffee, and during our discussion he occasionally elides his way out of anything remotely resembling an impasse by alluding to these eatables: 'This is such great coffee,' he pronounces at one point, and when I ask him what's on his mind he replies: 'This KitKat.'

These are just the sort of tropes Morrissey comes up with from minute to minute, turning phrases as he does, like rotating signs outside petrol stations. Morrissey is for many people irredeemably associated with the 1980s – and even to say this brings that decade into sharper focus. In the 1980s a particular kind of male adolescent angst and self-pity infused the zeitgeist, and Morrissey was its avatar. He was the first male pop star to address a whole generation of boys who were growing up with feminism, a heavy underscoring to a period of natural inadequacy and uselessness.

His miserabilism came from that archetypally grim, ravaged provincial city, Manchester. Cut off from a supporting popular culture with any remotely intellectual element, or political undercurrent, Morrissey forged the Smiths, the pop band who were to be spokesmen for the Miserabilists, and penned their national anthem 'Heaven Knows I'm Miserable Now'.

Morrissey's hipness and artistry was always wedded to an exquisite taste for the most subtle kitsch of the recent English past, and slathered in Yank worship. But mixed in with all this came his ambiguous campery.

Among the train-spotters of the music press, his break with Johnny Marr, his songwriting partner in the Smiths, has been insistently viewed as a creative death for him. Yet some of the solo material he has recorded is just as strong as anything they ever did together – and by the same token, who outside the music press has heard much about Johnny Marr in the past five years?

Suited darkly, booted sturdily and wearing one of those jerseyesque shirts that almost define the retro-committed, Morrissey is very attractive in the flesh. The deeply-set blue eyes coruscate from beneath a high, intelligent brow, and given his self-professed celibacy one of the first things any conscientious interviewer does is to try to assess the quality of his physical presence, his essential heft.

Is this a man tortured by his own sexuality and that of others? Is this a man about whom lingers a faint scent of fleshy revulsion? No, on both counts. His handshake is firm, warm even. His body language is far from craven. Indeed, there is something quite affectingly embodied about him. At one point in our conversation he commented on my face: 'You've actually got the face of a criminal that I've met . . . a very strong face. A very determined face.' Setting aside the content of this remark, it struck me that this was not the sort of thing that someone intent on denying corporeality would be likely to say.

And of course, while his well-publicised encouragement of the excessive and physical devotion of his fans has a double-edged quality about it (you can touch, but only in this contrived, aberrant way), in person he lampoons his own self-created shibboleths, again and again and again. When I suggest to him that stage invasions puncture the surface of stardom and confront him with fans who are 98 per cent water, he replies: 'Let it be punctured, let it be punctured, that's my motto.'

The following week at Wembley Arena, the star goes so far towards puncturing that he almost bodily hauls a would-be stage invader through the arms of bouncers, past the rank of monitors and into his arms. He receives kisses on both cheeks as no more than his due. He also bends down into the thicket of arms waving towards him and as much takes as gives out the benediction.

There's a submerged incongruity here, but one that works in his favour. Perhaps one of the central ironies about this most ironic of performers is that he clearly seeks adulation from those most indisposed to give it – the Dagenham Daves and Rusholme Ruffians who people his landscapes – and eschews the advances of those who regard his talent as essentially poetic. When I ask him if he's ever been attracted to the world of the intelligentsia, he is emphatic: 'Absolutely not. In fact, scorn is perhaps all I really feel. I feel quite sad for such people. I think that everything there is to be lived is hanging round the gutter somewhere. I've always believed that and still do.'

Which rather begs the question, exactly how much hanging around the gutter is involved in researching his marvellously deadpan little word pictures? He mentions 'Certain pubs around north and east London. But I'm not the sort of person you're likely to spot because I don't go about wanting to be noticed . . . I'm just slipping in and slipping out, and if you were looking for me you'd never find me.'

He tells me that performance for him represents 'exuberance', and when I tax him that this goes somewhat against his self-styled anti-fun posture, he grins and admits it. That being said, Morrissey's idea of post-gig kicks is not exactly what we expect from a pop star: 'Just pure silence.' I found this attitude refreshing, but it did act as a springboard for Morrissey to trot out some of his more passe attitudinising: 'Life's incredibly boring. I don't say that in an effort to seem vaguely amusing but the secret of life is that there's no secret, it's just exceedingly boring.'

I got the feeling that these kinds of sallies are a form of bluff for Morrissey, and that he throws them out in much the way that aircraft in World War II dropped strips of metal to fool radar. If his interlocutors rise to such chaff, then they're not really worthy of consideration. But he's also an adept at sidestepping the conventional psychoanalytic thrusts of the interviewer.

When I mention the 'vexed question' of his sexuality, he replies: 'It doesn't vex me. I don't exactly think it vexes other people at all. People have their opinions and I don't mind what they are. I mean, there's a limit to what people can actually assume about sexuality, and at least I'm relieved by that. I don't think people assume anything any-more about me. I'm sort of classified in a non-sexual, asexual way, which is an air of dismissiveness which I quite like.'

The interesting thing about this speech is, of course, that the exact opposite is the truth: it does vex people, he does mind, there are no limits to what people can assume about sexuality (which is far from being a relief), and it is he himself who has struck the asexual attitude. It's worth remembering at this point that it was one of Morrissey's heroes, Oscar Wilde, who defined celibacy as 'the only known sexual per-version'.

Perhaps it would be too trite to suggest that the plaintive refrain of 'The Teachers Are Afraid Of The Pupils', the lead track on his latest album *Southpaw Grammar*, is in some way an echo of this posture: 'To be finished would be a relief,' the singer pro-claims, again and again and again.

The sting really comes when I say: 'Do you think you've pulled that one off?' And with another smile he replies: 'Yeah. Quite well. I think the skill has paid off quite well. I've managed to slip through the net – whatever the net is.' Then there's a neat little bit of wordplay, analogous in the Morrissey idiolect to a boxer's centre-ring shuf-fle. I interject: 'But – ' and he overrides me: 'I know you're about to say "but", but so am I. It's not really an issue, there's nothing to say, and there's nothing to ask, more to the point.'

He's right. Unless I choose to be a boor and attempt to crash into his private exis-tence, there really is nothing to ask. This is the 'skill' that Morrissey has perfected and it's a skill that in anyone else would be described as maturity.

Yes, that's the only revelation I have to give you about Steven Patrick Morrissey: he is, against all odds, a grown-up. How exactly he has managed this growing up it's hard to tell. The lineaments of the biography give the impression of a direct transferral from air guitar in front of a suburban Manchester mirror, to air guitar in front of hys-terical crowds at the Hacienda, followed by thirteen years of – albeit anomalous – stardom. Where exactly did he find those normal interactions, normal relationships, necessary to affect maturation?

Of course, it's no secret in the business that his 'no-touch' persona bears little rela-tion to a man who closely guards his close friendships; and quite clearly something is going on here. It was once said of Edward Heath that if he did have sex at all, it was only in a locked vault in the Bank of England. I don't wish to speculate about whether or not Morrissey has sex, but if he does I think it's fairly safe to assume that the 'locked vault' is a function of two things: an unswerving dedication to maintaining a genuine private life, and a capability for generating immense personal loyalty – a loy-alty vault, if you will.

When we discuss the issue of camp, which informs so much of his artistic sensi-bility, right down to the title of one of his solo albums: *Bona Drag* ('bona' meaning attractive or sexy in gay argot), he veers off into the Kenneth Williams diaries: 'It was quite gruesome, quite gruesome. I've read it a couple of times and each time it's been like a hammer on the head. An astonishingly depressing book. It's incredibly witty and well done, but the hollow ring it has throughout is murderous, absolutely murderous. I think he was always depressed, because the diaries spread over a 40-year period and even at the beginning of them he was saying, "why am I alive, what's the point?" And this was 1952. It's astonishing that he lasted so long.'

I tax him that some people might view his life as being a bit like that, and he replies, 'it's not. It definitely isn't,' with a deeply felt emphasis. So deep that I'm moved to put to him the most extreme contrast to Williams's life of emotional and sexual barrenness: 'Have you ever considered having children?' 'Yeah,' he says flatly, in his burring Mancunian voice. When we tease out this issue it becomes apparent that what bothers him about having kids is to do with this quite legitimate fear of over-identification with them: 'I wonder what they'd do. I mean, what do they do when they're eleven? What would they do when they were seventeen? What happens when your child turns round and says: "Look, I don't like this world. Why did you bring me into it? I don't want to be part of it. I'm not leaving home. I'm staying here, I refuse to grow up"?'

But if there are shades of his own (allegedly) willed infantility here, there are also discernible the lineaments of grown-up Morrissey, Morrissey whose 'skill' has served him well. He seems to understand only too well the impact of the ambiguous image he has created.

Morrissey, it became apparent to me, is someone who finds his love for other people painful and overpowering. In this he is, of course, like all of us, but perhaps more so. He has given up on his favourite soap, *Coronation Street*, but when discussing its replacement in his affections, *EastEnders*, he lets slip a yearning for a very populated, very unmiserable arcadia: 'I think people wish that life really was like that, that we couldn't avoid seeing 40 people every day that we spoke to, that knew everything about us, and that we couldn't avoid being caught up in these relationships all the time, and that there was somebody standing on the doorstep throughout the day. I think that's how we'd all secretly like to live. Within *EastEnders*, within *Coronation Street*, there are no age barriers. Senior citizens, young children, they all blend, and they all like one another and they all have a great deal to say, which isn't how life is.'

Perhaps here the complex mask of ritual, signs, signals and cultural references Morrissey has devised to obliterate the very non-contrived human character beneath, slips a little. But I'd be wary of pushing it. To me he said: 'I wish somebody would get it right. I don't mind if they hate me as long as they get it right.' And yet 'getting it right' would be wholly destructive for the image, if liberating for the man.

Throughout the solo career there has been a strenuous conflation of the notion of 'Englishness' with that of a camp, Ortonesque liking for 'rough lads'. Was Morrissey, like William Burroughs, I wondered, possessed of an eternal faith in the 'goodness' of these rough lads? Was this atmosphere, so vividly captured in *Southpaw Grammar*, one he saw as an arcadia or merely one of nostalgia?

'It's pure nostalgia, really, and there's very little truth in it. I'm well aware of that. I know that it's all pure fantasy really, and 50 per cent drivel. Everybody has their problems and there is no way of being that is absolutely free and fun loving and without horrific responsibilities. It just isn't true. And I think I've had the best of it personally. I don't think I'm missing anything because I'm not a roofer from Ilford.'

Did we really expect anything else? Every alleged 'arcadian' image Morrissey produces is in reality shot through with irony. The eponymous hero of 'Boy Racer' is described thus: 'Stood at the urinal/He thinks he's got the whole world in his hands.' And as for poor 'Dagenham Dave', 'Head in a blouse/Everybody loves him/I see why.' Yes indeed! But then, by the same token: 'He'd love to touch, he's afraid he might self-combust/I could say more, but you get the general idea.'

The implication being one of what? Chronically repressed homosexuality? Or merely the singer's own tedium vitae in the face of the exhausted husk of English working-class culture? The rubric here is one of subversion, subversion and more sub-version. This being most graphically shown when Morrissey, 37 and rising, comes on stage at Wembley Arena (where he is supporting David Bowie) with his somewhat younger fellow musicians. Either it's *Happy Days* with Morrissey as the Fonz and the vaguely bat-eared guitarist as Richie, or else something altogether more sinister.

The backcloth is a giant projection of the cover of *Southpaw Grammar*, the face of an obscure boxer which Morrissey himself plucked from the anonymity of an old copy of *The Ring*. There's a wheeze and a creak from the massive bunches of speakers dangling overhead, and 'Jerusalem' starts up, being sung by some long-gone school choir. The effect, in tandem with the suited, cropped figures striding about the dark stage is extremely unsettling. Is this the start of some weird fascist rally?

Then the band crashes into the opening chords of 'Reader Meet Author' and Morrissey begins to flail at the air with the cord of his microphone, pirouetting, hip-swivelling, for all the world like some camp version of Roy Rogers. He'd be run out of the British National Party in seconds if they caught him swishing about like this! Again he has subverted the political in a peculiarly personal way.

Later on in the set, Morrissey and the band perform the dark and extremely depressing song 'The Operation'. Like many of his songs this one is addressed to an unnamed person. Morrissey must be one of the few songwriters who uses the second person more than the first. 'You fight with your right hand,' he yodels, 'and caress with your left,' and as he joins up the couplet he wipes the arse of the air with a limp hand. This is presumably what he means by *Southpaw Grammar*, and the manifest and ongoing preoccupation with 'the other' in his work is so antithetical to his pos-ture of bedsit isolation that I wonder again just how truly protean a person this is? To me he said: 'I don't feel trapped in your tape recorder and on those CD's. I don't at all. I can do whatever I like and I can become whatever I like, and if next week I want to have thirteen children and live in Barking, then I can and I will, and nobody will stop me.'

This is all very double-edged, very southpaw. On one reading it smacks of an arrested, adolescent will-to-omnipotentiality, but on another it's an indicator of great sanity, and a refusal to believe wholly in the image he has created. While in his first incarnation, as the taboo-busting frontman for the Smiths, Morrissey was prone to using his platform for issuing diktats on all manner of issues unrelated to popular music, his fame now appears to have been well worn in, like a favourite old overcoat.

He confirmed this when I asked him how he managed to keep such tight control over the empire he has created: 'I only manage it by repeatedly saying "no". And then the obvious reputation gathers around you that you are a problem, because you are awkward, you are difficult, and you don't really want to be famous. But I just don't want to be famous in any way other than that which naturally suits me.'

I wonder what's going to happen to Morrissey. My hunch is that he may well find iconic pop status an increasing drag. He is a very funny man to be with, but he keeps his wit well reined in. Just on example of this came when we dissected the 'vexed question' of my not having a television. 'Is that a political statement?' he asked me, and when I said it was he rejoined: 'Do all your neighbours know that you don't possess a television set?'

I think the wit is reined in because it's so destructive of the ironic edifice he has created. Stardom requires a certain kind of stupidity to sustain it, and Morrissey is far from being a stupid man. He is responsible – among other things – for encapsulating 200 years of philosophical speculation in a single line: 'Does the body rule the mind or does the mind rule the body, I dunno.'

His ambitions as an artist clearly don't require him to feed the Moloch of celebrity with more creative babies. He once memorably sang, castigating yet another of his numinous others for their sexual peccadilloes: 'On the day that your mentality/Catches up with your biology.' But I think the comparable day of reckoning for Morrissey will come when he allows his sense of humour to catch up with his irony.

Even at Wembley Arena it looked as if the band had invited their uncle to come along and do a turn with them. Morrissey has too acute a view of himself – one hopes – to become one of those granddads of pop, perambulating around the stage in support hose, permanently marooned in some hormonal stretch limo. He told me he could 'do anything', I certainly hope he does. England needs him.

Life/The Observer, December 1995

THE IMPORTANCE OF BEING MORRISSEY

BY JENNIFER NINE

'I'm *completely* unpredictable,' he says at one point, smiling ' . . . *especially* on Friday nights.' And then, of course, he says absolutely nothing more about it.

It's called Being Morrissey.

And in fact we've all thought about Being Morrissey. The bands – some, like Gene, obviously, and some, like Radiohead, not – who wouldn't have been quite the same were it not for his songs of defiant self-love and self-loathing. The professional tough guy Henry Rollins, who's been mocking him so long you start to wonder if it's actually envy. The journalists impressed, exasperated, and outfoxed by the weary grandness with which he controls the game every time a tape recorder is switched on. The hundreds of fans at a recent gay and lesbian Morrissey convention which culminated in a mass singalong of 'The Queen Is Dead' at Buckingham Palace gates. Every introspective teenager *ever*, or at least circa 1982 to the present. And, erm, Vic Reeves' Morrissey the Consumer Monkey.

From the sublime to the ridiculous. And then me.

All of which makes meeting Morrissey himself – seven years after he last spoke to the *Maker* – all the more unnerving. And here he is, larger than life. Unexpectedly tall, unexpectedly handsome, unexpectedly fit-looking ('most people my age look dreadful; I'd say I'm probably "not bad"') lounging opposite me, and speaking softly in the manner of someone used to being listened to.

And he's on form. He's got a new set of record labels in the UK and America. He's got an effortlessly lithe and quite clearly Superior Quality Moz new single called 'Alma Matters' on the radio, where it sounds great, and in the charts. And he's got the imminent new album, *Maladjusted*. (The devoted and the nosy might wish to note that there's a slightly different track listing in America, where it includes a song that might very well be about former bandmates. It isn't particularly forgiving.)

Two things strike me. The second is that I'm determined not to burst into tears, even when I joke that he really should have a trapdoor to get rid of interviewers who stay too long and he says sweetly, 'Well, there is one, but it didn't work; I've been pressing the button for the last fifteen minutes.'

The first, of course, is how good Morrissey is at Being Morrissey. Meticulously gracious; carelessly articulate; effortlessly self-mocking . . . and sharp as a case full of stilettos and never missing a single trick. He smiles, laughs, dispenses small tokens of praise – 'you're absolutely right,' he nods indulgently, at one point – and then interrupts me with an unnervingly peremptory, '*What* was the question?' Or smirks, as I try to draw conclusions from his comments, and says, 'Yes, but *my* reasoning was much more interesting.'

Which, Being Morrissey and all, it probably was.

'But I *am* box office poison here,' he says when I ask why he applies the term to his UK status, despite a ten-year solo career – never mind the five in the Smiths – that includes two Number One albums and a busload of chart singles. 'I sell, but not a great deal, compared to your average Top Twenty person. A lot of people expect the worst of me, and that's why I'm box office poison. Though God knows it's a great thing to be. If I was in the pack there wouldn't be room to move. I'd hate to be everybody's friend. I'd hate to be in *Melody Maker* every week photographed with someone, smiling, somewhere. I always liked artists who remained aloof and who felt somehow superior.'

I ask if he has sympathy for the people who play that fame game.

'I don't have sympathy for *anyone*,' Morrissey tilts his head back. 'It's such a wasted emotion. I'd rather keep it all for myself. God knows I *need* it,' he adds, Being Morrissey again.

But surely your songs wouldn't have meant as much to so many, if they hadn't been imbued with sympathy?

'Well, maybe they mean more than they're *meant* to mean,' he retorts. 'Anyway, I prefer good old-fashioned spite.'

And what of the song 'He Cried'? When did you last cry?

'Not for a long time. I used to cry very regularly. And it's a fantastic cleansing process; I feel three stone lighter afterward. But I haven't recently. I've had cause to – we all know that,' he says, Being Morrissey again. 'But I truly haven't cried in a long time.'

Do you cry alone, or in front of other people?

His eyes widen. '*Alone*, of course. I have some dignity.'

But I'm sure there are people who would comfort you.

'Yes, but they're all on death row.'

Ah. But aren't the airmail stamps to America costing you a small fortune?

'You've tried it too, obviously,' he smirks.

Ah, the vagaries of fame. When was the last time you met someone who didn't know who you were?

'Possibly two days ago. I was trying to rent a car and was asked what my profession was. A lot of people don't know why they know me but recognise my face. I don't strut around hoping people recognise me. I don't walk down the street trying to score points seeing how many people recognise me and I don't burst into tears if they don't.'

Does fame induce agoraphobia?

'Slightly. There are certain days when it seems that people are really looking at me. And when you have that for 35 minutes in a day, you begin to think, "Well, should I go there, should I wear that hat, should I get on this bus?" and eventually you think, "To hell with it," and go back home. There's something about eye contact on the street that if you're staring at the people coming toward you, you think they think you're looking at them wondering whether they recognise you. So you begin to avoid people's face and eye contact.'

Maladjusted has one of the all-time great, swirling, angel-voiced Morrissey songs on it, 'Wide To Receive'. It's a love song, isn't it?

167

'Yes, it's supposed to be, but I'd never dash out on a limb. It's supposed to be an internet song. You know, lying by your computer waiting for someone to tap into you and finding that nobody is, and hence being wide to receive. How *awful*, of course, to be wide to receive and finding there's no reason to be.'

Do you have a computer?

'That's a trick question, and I refuse to answer,' Morrissey huffs.

Any interest in computers?

'I'm a Luddite,' he retorts.

But even Luddites know . . .

'No, they *don't*,' Morrissey contradicts.

So you've written a song about the internet, but you won't tell me if you have a computer.

'I'm not going to *cater*,' he says, mildly incredulous.

Is it just possible that you're always conscious of what things you do that are Being Morrissey-like, and which aren't, and only giving me the Being Morrissey bits?

'No.'

It's not just anoraks who use computers, you know. Some good-looking people own them as well.

'I've yet to meet one,' Morrissey snickers.

Time to log out of that area, then.

Are you enjoying getting older? Or at least more than you expected?

'The beauty of being seventeen is that you can never believe that time flies and that soon, very soon, you'll be 38. I never expected to get this old, but it's very comfortable . . . in an edgy sort of way.'

Is there anything you feel too old for?

Morrissey sighs a very well-timed sigh.

'Yes, I felt too old for Britpop. But maybe I just didn't like it. The Little Englandness stuff of, "You're too old to be here," even though people in their thirties are getting younger is all part of British snobbery, isn't it? "Where are you going?" "You're not allowed to be there." "What right do you have?" They'll say it about age, and they'll say it about using the flag,' he adds, referring both to the inflated 'Is Morrissey a Racist?' controversy of a few years back when he performed onstage with a Union Jack backdrop, and to the subsequent lack of controversy when a host of later artists from Noel Gallagher to Geri Spice employed exactly the same emblem. 'I wasn't the first to use it, and I *certainly* wasn't the last,' he observes pointedly.

And he's got a point.

I have colleagues in the music press, who seem to believe that seventeen-year-olds should only listen to seventeen-year-old musicians.

'Oh yes, that sort of snobbism is extraordinary,' he shrugs. 'When I was younger, should I therefore have felt that I had nothing to say to people who were older than me? That just wouldn't make sense. If you were simply singing for people who were all born in the same month and the same year that you were, what a very narrow aim.'

But it's still easier to feel a closer affinity to people in your own age group. Would you be alarmed at the prospect of going out with someone much older or much younger?

'I'd be alarmed at the prospect of ever going out with someone. So that ends *that* question,' Morrissey retorts, lightning fast and suddenly very, very alert.

But you must be breaking someone's heart by saying, 'I've never gone out with anyone.' There must be someone out there who will read this and say, 'But I saw him for four years – how can he say that?'

There's a chilly pause. 'There's nobody living on the planet who can say that. So *there . . .*'

Well, I don't *believe* you haven't ever gone out with anyone, Steven.

'Well, I haven't, so put that in your Sony cassette and . . .' He laughs sharply, almost harshly. 'I really haven't.'

But you're a human being.

'You've got no evidence of that,' he rejoins. 'Artists aren't really people. And *I'm* actually 40 percent papier mache.'

Have you been in love with people?

'Oh yes. Real people with flesh and bones and eyes. But I'm so used to fantasy and everything being rock 'n' roll, I could never quite come out of the cinema and relate everything to the hard world. It was always at a distance. Always a dream. And I'm used to that now. I understand the life of books and films and music.'

When's the last time you walked down the street holding someone's hand?

'I've never done that.'

Ever?

'No! My mother, when I was one, perhaps.'

When's the last time you snogged in the cinema?

'Never. You really do overestimate me, don't you? Can you really see me sitting in the back of the cinema snogging? Well, you should stop reading *Cosmopolitan*. It's not one of my strong points. You may bang your head against the hotel wall but there's *nothing* to tell. Nothing at all.'

Fairly icy silence.

Did your friends ever suggest that by the time you were in your late thirties you'd want to settle down?

'No.'

I'd think they'd want to see you happy.

'Maybe they do. I don't know. But they don't say.'

Because they're not that crass?

'That's it. They're not that crass.' He pauses and looks at the ceiling. 'You know, this conversation has devolved dramatically.'

Perhaps we might talk about being – sorry, about the new album – *Maladjusted*, then.

'The process used on this record was very, very spartan,' Morrissey says, still Being Morrissey, of course, but enjoying himself more. 'And what's always been most important to me are the vocal melodies, even more so than the lyrical content. That's really the key to the songs surviving. For better or worse what I do is distinctive. And that's a very unusual thing to be able to say in nineties pop, because most people sound exactly the same, and you can be with somebody and they can be speaking in a perfectly normal English accent and as soon as they stand behind a microphone they develop this swirling West Coast twang. They can't just sing as they speak. And I *completely* sing as I speak.'

And you must feel you're growing stronger as a vocalist.

'Yes. When I listen to the early records, they sound very thin and shrieky and the voice sounds marginally hysterical, like I was balancing on a ledge. But now my voice is so much stronger, and I'm sure it has something to do with the oesophagus. Or physical strength; in the days of yore I was extremely undernourished. Though that didn't impede Edith Piaf, I suppose.'

It's a more *soulful* voice than it was.

Oh yes, I think so too. And I don't mean, "I think it's the best record I've made this week." I know I've made quite a few stinkers,' he adds. (When I ask him later, he'll admit to 'Pregnant For The Last Time' and a few other 'pretty ropy' singles.) 'But *this*, I think, is the best of me. And people inevitably say, "Ah, but the Smiths . . ." I think that's so tedious, so boring. Nothing against the Smiths, of course, but I *have* been away from them for a decade.'

But why don't you sing any Smith songs live? They were great songs.

'They *are* great songs," he amends meticulously. 'You know, occasionally, as I'm rolling out pastry, I find myself singing "Death Of A Disco Dancer".'

I suspect both of us are pleased at how very deliciously Being Morrissey that last line was.

But why deny your back catalogue?

'I'm not sure. It's certainly not a pained decision. I don't close the curtain and say, "I'm not singing any of those horrible old songs that belonged to the Smiths." Because I feel that those songs are still me. But I like to sing the songs I've recorded recently, because I think they're wonderful. If I met a complete stranger today and wanted them to hear the best of me, I would quite truthfully play *Vauxhall And I*, or *Maladjusted*, or *Your Arsenal*. I actually wouldn't play *Meat Is Murder*. And that really is the truth.'

Which brings us to another prickly topic. Much to my relief, however, Morrissey's much happier having his say about the law – and specifically the judge who called him 'truculent and devious' – than he is talking about dating.

Was the court case in which Mike Joyce successfully sued you and Johnny Marr for a greater share of the Smiths' profits a matter of finance or revenge?

'Well, it was both. It was entirely to do with finances on Mike Joyce's part. He says it's nothing to do with money, but I'm sure he won't donate any of his gains to charity. Really, I'll never forgive him and to a lesser degree Andy [Rourke], because it was horrific. I thought it was shocking, and if I was a weaker person or less intelligent, it would make me despise the Smiths and everything they stood for.

'And the judge was horrendous, and all the scrawly snivelling little extremely physically ugly people involved, who viewed me as some kind of anarchic, and semi-glamorous if you don't mind me saying, free spirit.'

Was it a case of 'He thinks he's better than anyone and we'll knock him down'?

'Exactly. It's actually that simple. It's pure unadulterated jealousy, nothing more, nothing less.'

And Mr. Marr?

'The court case was a potted history of the life of the Smiths. Mike, talking constantly and saying nothing. Andy, unable to remember his own name. Johnny, trying to please everyone and consequently pleasing no one. And Morrissey under the *scorching* spotlight in the *dock*' – Morrissey is warming to the narrative, as you might have noticed – 'being *drilled*. "How dare you be successful?" "How dare you move on?" To me, the Smiths were a beautiful thing and Johnny left it, and Mike has destroyed it.

'There were so many creative ideas around the Smiths that came from my head and no one else's. Apart from singing, creating vocal melodies and lyrics, and titles, and record sleeves, and doing interviews, there was always more to consider. Most of the pressure fell on my shoulders. And this is what the judge couldn't possibly have comprehended, or didn't want to. And was totally unaware of how pop music works. Didn't understand the word gig. Had never heard of *Top of the Pops*.

'It was like watching a plane crash. And I'd look down at Johnny's face and I would look at Mike and Andy and think, this is probably as sad as life would ever get.

'There is no justice, I'm afraid,' Morrissey adds, very quietly. 'I came away from those courts feeling more convinced of that than ever.'

Perhaps not in a court of law. And I'm not sure if Morrissey, the man fond of spite and not at all fond of sympathy, would consider poetic justice to be an adequate replacement for legal justice. But if there's any consolation at all, it's worth remembering that Morrissey's still here, a decade after the Smiths. Still making records of wilful greedy grace which, even if greater familiarity will always make them less astonishing than 'Hand In Glove' was at the time, are still things of rare beauty.

And with better vocals.

And what's more, the awkward, introspective, 'undernourished' boy Morrissey looks, well, like a lithe, healthy and self-assured man. You know, you look *comfortable dans votre peau*, I tell him impulsively.

'Hmmmh!' he exclaims, faintly surprised, in his best 'well-I-never' fashion. 'I don't speak Arabic, actually,' he adds, but not unkindly.

It's French. For 'looking comfortable in your own skin'. You look at ease with yourself.

Morrissey, Being Morrissey, is either touched or gracious enough to pretend to be.

'Thank you. That really *is* kind.'

I have a theory, you know, I say as I pack up, that we'll always judge your recorded work more harshly than anyone else's because you've always meant so much more. Because, in some way, you broke all our hearts and never said sorry.

Morrissey smiles.

'That's because I never *was* sorry.'

Are you a bad man?

'Only inwardly.'

I look at the man who not only invented Being Morrissey but is still the unchallenged world champion. And I start to laugh. You're really good at this, you know, I giggle helplessly.

Morrissey rolls his eyes. 'Ohhh, you can't keep an old pro down.'

Big Mouth Strikes Again (slight return)
Moz the Mouth on:

Gene

Are you flattered by what Martin Rossiter does?
What does he do?
He's the singer in a band called Gene.
Well. God bless all who sail in him. In her. In it.

Actually, I think he can sing. That might sound like a very simple thing to say, but most people in pop music can't sing. But he can actually sing, so he deserves more attention than most.

Spice Girls

I'm not one of them.
Do you see them as . . .
As competition? I'm hugely indifferent. And we don't have the same hairdresser.

Blur

I'll never be one of them. But I liked 'Charmless Man'.

Oasis

We definitely don't have the same hairdresser. I think the single is . . . almost awful. Very disappointing. At a time when they have the spotlight of the world on them, they should have made the most revolutionary, creative record and instead it's practically awful. For a song which is trying so hard to create hooks, it doesn't really have any. Apart from the 'Pictures Of Matchstick Men' by Status Quo middle – am I the first or the last person to say that? – there's nothing there. I liked 'Round Are Way'. But I like music which is slightly more anarchic, violent, confrontational. Oasis are very tame to me. God bless Noel; I'm sure he'll always have a spot on *Bob's Full House*, but I search for something with more bite and rage.

Echo and the Bunnymen

I can't think of a reformation that's ever worked. Can you? Well, there's your answer.

Elcka

They're astonishing. I went to see them recently and it was one of those gigs of a lifetime. One you never forget. They're really special. I wouldn't like to praise them because the press will hate them if I like them. Possibly. But that's the way the hamster wheel turns these days.

Melody Maker, 9 August 1997

THE MAN WITH THE THORN IN HIS SIDE

———•— BY LYNN BARBER ——•———

The Colorado Music Hall. How glamorous it sounds! How dismal it is! A bleak, concrete shed off the highway a few miles out of Colorado Springs, it looks as though it might have been built originally as a cattle pen. It has a neon sign outside, but the neon doesn't work – I can dimly make out MORRISY in straggling letters. In the foyer there is a long bar with people fighting for polystyrene beakers of beer; there is a trestle table with 'Morrissey Merchandise' which consists of an old poster and a few grey T-shirts. No one seems to be buying.

Backstage, Morrissey's dressing room is hardly more than a lavatory with a couple of plastic bags on the floor (there is no table) containing sliced bread. In his eighties heyday, with the Smiths, his contract used to stipulate that his dressing-room should contain vegetarian food, wine, fruit juice and 'flowers to the approximate value of £50 sterling, including gladioli, no roses or flowers with thorns', though later he replaced this with the demand for 'a live tree with a minimum height of three feet and a maximum height of five feet'. The tour manager used to carry a saw in his briefcase in case the tree provided was too tall. But there is no tree in tonight's dressing-room.

Morrissey's set begins with a recording of John Betjeman reading his poem 'A Child Ill', which might as well be in Urdu for all the impact it makes. Morrissey wanders onstage, looking portly in a long, brown cardigan. A few fans in the front cheer, but most of the audience are still milling round buying beer. Then he sings – and suddenly I see the whole point of Morrissey which was a mystery to me before. He is amazing – not just the lyrics and the voice, and the weird barks and yelps – but also his strange movements, the diva-like caressing of his body, the writhing on the floor, the almost Greta Garbo way he arches his neck. It is wildly camp, insanely provocative for Hicksville, USA. When he sings his vegetarian anthem, 'Meat Is Murder', you think all these beef-fed cowboys in the audience might rush the stage and kill him. The grandeur, the sheer courage of his performance, completely transcends the dinginess of his surroundings. I am quite seriously tempted to run onstage and kiss his feet.

I had been warned that Morrissey could be flakey and difficult. But when I'd interviewed him earlier in the day, I found him exceptionally polite, friendly and tolerant of my ignorance of pop music. He went to great lengths to explain to me why Jarvis Cocker was not a patch on him – basically, he said, because he can't sing – while also claiming that he never listened to Pulp. He made good jokes, including jokes against himself. When I asked why he was so anti drink and drugs, he said, 'It's really self control, isn't it? I don't mind getting drunk, but it's not something I do very often. I mean – I am quite human. From a distance.'

He is 43 and looks it – a bit thickening around the middle, a bit greying at the temples. He is wearing a denim suit so ludicrously tight and pintucked it must be by some famous designer, but otherwise he seems quite normal. He has a Manchester accent and a dry Mancunian wit, but he also often says 'Bejaysus!' which presumably he gets from his Irish parents. He explains that he is in the middle of a three-month tour, going round American towns, then to England for two concerts at the Royal Albert Hall, and on to Australia and Paris. He likes to tour, he says, because he likes singing in front of audiences – simple as that. He admits that Colorado Springs is a bit off the beaten track, but 'I think it's a test of one's own private strengths that you can go to the more obscure markets.'

His career is at an odd point. He always tells the British press that he is 'big in the States' but actually no one I met in the States had even heard of him. On the other hand, his two concerts at the Royal Albert Hall next week are fully sold out, which suggests that he still has a good fan base in the UK. But are these merely old Smiths fans, still holding the torch? He says not – he says he attracts teenagers who were barely born when the Smiths were around. But if so, it's a bit of a mystery how he gets them because he hasn't had a recording deal since 1996, when Mercury signed him for three albums, but dropped him after the first.

He still goes to see record companies in search of a deal: 'But they all ask me how much I'm prepared to compromise, and I say, "Nothing." One company said, "Yes, we'll sign you, but we'd like you to make an album with Radiohead" – which doesn't mean anything to me. And several labels have said, "Yes, we'd like to sign you but we don't want to sign your musicians." There's always some absurd condition which makes absolutely no sense. And all the labels in America have said: "Will your music fit in with what is successful in the American charts?" To which I reply: "Bejaysus, I hope it doesn't!" And then I'm out on the street immediately. If you saw me at those meetings, you'd feel really pitifully sorry for me.'

So no record deal then. Which means no radio play. Which means no new fans. Which means that his career – which already looks pretty flakey in Colorado Springs – is bound to dwindle. Of course at present, he still gets a good income from the Smiths royalties but he admits, 'I don't know whether it will keep rolling in – it's not for me to say. I don't really try to make anything happen – I don't force anything at all. I don't feel that I'm in the midst of a career and I don't feel good grief, I must make money – that never occurs to me. Everything evolves quite naturally, as if some unseen guiding hand is in the background.'

Anyway, he can still afford to live very comfortably. He has a house in Ireland, but for the past four years he has lived in Los Angeles, off Sunset Boulevard, in a house that was built by Clark Gable for Carole Lombard. When I ask if he lives next door to Johnny Depp, as the press always says, he corrects me, 'No – he lives next door to me.' Los Angeles suits him, he says, because 'it's a particularly sexless city. Everybody's bodies are so sanitised, so caked in every conceivable exfoliation, cologne and mousse, they have no trace of any kind of sexuality, nothing real and earthy. So I blend in very well!'

Nowadays he is a fairly rare visitor to Manchester – he pays flying visits to see his mother, sister, and father who all live in the area, but never for very long. 'I feel a cavalcade of very strange emotions when I go there – a city that turned me away and then accepted me under very peculiar circumstances. When I was a teenager it was always very difficult. At the age of twelve, I would go and see David Bowie and Roxy Music, and that's very young to be wandering about Manchester by yourself. I saw all the important concerts at the time, but it was a very solitary experience, there was no gang, no camaraderie, no union of any kind. Nobody really understood the music that I liked. People forget how austere the early seventies were. There weren't that many people who would confess to liking David Bowie, let alone the New York Dolls, certainly not among the hard cases of Manchester.'

He was a classic bedroom pop obsessive, but of course even more obsessive than most. From the age of ten he bought all the music papers and would be 'inconsolable' if one of them was missing. He also wrote endless nitpicking letters – sometimes 30 a day – to the *NME* and other music papers, correcting their mistakes and lambasting their opinions. Before he was even a teenager, he was a walking expert on pop music. 'I never fell in love with people or places: I always fell in love with seven-inch singles. I took pop music very seriously. I thought it was the heart of everything, I thought it affected everybody and moved everybody. It started me as a person. As a child I would sing every single night – and the neighbours would complain – because I had this insane desire to sing. I was obsessed with vocal melody – and remain so. So it's been a lifetime's preoccupation really. And at the expense of everything else you could possibly name.'

But despite a brief involvement with a group called the Nosebleeds, it seemed he might be singing to his bedroom wall for ever. Until, in 1982, Johnny Marr walked into his life. Marr was four years younger than Morrissey, but already had good contacts in the Manchester music scene. Morrissey showed him the lyrics he had written; Marr set them to music; they went out and hired two other musicians, called themselves the Smiths (an odd choice of name, given that most of them had Irish parents) and within a year they were famous. 'It was a very overnight success,' Morrissey agrees. 'And to step from the huddled shyness of my life – I had never had a life, I had never had a bank account, or a car – and to be the one stepping forward, explaining this magnificent game plan, which only ever existed in my head, was a fantastic learning process.'

In their five-year reign, the Smiths produced five bestselling albums and fourteen hit singles. It was, as Morrissey says, 'a very, very pure success story'. But in 1987, Johnny Marr announced that he was leaving and that was the end of the Smiths. Morrissey was devastated – it came out of the blue as far as he was concerned. He has not seen Marr since, except in court, and claims he has no desire to see him. 'Why would you want to see someone who'd said bad things about you? It doesn't occur to me. He's never said anything nice about the solo music I've made. And he knows that at the end of the Smiths I was in a very depressed state – and that possibly the fact that he broke the Smiths up could have killed me. But, instead, I triumphed somewhat – and he's never said well done.'

Morrissey claims 'nobody was more surprised than I was' when he successfully started a solo career. His first album, *Viva Hate*, was a hit. But then successive albums did less well, and his last one, *Maladjusted*, hardly sold at all. It didn't help that he kept switching managers, and walked out of a tour with David Bowie in 1995. His then assistant Jo Slee said it was because 'he was very ill with depression. He was coming apart at the seams.' But Morrissey says it was because Bowie kept badgering him to sing one of his songs.

And then there was the court case. I made the mistake of raising the subject by asking – in passing, I thought – whether he'd now settled his long-running lawsuit with Mike Joyce, the former Smiths drummer. Suddenly Morrissey was off, galloping into a monologue which became increasingly weird as it went on. He said he'd 'never come face to face with human evil' until he encountered the judge, John Weeks. He uses the name John Weeks like an incantation or a curse.

The court case arose because, after the Smiths ended in 1987 and Morrissey and Marr went their separate ways, the two other Smiths, Andy Rourke and Mike Joyce, began thinking they'd been underpaid, in that they only got ten per cent of the Smiths earnings, instead of 25 per cent. (This is performing royalties, not composing royalties, to which obviously only Morrissey and Marr were entitled.) The situation was complicated because Joyce and Rourke had never had a contract – in fact, legally, they didn't exist. Anyway, Rourke and Joyce sued Morrissey and Marr for back earnings. Rourke soon dropped out, but Joyce persisted and the case came to the high court in 1996. Summing up in favour of Joyce, the judge pronounced Morrissey 'devious, truculent, and unreliable' and ordered him and Marr to pay Joyce £1.25m in back earnings. Marr paid up, but Morrissey pursued the case to appeal – where it was dismissed.

Obviously it must have been a blow – but it was six years ago, you'd think Morrissey would have got over it by now. Ha! 'It was an extraordinary miscarriage of justice,' he rants. 'The whole point of this court case was to say Mr. Joyce is a poor shambolic character in desperate need of money who has been treated abysmally by Morrissey and Marr – when the fact was he had been treated with absolute generosity, considering the minor role that he played. He played his instrument and went home. He was always in search of more shags. Now Johnny Marr and myself, throughout the history of the Smiths, never slept with anybody, and took the Smiths very seriously. We stayed up till the small hours perfecting and shaping everything. Joyce was the exact opposite – he had no sense of duty. So when this person therefore, ten years after the group has ended, starts demanding £1m . . .'

Marr and Morrissey were in court together, but didn't speak except through their lawyers. At the end, Marr accepted the judgement, but Morrissey took the case to appeal where he fared no better. 'You go to the appeal court and you come across three judges who are the same age, colour, background, demeanour, as the judge about whom you are complaining. And their attitude is, "How dare you disagree with one of our friends?"' So Morrissey complained to the Prime Minister, the Queen ('Tony Blair was not at all interested; the Queen was very nice'), the Lord Chancellor, the ombudsman, the Law Society, the Bar Council – 'But they just collect complaints in order to protect the judges.' Joyce meanwhile put a charge on Morrissey's mother's house and his sister's house, (presumably because Morrissey has no property in the UK) which makes them unsellable until the claim is settled.

Morrissey is now taking the case to the European Court of Human Rights, though he admits it is costing him a fortune – 'because with each new solicitor that I get to defend me, they view the overall situation and find it so extraordinary that they immediately place a bill before me for 100 grand before they do anything.' Wouldn't it be healthier, saner and cheaper just to cut his losses? 'No. I will never give up. I will fight till the last fibre of my body is spilled. I will go down with the ship. And my mother as well. We will never be beaten, not at all, because we have right on our side.' But meanwhile, the case seems to be blighting his life. 'No. It has strengthened my resolve. I'm not shrivelled up in a box in Manchester surrounded by empty beer bottles. They're going to have to fight long and hard to bring me down.'

Phew. I'm sorry I ever raised that subject because it was half an hour of almost undiluted venom. And I noticed later, when Morrissey's assistant Blossom asked what we talked about and I told her, 'The court case quite a lot,' her face fell. I bet all his friends – not that he has any friends according to him – know not to press that button. Anyway, I was glad to change the subject and ask about his nonexistent love life, which he always seems happy to discuss.

Does he have relationships ever? 'Not physical relationships, no. I mean there are some people on this planet who aren't obsessed with sex, and I'm one of them. I'm not interested. And I'm not cloaking something, I'm not going somewhere under cover of night and existing in some wild secretive way. I wasn't interested when I was seventeen, I wasn't interested when I was 27, I was less interested when I was 37 and I'm even less interested now. I really enjoy my own company enormously, so I don't feel a great gaping hole. I sit at home at night and I feel absolutely honoured not having to cater for anybody, or listen, or put up with anybody. I feel it's a great privilege to live alone.'

Who is his best friend? He laughs derisively, 'My best friend? At the age of 43? My credit card!' Not even a cat? 'No. My best friend is myself. I look after myself very, very well. I can rely on myself never to let myself down. I'm the last person I want to see at night and the first in the morning. I am endlessly fascinating – at eight o'clock at night, at midnight, I'm fascinated. It's a lifelong relationship and divorce will never come into it. That's why, as I say, I feel privileged. And that is an honest reply.'

I believe him. But given his admitted self-obsession, it seems extraordinary that he is in an industry like pop music, which by definition entails being popular and communicating with other people. 'Yes,' he agrees. 'It's an enormous contradiction really. But the fluffy elements of pop stardom, if you like, are not why I'm here. I'm generally very interested in the written word and changing the poetic landscape of pop music, and I think I've achieved that. I think, with the Smiths, I introduced a harsh romanticism which has been picked up by many people and which didn't exist previously. And it's nice to be a curious footnote to the whole story of British popular music. And not to be compliant, smiling, bland.' And with that, he goes off, smiling, to his concert at the Colorado Music Hall, where I suddenly – too late – discover the point of Morrissey.

The Observer, 15 September 2002

WHO'S THE DADDY?

——•••—— BY KEITH CAMERON ——•••——

Morrissey is sick. By his own estimation, he is sick of the sound of his own voice. In a suite at the Dorchester Hotel on London's Park Lane, he apologises to *Mojo* for what we are about to receive, as it were.

'I warn you, I'm at the gab gab gab stage – I just sit here and my lips are moving and I can hear the sound of words coming from somewhere and I realise that I'm actually forming them. I'd love to be able to stand back or from the side and shout back at myself! The unfortunate thing is that simply because you happen to hobble together an album that you're terribly proud of, people assume you have the answers to everything, and you can explain everything with *fantastic flow.*'

He gives a little bronchial chuckle, avuncular, self-deprecating and, to *Mojo*'s ears, strangely reminiscent of the crumbly tones of John Arlott, the legendary cricket commentator and poet; a protégé of Betjeman, a connoisseur of wine and words, and notably, given the conservative milieu he inhabited, an early anti-apartheid campaigner. A man regarded as quintessentially English, who also betrayed a profound anti-establishment streak, Arlott grew up of humble stock in a Basingstoke cemetery superintendent's lodge. Perhaps the resemblance isn't so strange after all.

Two months shy of his 45th birthday, age and the concomitant slight thickening of the girth become Steven Patrick Morrissey. He looks in terrific nick, if a little wearied by the rigours of his promotional campaign. It's been seven long years since his last 'hobbled together' album, the underwhelming *Maladjusted*, slipped out and past the gaze of most, around which time he left England and relocated permanently, via Dublin, to Los Angeles, where he still resides, a status that from a British perspective increasingly seemed like exile. Without a record contract after his relationship with Mercury disintegrated in 1998, he worked his way through various managers (including Elliot Roberts, who has ministered to Neil Young for most of the last 35 years), and communed with his public via world tours during 1999-2000 and 2002. The extent of these demonstrated that Morrissey still enjoyed a considerable fan-base – particularly in the US and Latin America, where his personality cult borders on religious idolatry – spanning a whole range of demographics, be it gender, age or nationality. Yet still the music industry shunned him. In September 2002, with no pre-publicity, he sold out two nights at the Royal Albert Hall. How was it possible that the man who had sung the songs of the Smiths, the band which more than any other after the Beatles and the Sex Pistols had infected the vocabulary of British pop culture, couldn't make records? This simply didn't make sense. This was Morrissey, the voice that proclaimed 'This Charming Man', 'William, It Was Really Nothing', 'How Soon Is Now', 'That Joke Isn't Funny Any More', 'Meat Is Murder', 'The Queen Is Dead', 'Bigmouth Strikes Again', 'Panic', 'Shoplifters Of The World Unite', 'Last Night I

Comfortable in his own skin: Morrissey at the turn of the millennium, with the suave look of an early 1960s London villain. (Discounting the 'Famous When Dead' badge.)

Dreamt Somebody Loved Me', 'Everyday Is Like Sunday', 'November Spawned A Monster', 'The More You Ignore Me The Closer I Get', 'The Teachers Are Afraid Of The Pupils', 'Satan Rejected My Soul' . . .

It must have been something he'd said.

Following the half-hearted release of *Maladjusted*, aside from a very occasional press or radio interview, to the casual UK observer Morrissey's was a merely spectral presence in the entertainment ether, sustained by the ongoing repackaging of the Smiths' back catalogue and the attendant retrospective celebration of that most defin- itive of groups. In April 2001, *Mojo* ran a Smiths cover story, bolstered by a couple of articles examining three of the defining aspects of Morrissey's solo career: his vilifica- tion by elements of the press over allegedly racist undertones to some of his work; the 1996 High Court case in which a judge found against Morrissey and his fellow song- writing Smith, Johnny Marr, in a dispute over performing royalties brought by Smiths drummer Mike Joyce; and his incredible popularity in the US, where in 1992 he sold out two nights at the Hollywood Bowl in less time than it takes to make a pot of tea. In the same issue there was a new interview with Morrissey, where he pondered his ostracism by the music industry ('What it is about Morrissey that nobody wants to touch?') and explained his decision to walk away from the media accusations of racism ('absolute crap') as a means of retaining his dignity. When asked by writer Jaan Uhelszki, 'Can we talk about what you're doing now in terms of your career?', Morrissey replied: 'That will be a very brief conversation. I'm looking for a deal. I don't have a deal . . . I have an album which I'm aching to record if anybody on the planet will let me.'

More than two years later, somebody finally did. On May 20, 2003, Morrissey signed to the Sanctuary Records Group, the West London-based management and label agglomerate, under whose aegis Morrissey's original patron, Geoff Travis, cur- rently runs the revamped Rough Trade Records. In return for signing, Morrissey requested and was given the Attack imprint as his own personal domain – a ripely knowing gesture on his part, given that Attack was formerly the home of Gregory Isaacs and the Upsetters and that those 'racist' accusations rested heavily on Morrissey's one-time protest to *NME* that 'reggae is vile'. Two weeks after the Sanctuary deal was signed, Channel 4 broadcast *The Importance of Being Morrissey*, a 60-minute documentary that followed the main attraction around LA and London, watched him meeting his Hollywood neighbour Nancy Sinatra ('He's a great hug- ger'), and rolled out a quaint assortment of celebrity talking heads (Alan Bennett, Bono, Kathy Burke, Noel Gallagher, Will Self) to make good on the premise of the title. The subtext was clear: Morrissey is a national treasure and we renounced him, ignored him – and ultimately drove him away. In his last words in the programme, he proclaimed: 'I'm my own person, and that's good enough. And I stand my ground – that's good enough.'

And now he's back, with a new album, combatively titled *You Are The Quarry* – the sleeve depicts Morrissey with a tommy gun, contemplating the weapon rather too fondly for the comfort of some – and holding court at the Dorchester with regal poise, having his photograph taken in the tea room and on the outside balcony of the suite where President Eisenhower used to stay. The procession of interviews confirms his willingness to engage fully with the soul-sucking processes of the music business, a reflection of his opinion that his new record is 'absolutely the definitive Morrissey album'. But it's also the result of the fact that people are interested in him once again: a collective realisation that he's been sorely missed, and that he should never have been allowed to go in the first place. Typically for Morrissey, it's all something of a mixed blessing.

'I've been asked to do an excessive amount of talking, shall we say, and unfortunately interviews, for me, are always pretty intense cross-examinations and they become intensely personal, and they really drain me. I'm actually an *intensely* private person, so juggling that with revealing interviews is very, very difficult for me. Because to be honest, I'd rather say nothing. I'd rather absolutely let the music speak for itself and do what it can do. But I've tried that so many times and nothing happened. It actually simply disappears. But the label at the moment do want me to do a hell of a lot more, and I just don't think I can. I mean, Britney I'm not.'

So why is he here? Why is he doing this?

'It's 100 per cent a calling, it really is. Because, unfortunately, I don't really exist anywhere else in life.'

Three weeks later, Morrissey really is sick. On April 8, *Mojo* arrives in Los Angeles for part two of our interview, only to learn that Morrissey has been diagnosed with meningitis, and won't be seeing anyone, far less speaking to them, until he's recovered. Uncharitable it may be, but one's instinct is to feel sceptical. Pinning Morrissey down to a schedule hasn't been easy thus far, and he does have a history of dealing with inconvenient engagements by simply making himself unavailable. Just as his interviews are sparring matches, with this some-time boxing aficionado a master of the feint and the parry and the surprise counter – not to mention the sly dig below the belt – so Morrissey delights in leading the world outside his window a merry dance. For him, the importance of being Morrissey is ensuring no one knows who Morrissey really is, or what he does (and with whom). Which is, of course, one of the reasons for his enduring fascination. On the Smiths' debut album, he averred, 'I'm not the man you think I am' – and twenty years on, the obfuscatory intent behind those words still holds true.

On April 15, *Mojo* speaks to him on the telephone. A little croaky but otherwise seemingly fine, he explains how he caught a virus on the flight back from London to LA and subsequently developed a five-day migraine, throwing his plans into disarray, most notably the rehearsals for his US tour.

'It's annoying, because in 48 hours I'll be standing on a stage in Las Vegas, hopefully singing,' he says. 'So I'm a bit nervous. [Meningitis] was only part of it. I had two brain scans in two days. And then, in the final analysis, last Tuesday, when they were about to take some spinal fluid, I just stood up and said, No more, this is silly. Absolutely silly. Because American medicine, they absolutely don't know anything. They'll saw your leg off just to prevent you getting gangrene in the future. I'm not kidding. I ended up in hospital on a drip, which was hugely humiliating and embarrassing. And at one point I went for a brain scan and they left me in the room for fifteen minutes with this really loud hip hop music playing. But I was strapped to the bed and I was on a drip so I couldn't do anything about it. So here I am, with this intense migraine, listening to *hip hop*. It could only be America.'

And I'd come all that way to see you, too.

'Well I thought you'd be cursing me and generally putting my windows in.'

Oh I'd never do anything like that. Although the more cynical side of me did wonder whether you were indeed really ill.

'Ooh, *tut-tut-tut*. So what did you do while you were here?'

Not much. Walked around, felt like an alien, then decided to come home.

'Well you probably made the right choice. Otherwise you'd still be here, just wandering around.'

What's the game-plan for your return to the live arena?

'(*laughs*) You mean the "stage presentation", shall we say? There's never been anything like that. I could never be part of anything that remotely resembles a performance. And when people say to me that I'm a "good performer" I'm absolutely horrified, because it's such a dreadful expression. For better or worse, I just stumble on and stumble off. I also find it's 50 per cent reliant on the audience and how they respond. If they're enflamed, the night takes very interesting twists and turns, but if they're not then . . . it doesn't.'

Brain scans, eh? Serious stuff.

'A day in the life, believe me. (*surprised*) You've never had one yourself?'

It was Morrissey's muse Oscar Wilde who reputedly opined: 'Consistency is the last refuge of the unimaginative.' It's worth bearing those words in mind when you hear – as you assuredly shall – that *You Are The Quarry* is a 'triumphant return to form', or suchlike. For sure, it's auspicious. Morrissey hasn't made an album anywhere near as good since 1994's *Vauxhall And I*. The instrumental textures and arrangements are rich and varied, the production – by Jerry Finn, noted for his work with Blink 182 and other young(ish) brats of repute – tough yet sympathetic, while Morrissey's voice is simply magnificent, its tawny baritone never so perfectly pitched and phrased. But stylistically and in many of the specific lyrical concerns and thematic obsessions, it resembles no massive departure from *Maladjusted* or that album's predecessor, 1995's *Southpaw Grammar*, which was similarly disdained by critics and received with reservation by all but the most diehard fan. Far from the artistic catastrophes received wisdom would maintain, these two albums are fascinating, inasmuch as they document a mid-nineties mid-life crisis for their author: flitting from one new label to another (RCA then Mercury/Island), dejected at his treatment by the press, his defeat in the Smiths court case and heaven knows what deeper personal traumas. In places, both Morrissey and the music sound muzzled, uncertain. For someone who wears his heart on his record sleeves, there were clues in the artwork: discounting the *World Of Morrissey* compilation, *Southpaw Grammar* was the only Morrissey solo album not to feature his own face on the cover – in a retreat to the iconic nostalgia of the Smiths, the honour went to a fuzzy snap of sixties boxer Kenny Lane – while *Maladjusted* was perfunctory beyond belief, an unflattering black-and-white cut-out Moz slapped onto a silver background. Significantly or not, Morrissey gave relatively few interviews around the time of either record.

'I was presented [by RCA] with lots of media hoops,' he says. 'And I couldn't do it, I couldn't jump through them. I didn't want to be exposed and didn't want people to know too much about me. And they took the view that if that's your attitude then we too will back off. So overnight it sort of deflated itself. I'm very, very proud of *Southpaw Grammar*. The sleeve was terrible and that's my fault. All the artwork was atrocious, and unfortunately there's no one else I can blame.'

Why was the artwork bad?

'Well I liked the artwork for about three days. Unfortunately they were the three days when everything was going to press. But then a few weeks later I looked at it and went, What the hell have you done? And I still don't know, but it certainly was not Tate quality. I made such a holy mess of *Southpaw Grammar* that I left *Maladjusted* to be pieced together by the record company – and it was even worse than *Southpaw Grammar*. I've got Tony Blair's hairline and I look as if I'm sat on the lavatory crying my eyes out. Nothing new there, then . . .'

So a mere glance at the opulent sleeve to *You Are The Quarry* is enough to suggest that the force is with him once more. It could be argued – and quite reasonably, too – that if Morrissey didn't return with something approaching his very best after a seven-year hiatus then he really wasn't the man he's said we thought he was after all. But he's really outdone himself. While veteran Morrisseyan scholars will enjoy a clutch of vivid case studies to dissect in their endless futile quest to ascertain what s/he's *really* like (viz, 'I'm Not Sorry', where Moz admits, 'The woman of my dreams, well, there never was one'; or 'All The Lazy Dykes', a genuinely affecting plea to an unhappily married woman to 'free yourself' . . . 'and join the girls'), what makes his seventh solo album such a treat is it has the musical flair to match his lyrical blunderbuss. With regard to the latter, not a bullet is wasted. If it's gung-ho, that's because he clearly feels wronged. There's wit and passion and pathos in every meticulously measured line. The single 'Irish Blood, English Heart' is an impressively cogent declaration of his patriotic self ('I've been dreaming of a time when/To be English is not be baneful/To be standing by the flag not feeling shameful/Racist or partial'). 'How Can Anybody Possibly Know How I Feel' states, 'I've had my face dragged in fifteen miles of shit/And I do not/And I do not/And I do not like it.' And the staunch closer, 'You Know I Couldn't Last', is the sound of a seriously conflicted man entering the last chance saloon and leaving with all guns blazing. He takes out his fans, the critics, the business suits, former bandmates ('the Northern leeches go on removing') and is ultimately left staring at what's left of his own reflection, beseeching: 'Your royalties bring you luxuries/But oh – the squalor of the mind.' In its florid grandiosity – that, and the use of the word 'gelignite' in a pop lyric – it recalls no one else but Queen. In addition to 'definitive', to the pre-meningitis Morrissey sipping tea at the Dorchester, 'it's so perfect and resolute that my work on this planet is over.'

Do you see lots of unsettled scores out there?

I do, because I have been quarry for so many years. And people have taken so many repeated pot-shots at me. So yes, I feel heavily bruised. But this time around I feel that the album represents something which is actually deeper than mere revenge and manages to rise above settling all those old scores. I do feel as if I have been been somewhat victimised. Which really isn't amusing.

Do have any conception as to why that happened?
The base of it is nothing more sinister than jealousy, really. And I do have a lot of ene-mies. And I seem to stir within people a reaction. There's nobody on the planet who thinks I'm OK. They're either extremely for or extremely against. I'm not the kind of person who tends to pass through unnoticed.

Surely that's not necessarily a bad thing?
It is when you're passing through a crowd of people who don't care that much for you – you would rather slip by unnoticed.

Why do you have so many enemies?
I think it's because I'm a strong person, and I don't rely on other people. And I don't ask for help. So therefore I'm not pitied.

But you'd like to be, in a way?
No, not at all. And it's an industry of massive egos. If you turn away from people they seek revenge for the rest of their lives against you. And I've been through so many managers and so many record companies and so many musicians – and they never let go, even though they may walk away of their own accord, they never let go. And they will do all in their power to stop you from fulfilling your dreams. I have a lot of ene-mies. But let it be. So be it.

You hate the music industry, would that be fair to say?
Yes.

And yet you still conjoin with it.
I'm trapped.

But are you? Why continue to do it if you dislike the apparatus so much?
It's throbbing through the veins, and there's nothing I can do about it. I am one of those born-in-a-trunk people, one of those old-fashioned . . . I mean, I simply do love to sing. All the entrapments, some of them are necessary. And if you do make a good album you do want as many people to hear it as possible, because you do want peo-ple to . . . like it, really. So it is very, very difficult, because a lot of things that I'm called upon to do, a lot of the things on the sidelines, I approach with abject horror – but what can you do?

You don't have to release records in the conventional sense at all.
Mmm. But then you end up like Robert Wyatt, don't you?

What's wrong with that?!
Well I don't know. I mean, his hair isn't too fantastic, is it?! (*laughs*)
But he does release records in the conventional sense!

Well he does, yes, but he sort of potters about in his potting shed, recording. Maybe that will happen to me eventually, I don't know, but there's a streak of intolerable glamour within me as well.

You like the bright lights . . .
Well, I can't *see* the bright lights, but . . . I like the scream of the greasepaint.

A few years ago, Paul Weller, expressing similar distaste for the machinations of the music industry, said he was seriously thinking of giving up dealing with it, and just playing once a week in his local pub . . .
It's interesting. Because he's probably gone as far as he can go – I would say. And the trouble with all the machinations of the music industry is that if you don't have a bubbly personality, as I don't, as the *world* knows Weller doesn't (*laughs*), then you can't really get on with the machinery, and therefore if you're not prepared to try to get on with it the record company are not really gonna bother trying to shove your new CD around. It's all a hideously delicate balance.

Who are the 'Northern leeches' you refer to?
You know exactly who they are.

Mike Joyce must be one of them.
Mmm. He would certainly fit the bill, wouldn't he?

Once the subject of Joyce and the court case is raised, Morrissey's demeanour changes quite palpably. Gone are the playful jousts and waspish asides, replaced by long, lucid soliloquies on the perceived injustice of what occurred in the High Court under the jurisdiction of Judge John Weeks at the end of 1996. 'Devious, truculent and unreliable,' was Weeks' assessment of Morrissey in his summation to the court. As one of Morrissey's old Smiths lyrics would have it, this story is old, but it goes on – because, he claims, Weeks made a flawed judgement, awarding Joyce £1.25 million, having decided that Joyce was a 25 per cent partner, but making no provision for how Joyce should receive the money. 'And because Joyce was never on any Smiths contract of any kind then none of the sources will pay him money because he's not entitled to any under the contract.' Thus, says Morrissey, every time he plays in England, Joyce issues legal orders to try and extract money. 'He will go on for the rest of his life, a pest to everybody that's in my life. That defines him now, that's what his life is. And it allows him to continue and be a part of my story. It has become a complete farce and there is only one victim and the victim is me.'

How can you account for this? Just because the judge didn't like you? He said as much.
He did say that much, which is fair enough. I mean, a judge has a right not to like me, but a judge doesn't have a right to dismiss the facts and dismiss what is obvious. The judge should not pass personal judgement. Because I may very well be a dislikeable person, but that doesn't mean that I'm not reliable in court. Obviously the judge was repaying me for all the things I'd ever said about Thatcher or the Queen or fox-

hunting, because this judge is obviously a lord of the hunt and there is obviously a private file on people that gets passed around.

I love a good conspiracy theory, and I'd like to believe you in that regard, but . . .
You must, you must, it really is that simple and devious. If you examine the court papers it's glaringly evident that this Morrissey character must be pulled down. Why did the entire case become about Morrissey? Not about Morrissey and Marr, who were partners, but it just became about Morrissey and the destruction of Morrissey. So, it's really obvious to anybody of any basic intelligence that it was victimisation.

How did you cope with this at the time?
I coped by believing I would have enough resolve to pull myself out of the situation. And get away from it. Kick it away. And I always believed that this wasn't it, and even though I was with dreary useless record labels I always believed there would be a better time ahead. And there was and there is.

Do you think the work you did for those labels was your strongest?
Erm . . . Nnooo, I don't. But I don't hang my head with shame. These are happier days. And I don't have any of those old forgotten people, those left-over people to thank. It's a situation which I think Frank Sinatra went through twice in his life, when he was in a lofty position musically and then he plummeted, and he seemed not to have a friend in the world. And all the people that he had worked with and had associated with him turned against him, and joined in the trend of debasing him. So I think that's what ultimately made him quite a hard character. Because he had been down. And he knew what it had been like to have been kicked aside and people that he had helped criticised him. And to a lesser degree I felt there were direct parallels. (*long pause*) And that's my tatty explanation. I just heard you snoring. Either that or you have kidney failure.

My stomach may be rumbling, it's true.
Last night's tandoori special. But on a brighter note . . .

Do you think the Smiths had to die? Was it inevitable that it would stop?
Erm, it wasn't to me.

So it was the choice of other people that the band stopped?
Yes it was. I thought that we'd be *at least* as big as Queen. (*pause*) You're laughing.

I'm not! That's a noble aspiration . . .
I mean, people often say to me, 'Well, REM . . .' And I think, No, not at all. I think we were heading in Queen directions – capital 'q' of course.

So you were genuinely disappointed when it finished?
I was horrified. I was absolutely horrified. But I'm over it now! (*laughs*) I've had the time to get over it, and I've had excessive counselling and I've picked up the pieces of

my life and I'm marching on into . . . the abyss. But lots of people won't let the Smiths die. I hear *Q* magazine are doing a Smiths magazine, rounding up all those little left-over people who met me on the stairs in 1986 for an hour, for those in-depth valuable observations. So boring. With all these retrospectives, whether it's television or magazines, they always interview the same ring of people, the same faint claims, and there's a whole glut of people who were involved who are never approached. Absolutely the same cast, all the time, of the same, shall we say . . . *people.*

So who should be approached?
Oh, well that's another story. I don't want to give them any guidance.

Was there anything you could have done to persuade Johnny Marr to stay?
Well, we did never have a conversation about it. He did just tear away, and I think he immediately went into sessions with Talking Heads and Bryan Ferry. Which is *fine.* But, I think he had it in his mind that he would elevate himself immediately out of the situation, which did not happen. And that's when the bitchiness set in.

Do you still speak to Johnny?
We spoke last summer for a while. In very friendly terms. But it's very, very difficult with the court case, because it's such a monster and it just goes on and it's very detailed. But the Smiths' legacy is dreadful. I mean, I think it's the worst legacy of any group in the history of music. The whole story is so black and twisted, I'm convinced the story will only end with . . . a murder. And, you're talking to the potential corpse (*laughs*)! I am quite serious. It's reaching that stage. I mean, who was it that said, 'Viva Hate'?

But I presume you're proud of the musical legacy?
Yeah, I'm extremely proud of the music, but people don't really talk about that. And when Marr, [bassist Andy] Rourke and Joyce go on television they never talk about the music, they just talk about the overall *dreadful* experience of being in the Smiths. And I find that very sad. (*breezily*) Nothing we can do about it now!

Perhaps, in a perverse sense, Morrissey rather relishes his experience of rough justice in the courts. Here is justification for all the vitriol and spleen he's vented at the British establishment, and of a rather more intense measure than merely having a rotten time at school. The eternal outsider, victimised by the country he's eulogised and castigated from the very outset, as in the Smiths' 'Still Ill': 'England is mine – and it owes me a living.' In this context, 'Irish Blood, English Heart' is a most personal *cri du coeur,* clarifying his ambivalent attitude towards nationality far more succinctly, and less contentiously, than past efforts such as 'Bengali In Platforms' ('Life is hard enough when you belong here'). Raised in working-class Manchester in the sixties, the son of two Irish immigrants, Morrissey was made very aware of Britain's mongrel pedigree.

'Obviously the Irish feel resentment towards England because England has historically been so appalling to Ireland,' he says. 'So it was somewhat confusing for me growing up.'

Did you experience prejudice because of your background?

'Not particularly. At school I would be called "Paddy", and it was considered not to be friendly to say that. I can't think why, 'cos it's a nice word and a nice thing to be. But of course, the English laugh at everybody and ridicule everybody. Which is often quite funny. But do you, being Scottish, come across any racism here?'

Only in the trivial sense.

'So not really? Nothing hurtful . . .'

I've not been physically attacked. Maybe if I were a black Scot I might not have been so lucky.'

'Yes. Hmm.'

A lot of Scottish nationalism is the politics of resentment.

'Against England?'

Yes. In the seventies it was perceived that certain resources were being siphoned off, in the case of the oil, quite literally. You could just as logically despise the American-based multinational companies for that.

'Which we do . . . but also England has been a bully, and is a bully.'

So why do people still cling to nationality, if it's so problematic? Why do people want to feel proud of being whatever nationality they are?

'Because here is the spot where you are born and where you live and where you continue to live. Where you build your life. And it's inconvenient to feel shame towards that. I mean, we all like to feel as if we're living in a fairly decent place. And we all like to feel pride, if we can. But then, unfortunately, there is the monarchy. But perhaps not for much longer.'

Ever the optimist.

'Ever the dreamer (*laughs*).'

The place where Morrissey lives, of course, is not England, or Ireland, but Los Angeles, the city Michael Stipe once described as a lemming colony at the precipice of a continent, just waiting for an earthquake to sever it from the rest of the world altogether. Where better to embalm idealised notions of dear old Blighty? Morrissey says, 'I honestly begin every single day only with the intention of avoiding people,' and to that end LA is certainly the place to be. He likes the architecture, the land-scape, the weather ('The sun makes you expand and makes you walk taller – which is a relief'). And this accomplished voyeur finds Americans endlessly fascinating-though he does miss the 'simplicity' of British TV.

'I could quite easily have stayed,' he says, staring at what's left of his Dorchester tea. 'But it was simply time to change the furniture and change the landscape. It had to be somewhere, and I had stayed in Dublin for a long time, and enjoyable as it was it wasn't an extreme enough change. I had to go somewhere reasonably far flung. To meet my undiscovered nature. Which I did. (*smiles broadly*) And what a shock that was! That's truly the best explanation I can give.'

Though he loves returning to England and being able to walk down the street and bump into people, he doesn't envisage a time when he might come back for good.

'I'll leave that decision to fate, really. I'll simply follow fate wherever it drags me. There is a saying – I'm 92 per cent certain it was the writer Thomas Mann – that you can never go home again. Every second of life is about timing, and the atmosphere of the present. And you think the past is a place you can return to but it isn't. Even though, they do say, don't they, also that it's never too late to have a happy childhood. But I suppose you could have that without returning to anywhere. You can have your childhood in a different place. It's never too late to rectify those nightmares in your mind.'

What's it all about, Morrissey? What keeps you going?

'Well, I'm possibly no different to anybody else!' he laughs. '(*sighs*) Wish I hadn't laughed when I said that. But life, this strange life, is simply something we have to go through on our way to somewhere else. It's just something you have to sit through. And we just hope that somewhere along the line something exciting will happen to us. Most people hope for romance, and that's really all that keeps most people going.'

And you're not looking for romance?

'Mmm. Err, well it's not the thing that keeps me going, the hope of. No. I'm not that silly. And I find romance in inanimate objects (*laughs*)! Like carpets, standard lamps . . .'

He gets up. 'Do you mind?' There's a phone call for him next door. It's Chrissie Hynde. As the curator of this year's Meltdown Festival on London's South Bank, Morrissey is reassembling the surviving members of his original pop epiphany, the New York Dolls, and is looking to recruit people to take the place of those Dolls who have passed away. He wants Hynde to be 'Chrissie Thunders'. 'She just needs to be tickled, but I think she'll do it. 'Cos she is yet another person who *loves the Dolls*. Did you ever care for them yourself? Hmm . . . So, you're actually going to fly to Los Angeles and ask me questions about England? There must be an easier way to do this!'

Mojo and Moz shake hands, and we take our leave, fully expecting to meet again on his home turf in a few weeks. But it isn't to be. Instead, his last words are cackled down the phone line at the news that he's one of the famous Mancunians in the frame for the proposed re-branding of Manchester Airport.

'Wow. That's just absurd, isn't it? Fantastically absurd. Life is out of control, really. I mean, what's going to happen next, do you think? So, is "Irish Blood, English Heart" being played in England? It is, really? The single is receiving blanket American airplay, which has never happened to me before. And it's astonishing, absolutely astonishing. It's quite a time for me.'

Do you ultimately just want to be loved?

'Well, I'd like to be liked as well. But I'll settle for loved, if that's all that's on offer. Do you have any advice for me?'

Be yourself. Free yourself . . .

He chuckles. 'I'll give it a go.'

Mojo, June 2004

HAPPY NOW?

—·— BY ANDREW MALE —·—

Morrissey doesn't look happy. But then, of course, appearances can be deceptive. He's sitting in the bar of Rome's Hotel de Russie (grand nineteenth century façade, modern interior), sipping a Grey Goose vodka and tonic, and pondering the *Mojo* photographer's suggestion that, tomorrow, we might shoot him next to John Keats' grave in the city's Protestant cemetery. It's striking how, in the flesh, at 46, Morrissey bears almost no resemblance to that gauche, willowy eighties Catholic boy in the Evans shirts and baggy jeans who wondered exactly when nature would make a man of him. Today, heavy-set, sharp-eyed, sporting bespoke shoes, tailored blue shirt, enviable cashmere jumper and dark blue jeans, he looks more like one of those square-jawed British leading men of the fifties like Anthony Steel or Kieron Moore, forgotten cockleshell heroes who sat out the uncertainty of a new swinging decade in a rented flat behind Harrods, armed only with a sharp quiff, the right profile and a wry, haunted smile. It's a look entirely in keeping with the pervading mood of splendid defeat when we last met him, in June 2004. After seven years of ascetic exile in Los Angeles, following the release of the bone-weary *Maladjusted* ('It's my life/To wreck my own way'), we were in the heady swirl of a Moz renaissance, on a new label, Sanctuary, with a new album, *You Are The Quarry* (his best since 1994 masterpiece *Vauxhall And I*), and a Channel 4 documentary that saw a cavalcade of top-drawer celebs (Bono, Nancy Sinatra, Alan Bennett, Noel Gallagher) singing the praises of this jammy Stretford poet. It should have been a celebratory homecoming, but it all went a bit Pinter. Talk soon turned to unsettled scores, hatred of the music industry, and grand conspiracy theories, all arising from the Jarndyce and Jarndyce-like machinations of the 1996 high court case where Judge John Weeks ordered that Morrissey and Johnny Marr pay former bassist Mike Joyce £1.25 million in back earnings. Struck down by migraines and meningitis, here was an artist not at full fighting strength, flinching from praise like a wary rescue-dog receiving a kindly pat on the head.

Then, in May 2005, following *Quarry* sales in excess of one million, a series of stunning live dates and the release of definitive Morrissey live album . . . *At Earls Court*, Sanctuary announced that Morrissey was scheduled to play, and then would not be appearing at, June's Isle of Wight Festival. The singer issued a statement asserting: 'I have not ever, at any time, agreed to play the Isle of Wight Festival. The announcement that I would play was made by Sanctuary – and it was their error. I am very angry about [this], but I can't control Sanctuary. There will be a new signing for the new album, so please wait until you hear the news from my lips. Everything else is just gossip.' The impression was, as ever, that you cross Morrissey at your peril.

And now, in the manner of politicians, popes and gangsters, he is having a soft, conspiratorial whisper in the ear of an *aide de camp*. Keats is on our side but then

No fur but his own: Morrissey flashes his chest at PETA's 'Antidote to Fashion Week' event in 2000, one of their celebrity signatories against the fur trade.

. . . another secretive exchange. 'It's very beautiful there,' he avers. He'll be happy to do it. Oh yes, 'Happy'. Odd as it may seem, that's a word we'll be seeing a bit of over the next few pages. He leans in to *Mojo*. 'Have you been to Rome before? It's incredibly beautiful, every corner you turn.'

Maybe it was Keith Cameron's parting words of advice to Morrissey in that last *Mojo* feature – 'Be yourself, free yourself' – but something has happened since those tormented times of 2004. One listen to the new album, *Ringleader Of The Tormentors*, is enough to convince. Recorded at Forum Music Village in Rome with legendary T.Rex/Bowie producer Tony Visconti, *Tormentors* is certainly the ex-Smith's most uncompromising full-band record since *The Queen Is Dead*. But there's also an invigorating, if not downright shocking, freshness to Morrissey's lyrics. Gone are the wearying court case references and fecund images of exhausted defeat, replaced by songs of emotional uplift and generosity, attack and defiance, and on the Ennio Morricone-scored 'Dear God Please Help Me', disarmingly explicit references to, well, yer actual sex. As if to confirm that that old Morrissey is dead and buried, the album ends with a melodramatic, Shangri-La's drama, 'At Last I Am Born', which finds the Artist Formally Known As Unhappy informing us that, 'I once thought that I had numerous reasons to cry/And I did/But I don't any more/because I am born.' In that eternal Romantic battle between thought and feeling, *ROTT* finds a Morrissey who has finally escaped the prison of the intellect, and given himself up to fire, passion and – gulp – flesh. What's gotten into him?

'It's Rome,' explains Morrissey matter of factly, sipping on another Grey Goose and tonic. We're sitting in a typically austere hotel boardroom, all flipcharts and complimentary Hotel de Russie pencils, but the mood is surprisingly warm, Morrissey having already discovered *Mojo*'s previous employment as a film lecturer and enthused about Godard's *Bande a Part* and recommended a 1955 Jimmy Cagney and Doris Day musical, *Love Me or Leave Me* ('Oh, you can buy it anywhere for £3.99. His best ever performance!'). 'A year ago I came to Rome and became obsessed with the place. I'd been a few times before but it had never triggered with me. I just drifted through and saw nothing and noticed nothing but this year was completely different. I think it's because I'd spent the last seven years locked in Los Angeles, a very frightened city, everything geared towards avoiding human contact. I left the house I lived in because too many people knew where I lived. Every day there'd be people outside. Which is nice but . . . difficult. I just find everybody so free and stylish in Rome. Nothing really matters, tomorrow doesn't matter and people will bump into you in the street and not even say anything, whereas in Los Angeles it's a horrible infringement.'

There is one downside, the fact that Rome is the fur-wearing capital of the world. 'It spoils the city,' he says, 'and perhaps the country, because it's not *necessary*. But it's fascinating the way that the women who do wear fur just look really stupid.'

Fur aside, however, he was completely overtaken. The past, and Los Angeles, 'completely evaporated'. 'It all happened in north central Rome,' he says, 'where we are now. That's where the album was recorded. Everything just slipped into place.' The elements that slipped into place included Visconti, Morricone ('He'd said no to everybody . . . but he listened to the song and said, Yes!'), and Alanis Morissette's Texan guitarist Jesse Tobias who co-wrote five of the album's eleven songs. 'He's an incredible addition,' enthuses Morrissey. 'You were asking earlier about new muses? Well, of course, it's Jesse as well.'

Are you an easy person to work for?
Yes. Not looking for any jokes or silly punchlines, but I feel I'm absurdly easy, very undemanding . . . But so did Mussolini.

Now you said no jokes. You can't resist it can you?
Not really. I was born to be on *The Benny Hill Show*.

The new record seems influenced by the welcome for the last album. It's more confident, less defensive . . .
Well, when you're slapped about the face there is a weakening of spirit. And you don't feel welcome or that people are that keen on hearing what you're about to say. But when people make you feel more welcome you feel stronger and more confident.

How easy was that acceptance to come to terms with? Weren't you a little suspicious?
Of course. I couldn't relax entirely and I'm happy about that. I'll always remain suspicious. I'm not one to bask in any sort of good fortune. When things are going a certain way somebody has to break the spell.

On the whole Isle of Wight kerfuffle you issued a statement saying Sanctuary would not be the home for the next Morrissey album. What brought you back?
Somebody at Sanctuary said that I'd do the Isle of Wight. An understandable mess resulted from that and nobody from Sanctuary was speaking up for me. I'm not the kind of person you lead into certain situations. I know what I want to do and what I don't want to do and that was a mess, but I think it's largely forgotten now.

Did they say sorry?
Absolutely! But I was out of contract anyway. It was a one-album thing and I was basically finished with Sanctuary, but after the Isle of Wight they made an offer and, erm, here we are. But there's been a few messes in my life . . .

Do you ever wish you'd had the cigar-chomping, tough-line manager?
Yes, I do, to a certain degree. I've always wanted somebody I could really look up to who could walk ahead of me.

At one point you were looked after by Neil Young and Bob Dylan's manager, Elliot Roberts. I don't imagine they're easy rides . . .
I think he managed me for seven days, and he was terribly nice but there was just no point, really, because you can't mould me. I'm not what I'm not. And I can't help that. I'm simply me, unfortunately. I really can only follow my heart and do the things I passionately believe in and that's difficult in the music industry. It causes problems. I'm not trying to imply I'm above everything but . . . I feel it!

So, in the end, you just think, I'd be better off if I did this myself?
Absolutely.

My initial impression from this album is that this is a man who is . . . cough, 'happy'?
Well, I'm glad you coughed.

You've changed the way you write, there's more of a sense of openness . . .
Worldliness? Well, there it is. When I began I was horrendously parochial. A slave to England.

The legal case isn't referenced on the album. Is that exorcised from the soul?
It's reasonably exorcised. If I keep rabbiting on . . . I was finding that if I talked about it at all it became the central piece of the interview . . . Enough is enough. But it doesn't mean I've softened.

Are Morrissey lyrics like pages in a diary? 'Why should I stand by what I wrote in 1987?'
Exactly. The emotions were expressed. It happened. It was there, but I don't feel tied to it, or trapped, and I don't feel like the same person. I'm not carrying on a sequence of events.

But was there ever a period where you were carrying on a sequence of events? The accepted media image of Morrissey is that you have always been someone who thrives on unhappiness . . .
(*He interrupts*) Please, that's a compliment. They think they're criticising me and they're not.

OK, let me insult you then. You could argue that you've made your greatest albums when you are content and loved.
When was that?

Well, at the height of the Smiths, when you realised when you were working with a great band? The rallying round of people on the making of Vauxhall And I *and this album?*
Yes, yes. Is there something wrong with that?

No. So Morrissey works best when he's . . .
(*whispers*) Happy . . . there's a massive grain of truth in that. But only a grain.

The children's chorus singing, 'There is no such thing as normal!' on 'The Youngest Was The Most Loved' must have been a high point.
Especially when you see all these seven-year-old Italian children singing it, and quite happy to do it, full of meaning and not needing to have anything explained to them. A perverse joy.

Would the world be a happier place if we all embraced that idea?

I think we have to because we're all so obsessed with it and so obsessed with being it and it's an absolute waste of time.

Listening to this album was a bit like watching a Hollywood film after the relaxing of the Hays Code, a world of decorum suddenly awash with sex. I never expected Morrissey to say such things as [in 'Dear God, Please Help Me']: 'He motions to me with his hand on my knee . . . And now I'm spreading your legs, with mine in between . . .'
(*laughs*) It's funny to hear you say it . . . Well, I didn't really think there was ever something I couldn't write about, but unless it was a strip of me then I didn't really want to venture into anything. The song has to be true, otherwise it's pointless. And it is, it's very true.

Wasn't there a time when, even if it had been true, you wouldn't have written about it? That you wouldn't have gone there?
Well, previously I wasn't invited. I can't speak for everyone but it's been a gratifying journey and I didn't quite think I'd live to be this . . . old. At least I'm living proof that things can get better.

Why didn't you think you'd live this long? Death from boredom, exhaustion, or just wanting to pack it in?
All of those things. And more.

It's odd, isn't it? Right from the start with the Smiths you learnt to be flippant about the deadly serious so as not to sound tedious. Did you feel that you gave away too much of yourself in those interviews?
I did but I felt it couldn't be any other way otherwise we'd have been the Nightingales, the June Brides or the Jasmine Minks. Jolly as those groups were, the world didn't need another. I felt that I had to simply dive in and to hell with what might happen.

As a result, though, we'll talk flippantly about your depression . . . Were there genuine points where you thought, Sod it, I've had enough?
Well, I think there was a certain stage when so many bad things were written about me. The Smiths trial was certainly something to go through. And I think anybody of lesser steel would have slipped under. And so from that point onwards I thought, Well, just say it, just do it, just be it, just live it and, I am. I mean, when so many people tell you that you'll never dance again . . .

And you come back at the end of the last act, a star!
Oh God, am I really that trite?

What are your defence mechanisms?
Sudden illness. It never fails.

There's a great critical tradition in associating artistic creativity with depression. Would you take a pill that could make you happy all the time?

I'd take the bottle. You joke, but I'm no fool!

You wouldn't worry that you'd lose your edge?
To hell with the edge!

But what songs would you write then?
Oh, I wouldn't! I'd be too busy.

On 'You Have Killed Me' you announce, 'Pasolini is me!' and refer to two of his films, Accatone, *and Anna Magnani in* Mamma Roma. *What is it about this discontented Marxist Catholic . . .?*
Well, many things really . . . I've seen all the films . . . There's nothing flash about them. You're seeing real people without any distractions, just the naked person, with everything taking place on the streets. An extreme genius. But he also looked great and he didn't seem to be impressed by other people. He didn't have to be anybody else, he was being himself in his own world and even though he was obsessed with the low-life, that was all he wanted. He didn't want anything else.

Might there be another point of connection? Do you feel that even if you don't practise, you'll always be a Catholic?
I don't think you have any choice. It's sandblasted into you. And it will take one hell of a blowtorch to get rid of it. That will never happen, regardless of what your feelings are, regardless of what your intentions are.

Which songs are most obviously a result of your Catholic upbringing?
Everything. There's absolutely nothing else.

What's your attitude to psychoanalysis? Did you see a therapist out in LA?
Nooo, not at all. Well, I did before I left, because I was leaving for LA. And they said, of course, 'Please don't do it.' I don't see anyone now. I think we're all a mess. And it will all end eventually so there's not really any point wasting money on therapists. What is there to talk about? You're unhappy? Who's happy?

But that's Morrissey Now saying that. Surely there was another Morrissey who thought, It might help?
Did I ever say that? No, but I did actually see a therapist for a while. I wasn't very impressed.

They sat there and said nothing?
What else could they do? They just simply hand you a bill. But therapy is releasing and purging the self and allowing everything to trail out . . .

Don't you have that already?
Exactly.

Pursuit of love seems to be one of the key topics of the last two albums.
Well, sub-topic . . .

Have you found love?
Yes I have, yes I have. I mean, it's completely false of course . . .

What? All love is false or the love you found was false?
The latter. But everything's fine. Have you found love? How do you know it's love?

Because I feel incomplete without them.
Well, that's always the exchange. You have something I don't have and I have something you don't have. Which is OK.

There's still a cold rationalism there, isn't there?
Well, we overexamine it, I think.

Does that mean you will never fall in love because you will always . . .
I'm 80! There's not that much time left.

Don't you worry that you'll end up like John Osborne or John Fowles, one of those cynical diarists chronicling the decaying world?
God willing. God willing.

But how does that make the person you love, or fall in love with, feel? Because they must know that.
Well, yes, because I write to them and tell them.

The next day, in the lobby of the Hotel de Russie, Morrissey presents *Mojo* with 'a small present': a DVD of Jimmy Cagney in *Love Me or Leave Me*. Later, wrapped in heavy wool overcoat, Morrissey is walking with *Mojo* through the crumbling landscape gardens of Rome's Villa Borghese, a beautifully dishevelled world of seventeenth century rococo grandeur, natural decay and modern graffiti, gifted to the people of Rome in 1901 as a state-owned public park. 'If this were Britain,' murmurs Morrissey, 'we'd be looking at numerous "Keep Off The Grass" signs and lots of brooding teenagers. Tell people not to do something and they want to do it so much more. Here they're free so they don't care.' Morrissey has always taken a notebook on such constitutionals ('I never carry less than five'), jotting down snatches of overheard conversation. 'I'm a dreadful eavesdropper,' he admits. 'Every time people speak to me I see it written down.' Later, at the graveside of Keats in the Protestant cemetery, prior to the photo-shoot, Morrissey lingers over the gravestone inscription (relishing the line about 'the malicious power of his enemies') while a trio of benign feral cats, part of 300,000 *gatti* now protected by Rome city council as part of the city's 'bio-heritage', pad contentedly around his feet. 'Do you know how to tell if it's a genuine tabby?' he whispers. 'They have an "M" marking on their forehead.' Recently, on the True To You fansite, Morrissey was asked how much environment affected his work.

His reply? 'None of these things affect me. I am an island.' This, I suggest, is rubbish. The Smiths never sounded like an East Anglian band, but were clearly Northern, and this album is obviously a product of his love of Rome.

'Yes, that's quite true,' he concedes, 'but then I do feel like an island, to the extent that I could be almost anywhere, unaffected yet massively affected.'

Growing up in Sixties Manchester, Morrissey holds that the muse struck him when he was seven or eight. 'You won't believe me,' he explains later, back at the hotel, 'but I was certainly hatching something and I felt in my own misguided way like a little work of art. All the memories I have of life are not of people but of songs or films. When I was a child I was obsessed with "You've Lost That Lovin' Feelin'", the way the two voices were jumping around, and, when I saw it on *Top of the Pops*, the way [Bill Medley and Bobby Hatfield] would not look at each other and sing those two parts was extraordinary. All the things that influenced me, in film and music, were quite haphazard and strange, and I felt that they could be gathered, blended and the final result would be something unique.'

If a catalyst were needed it came with the November 1973 appearance on *The Old Grey Whistle Test* of the New York Dolls which spurred the teenage Morrissey to pen letters to the *Melody Maker* and *NME* in praise and defence of the much-mocked lower Manhattan glam heroes. 'I was a nuisance for a while,' he says. 'I'd write letters and long to be in the press but I was a complete failure. Of course, being a pop star when you're eleven and a half and covered in acne is also ludicrous [but] in those days it seemed such a powerful thing. I was incredibly clumsy, and determined, but knew, deep down, that I was reasonably glamorous, even if nobody else could see it.'

When 'This Charming Man' was released in 1983, many thought it was Morrissey, as opposed to Jean Cocteau protégé Jean Marais, on the cover. 'It was, spiritually,' says Morrissey today. Whether it was fifties British character actor Sean Barrett (on the cover of 'How Soon Is Now') or the late Patric Doonan, namechecked on 1994's 'Now My Heart Is Full', the impression was that this deep down conviction of his own glamour resulted in our hero seeking out 'the Morrissey look' in other faces, other people . . . 'Yes, I think I did,' he says, 'I think I do. Do you know much about Patric Doonan? He killed himself in a road in Chelsea called Margaretta Terrace, just off Oakley Street, number four I think. He gassed himself in the basement. I wrote to the people and (*laughs*) I said, Do you know anything about the fact that Patric Doonan took his life in your basement . . . ?'

And they said, 'How did you get this address? Please stop writing to us'? 'No, they didn't even bother to say that much, unfortunately. The feeling was that, surely, the things I feel, the people that I see great beauty, value and glamour in, can't possibly amount to nothing.'

Morrissey has never fallen out of love with his heroes. As host of the 2004 Meltdown Festival, he invited the surviving members of the New York Dolls to perform live. It appeared a true moment of vindication for the Manchester kid with the weird taste who'd never given up. 'Have you seen the Bob Gruen DVD [*All Dolled Up*]?' he asks. 'It's astonishing, and confirms what I've been saying about them for years. David Johansen was so clever for a nineteen-year-old; so witty, literate, unstoppable and here, finally, it is, on film. It was always frustrating to me, that the rest of the world wouldn't take the things that were setting me alight. So it's fascinating that in 2006 it all seems to make sense.'

Given how much your early songs were influenced by such inspirational writers as Shelagh Delaney and Elizabeth Smart, what was the first unfettered song you wrote, where you thought, these people have helped me but now I can fly free?
It's a good question and it probably didn't happen until very late because a spark of me was always very, erm, unsure and that's when I think you rely on other people's ideas. I mean, I know I overdid it with Shelagh Delaney. It took me a long, long time to shed that particular one. [But] no one is ever quite as original as they think they are. I always considered the great mesh of all of my influences had emerged in me as something that was unique *enough*.

The first significant piece written about the Smiths was by Dave McCullough in Sounds *in 1983. How did it feel to read that?*
Fantastic because he was ablaze with excitement and there was a fantastic run of photographs of me and I had always believed until that second in my life that I was . . . not remotely photogenic, so I was amazed to see this strange creature . . . I couldn't believe I inhabited this body and I was here doing this thing. It was just unspeakably exciting.

Daft question: Could the Smiths only have happened when they did?
Absolutely, while the rest of the world wasn't looking. That's the only way you can surprise people. You can't surprise people if your arrival is trumpeted by a record company. You have to tap them on the shoulder and catch their expression when they turn round. As I do frequently.

Is it time for your version of the story? The autobiography rumours . . .
Well they're not rumours. But, unfortunately you can't really do something like a serious autobiography if you travel and your time is constantly interrupted by a change of environment. I've agreed with myself to do it. But there's no deal at all. I read stories in the daily newspapers that I'd been given millions. And demanded more! That's absolute crap. I've never been offered anything! And I've never had any dialogue with a publisher.

How do you feel when these stories seemingly spring up by themselves?
It's always very annoying because, in my case, the wording's always so extreme and I always seem to appear to have an extreme reaction to something that, in the first place, is completely fabricated. It's infuriating but you reach a point where life just doesn't really belong to you.

In William E. Jones' film about US Morrissey fans, Is It Really So Strange?, *the fans were saying that because your lyrics in the past have rarely been gender-specific, it's allowed a wide variety of different groups to identify with them. Now, with something like 'Dear God, Please Help Me' on the new album . . . gender-specific.*
Yes.

Why?

Am I running scared now? Whatever people invest within you, that's what you are and there's nothing I can do about that. People can say what they like. I can't really control how people view a situation so why obsess about it? And why set out to correct everybody on the planet with the view they have about you? That would be exhausting. And it's impossible.

But does it take a strong and content Morrissey to now be gender-specific in such a beautiful, well, love song?

Many of the great love songs of all time are non-gender specific. Mine are, truthfully, innocent expressions of a somewhat primitive person. This innocence stops you from going any further. If you write in a non-gender specific way, you can be considered to be avoiding the bold truth, or speaking in code, or giving a knowing wink – I understand all of that, naturally. But I don't think I'd be any less of a conundrum to people if I actually wrote or sang in a deafeningly specific way. As I said earlier, I am simply inexcusably me.

What has maturity brought you?

Well, it's certainly surprised me. I always thought that the pathway to 30 was horrendous and the pathway to 40 was almost bearable but within recent years I feel that there's some kind of joy to be had in life.

That's probably a statement you never imagined yourself saying.

Never. But I never imagined being this age.

You would have decided to make an exit?

I would be asked to leave.

What would you compromise for?

Nothing. What would there be?

Someone else?

They'd have to be incredibly good at darts.

On the new album's 'To Me You Are A Work Of Art', you sing, 'I see the world/It makes me puke/But I know that somewhere there's a someone who can soothe me.' Is that the essential core of Morrissey today?

Yes.

I never thought I'd hear you say it.

Stick around, it gets worse.

So, does that mean you've finally met that special someone you'd wait outside the shops for?

Yes . . . Santa.

And in the future?
I never see beyond seven days. I can't understand why, but I never have.

Is it a coping tactic?
Well I try to care so much less than I once did. It's a fantastic defence mechanism.

Will you be staying in Rome for the foreseeable future?
Yes. It's in my nature to overdo everything.

*You once said you'd run a mile if confronted with the Steven Morrissey of 1983.
How do you think he'd respond to meeting you now?*
I think he'd be terribly impressed. I really do.

And that's it. Our time is up. I tell Morrissey that I really enjoyed it ('I bet you'd say that to Jimmy Krankie') and ask if there's a way to get in touch with him again. 'It's a punishing life,' he mutters, and the man who once only communicated with collaborators or management by fax, scribbles his e-mail address at the top of my list of questions. 'Keep it under your Stetson,' he says. It's all gone eerily well and I leave with my Cagney DVD, a passable knowledge of tabby cats and a strange hunch that the man I spoke to, the real Morrissey, is finally, cough, happy. More surprisingly, a fortnight later, as we go to press, *Mojo* receives nine different e-mails from Morrissey, apologising for lateness and happily answering a list of follow-up questions. Worldly, co-operative, content? Let's face it, Steven Patrick Morrissey would run a mile.

Mojo, April 2006

THE LAST TEMPTATION
OF MORRISSEY
———·— BY PAUL MORLEY ——·———

I first met Morrissey in 1976 queueing outside Manchester's Electric Circus in the rain. We were there to see the Ramones. I asked him if he knew that he was wearing odd shoes. 'Of course,' he replied. It was our first interview.

30 years later, I review Morrissey's new record very favourably, correctly diagnosing it as an emphatic, eloquent modern classic. He asks to see me, possibly just to check I'm not having him on. He greets me at the door of his fourth floor suite at the Dorchester looking nimble, vaguely wary and well scrubbed. He's plainly but expensively dressed in note-perfect charcoal jacket, cashmere v-neck sweater, freshly laundered jeans and exquisite, matching Italian slip-ons – the carefully considered purchase of a man who doesn't hate the idea of life as much as he might suggest. The famous quiff, the colour of a low cloud, now erupts playfully from an untouched receding hairline. It's as erect as it's ever been. 'It's good to see you,' I say, before I realise my error. 'Why?' he shudders, stretching the word around a few pained, persecuted syllables, shocked at my forwardness.

Morrissey answers questions quietly, with a kind of practised serenity, as if he is the sanest man on the planet. In many ways, he actually is, but the cost of maintaining this sanity has been a kind of insanity. (In much the same way, a sophisticated maturity is all tangled up with a seemingly incurable immaturity, robustness battles sickliness, niceness meets nastiness, and billowing self-assurance snakes around chilling insecurity.) His conversational style is funnier than it seems in print, and he laughs a lot, at/with/by himself, sometimes at the same time as seeming in terrible pain. He does not volunteer information easily. An interviewer has to dig for it, as if, in front of his very eyes, and with his help, even if you are being benign, or flattering, or very innocuous, you are digging his grave, and asking him to lie down in it so that you can bury him alive with his own utterances.

Consequently, after being almost buried in such a manner so many times over the past 23 years, he is understandably reluctant to willingly supply the material that might completely cover his body and face. He hands out just a little soil that he can easily rinse away later. And if he doesn't think that he's being buried, he might think that he is being stabbed. After a particularly stylish rebuttal or deflection of this, that or the other enquiry, he'll smile – ish – and say, keep stabbing away. It's an interesting way of looking at what, in the end, is just a few questions asked in the service of quite natural, raging curiosity about this individual who has made such a perverse success at being so individual. So, you keep stabbing, and he deftly manages to avoid being sliced open.

Certain questions – such as, is the new record your masterpiece, are you happy, do

Morrissey in concert at Alexandra Palace in May 2006. England's prodigal son:
Morrissey emerges from years of unofficial 'exile' in LA. Note the Snow White pendant,
symbol of its cultural capital, Disneyland.

203

you find yourself repeating yourself, what were the last three things on your credit card statement, what excites you these days, are you so desperate for our attention, is all of this an act of revenge on Marr, are you caught up in the saga of Preston and Chantelle? – receive one of the following replies, occasionally accompanied by a gloriously forced winning smile, a faraway look, a clenched pause and a subtle, sinister sneer: 1/ What do you think? 2/ I couldn't possibly comment. 3/ I can't imagine.

Occasionally, there's no sound, just a look, brutal and artistic, to indicate that the question is monumentally stupid or too profound or unstable to adequately deal with, a look containing elements of a weary, oddly happy acceptance, a faint smirk as if he might indeed be swooning, a faraway, slightly old-fashioned look, a flash of boredom and/or bad temper, a glimmer of contempt and a subtle, radiant sneer. In the following record of our meeting, I use the word 'face' to communicate this silence. Occasionally there is a peeved, but somehow polite sigh that seems to stretch from the beginning to the end of time. I signify this with the word 'sigh'. Also for the record, I visit the bathroom three times during our time together – just to check my expression in the mirror – and each time I return, Morrissey has moved to a different seat and is wearing a slightly guilty expression on his face that I can't quite pin down.

So you're going to be nice? (*face*)

You read my review of Ringleader Of The Tormentors . . .
That means no . . .

Just because I called you doggedly odd. It's not even something I would consider . . .
Of you being nice, or not being nice . . .

Oh come on . . .
I think you should be nice.

You're looking well.
I don't know why, considering all that I have been through.

Today in general, the last week, the last few years . . .
Since 1959.

How are you ageing, how do you feel about it?
Oh (*sigh*), it's an unanswerable question . . . because it's a mystery to me. I'm here. Still. Beyond that I'm quite clueless, to be honest.

The last few years – you seem to be enjoying them. You're as prolific as ever. You've got everyone's attention. Age suits you.
It becomes a matter of perseverance in the end. You just keep going. You have no choice once you cross the 40 threshold. Virtually nothing on the planet really matters anymore. It's too late to really worry about things because you are already in an unimaginable state.

Stunned by an overwhelming accumulation of experience?
Well, you would say that. It was always unimaginable to me that I would turn 40 and then suddenly be 46 and everyone in music is half my age . . . it's fascinating. And it's fascinating that people of seventeen will stop me in the street and go, 'Oh my God.' It's a curious place to be. You step into music and you are one of the apple-cheeked juniors and you are trying to impress everyone else who is older than you and suddenly, just like that, you turn fifteen corners at once and you are seen as an elder statesman or something, and the person above all who can't explain it is yourself.

I remember even at 33 you were a little shocked.
I thought that was such an unattainable age. I didn't think it was possible to live that long. I remember being interviewed on Radio One and I said that all pop singers should be shot at 30. The disturbing thing is I actually believed that with all of my heart. But not now, of course. Ah, those were the days.

What happened?
I didn't die. (*sigh*)

It's as simple as that.
Well that's quite complicated really. No, it's really that simple.

What happened to the idea of an early death?
Well, there's time. I haven't ruled it out yet.

Are you tempted to return to the beautiful north?
Absolutely. And as you know, Manchester is a completely new place. But an attractively new place.

What do you make of it?
It bears no relation to the place I used to know and the place you used to know. It makes me feel sad in a way, because not just the older generation have disappeared, but the generation down have disappeared, and walking through Manchester you don't really see senior citizens. Everyone is young all of a sudden. So I presume all the older Mancunians have been wiped out, all the ones that can remember the things that we'd like to forget. In that respect it's sad. But of course it wasn't a pleasant place in the Seventies. That's why you became a writer and I became whatever I became. Otherwise we would have been completely happy to live in Denton and . . . complete the sentence.

Wasn't this new modernisation what we wanted?
Yes. But I don't think that we envisaged it happening, and the reality is always a little unnerving, and seems to take as much, if not more, away with it as whatever it brings in replacement. It's quite sad that the entire satanic mill element of Manchester, the oldness, is melting away, because there's something about not having a choice in life that can be quite gratifying. There's something about being trapped . . .

So you wouldn't have wanted it any other way?
Well, nobody asked me, and I had no choice in whether there was any choice or not
. . . but there is something gratifying about being quite stuck, the way it feeds the
nervous system is quite a rush that I wouldn't imagine you get if you lived in a wing
of Windsor Castle.

In the Sixties and Seventies was your dream of a sophisticated life?
A comfortable life. And I don't mean Alderly Edge.

You were looking for some otherness?
Well, yes. I wasn't very good at being working class and so forth . . . There is
absolutely no reason at all on this planet why I should have any taste in any department. But I do.

*Has once wanting to be a writer about music coloured how you've engaged with the
music press . . . almost as one who escaped into the outside world, living out the idea
of being a pop star for real, leaving many bitter and twisted in your wake?*
Well I never was one . . . I tried very hard to be one, and as you know I was a complete nuisance for about twelve years, and feel absolute sympathy for anyone who I
burdened with those letters and pieces and so forth, but I was only three and a half
and I wanted to be part of something glamorous and that's how I thought I could do
it, but it just wasn't to be for me . . . for which I'm now grateful, because if I had
become a success in that field then perhaps I would never have played the ukulele.

When did you first want to be a singer?
When I was two years old. I saw the Righteous Brothers on television. Bill and Bobby.
I thought, fantastic. That's me.

Was Howard Devoto an influence in the late Seventies?
At the time he was because he was quite like me in temperament, or I was quite like
him. I remember seeing Magazine at the Russell Club, and they had come back from
London where things were going well for them, and it was all quite exciting and he
fell on the floor and I thought that was the height of intellectual glamour. I couldn't
really see many people like me in pop music. There was Ron Mael. I could identify
with him. But nobody else.

What was it about Mael and Devoto?
I thought they were both obviously quite shy and they were clearly grappling with
many complex issues. And they weren't smiling. But they were thinking. They weren't
on some happy pop roller coaster. Which I also appreciated in Nico. There was still
a belief in those days that to be, shall we say, a front man, you had to be very extro-
vert and ballsy and have shocking hair.

What finally triggered the move onto a stage?
Well, I didn't really have that much choice. I felt so despairing and so desperate and

I just couldn't bear to watch anyone else do it. I went through a period where I could not listen to music because I was so enraged and angry. And then suddenly, at just the right time, I found myself sound-checking.

What is it like now, this far in, when it comes to making a new record? After all the sound checks and the albums you've made, where you've been, how comfortable you are, what people are expecting, you don't need to do it but you decide to make an album . . .
When you say 'need', you mean financially; well it's not a question of that, and it never, absolutely never, has been. It's about making something that I can be proud of, and something to point to so that I can see that I'm still here. For myself, nobody else. And as a significant aside, making a record is always enjoyable. I like to be occupied.

That sense of wanting to be different – and there is a sense that the world wants to have you filed, sorted, boxed – and making a new album is a way for you to announce that you are still resisting being framed, that you are still different, and you see things differently.
There isn't any announcement. This isn't about that. It leads me. And I simply follow.

What leads you?
The compulsion. This isn't a job, or a vocation. It's a demand.

All the analysis, perception, scrutiny, the accumulation of information about you – how hard is it to keep going, resisting being set into concrete?
It's very difficult. It could once be believed that, even if something was burnt into print, it would disappear seven days later – and there would be no trace of it. With the internet now, that's not the case, and everything is there and it's a raging fire every single day, and it's alive every single day. For me it's difficult, because so much crap is written about me endlessly, and the interviews I do bear no relation in print with the meeting I've just had with the writer. That's something about me, unfortunately, that people feel they have to write something . . . noteworthy. They can't simply write a factual account of a meeting. There has to be something . . . astonishing.

You have become an opportunity for writers to demonstrate their own hoped-for specialness.
I'm afraid so.

The nerve of it . . .
And I can see it for days before I've even met the writer. There's nothing I can do about it. I'm just a key in the middle of it. In fact, I'm nothing. A mere key. I'm nothing.

You keep doing them.
They please people, sometimes. It's not something I can explain. (*sigh*)

By the beginning of the Nineties, the music papers' love for you had turned into something nasty, and there were all sorts of accusations and scandals, as if the great roman-

tic English hero had turned right-wing, nazi skinhead. Has any of that hostility stuck, do you think?

No. When it was at its height I released an album that entered at one, and I did no promotion. I think it was a measure of the *NME*'s self-importance at the time that they thought they were destroying me. And it was only two people, and two people who never liked me all through the Eighties, and they were using their position, their new position at the *NME*, to try and get rid of me. The *NME* had become so obsessed with me that they then were embarrassed by it, and wanted to get rid of me. I partly understood that . . . it had got a bit ridiculous, inventing stories about me and Charles Hawtrey, it was getting so ludicrous. I was not involved in the way I was so inflated and reported on, in much the same way that the Arctic Monkeys are not involved with their own particular escalation. They're probably bewildered by it, and feel some nervousness that it's too quick. Back in the glorious days of what people called the *New Morrissey Express*, I felt nervous, and was divorced from it. It was nothing to do with me, but it coloured how people perceived me. I wasn't at the *NME* offices saying write this about me, take this picture of me quick!

And now everyone loves you again.

This will also change. The neglect in the Nineties fairly trumpeted itself, and I've no doubt such a time will come again. Well, that happens in England, not really anywhere else. In England, most writers have a how-dare-you attitude towards me, even if they quite like me. The implication is that I must satisfy all their demands, even if they are not relevant to me. That's just something I've learnt to live with. I think it's because there's an impression that if you matter then you should be drilled, but if you don't matter then you can just fly away and do what you want, and collect the money and release dreadful albums and so forth. You are only targeted and crucified when you matter. So somewhere in the midst of all the assassinations I receive I have a twinge of satisfaction, from knowing that they care enough to be so concerned with me, even if that means toying with me, ripping me apart, making me out to be the freak, general character assassination. People never sit down with me and talk about the act of singing and the voice, and very rarely do they want to talk about the songs, but they will want to know about politics, and they'll want to know why I am still alive, and about my sex life, and God, even my love life . . .

You've asked for it . . .

Only a little bit.

Because you sing about very private things and this leads on to certain kinds of curiosity.

Don't the songs satisfy people enough?

Did you give producer Tony Visconti a brief for the new record? What did you ask for? Something alien and enterprising that You Are The Quarry *failed to capture?*

(*face/sigh/agony*) I told him I wanted . . . detail . . . comprehensive detail . . . I wanted a certain kind of something. Do you want to know the commas and the semicolons of that brief? Well, you can't. Let's not ruin the mystery. But put it this way, I'm not just a pretty face.

The first line on your new album – 'No one knows what human life is' – did that accidentally become the first line of the album, or was it always intended to be the first line?
Oh, it's absolutely the first line. I thought at the time, why write anything else, why not just leave it at that? That says it all. But of course, there were other things I decided to sing that also say it all.

Listening to the new record, it's one of the first things the listener will think – he's in love, and it's not nosiness to want to ask about that . . . well, it is . . . but it's also wanting to give the songs some kind of wider framework. So, in a situation like this, you being there, and me being here, together in this lovely room overlooking Hyde Park on the notable occasion of your new record, it seems right and fitting to ask: are you in love?
I'm in love with something. I often am.

Not someone.
Not a human being, no. And on these new songs, I'm in love with something. So, keep stabbing away.

You've moved to Rome?
I travel so much that I actually live nowhere. I live in the middle of the Atlantic Ocean. I left Los Angeles last year after seven years. I became an Italianophile, yes.

You moved to Rome to be with someone.
Something.

Because of someone.
Something.

Someone?
Something.

One.
Thing.

You met someone and you moved to Rome to be with them.
That's the tabloid journalist in you, as if there is no story worth discussing unless there is a greasy little tabloid element to it.

So you haven't.
I haven't. (*sigh*) I can't say anything other than I haven't if I haven't. Don't put the innocent face on me. Does it really matter in the end one way or another, whether I have, haven't, have never, have soon?

Something has happened with this record – a sonic discovery, a musical discovery, an emotional discovery, a reawakening, a new focus . . .
Maybe you know and I don't. Maybe that's the way it should be.

You must know that, as a listening experience, for people perhaps outside of the fascination with Morrissey, this album breaks outside the self-enclosed myth of you and achieves something atmospherically that you haven't reached before.
I'll take your lead on that . . .

You don't see it this way?
I've always been me, and whatever happens on a record, that's me, at whatever stage I'm at, in whatever state . . . I've always been inexplicably me, detailing every twist and turn in the sordid events of my life . . . Shall I keep answering that question by not answering how you want me to?

Suddenly . . . all this ice seems to have melted, there's an erotic charge in the music and the language.
I've always been erotic. This won't go anywhere, by the way. It might be because I consider you're not really that interested in the subject and are just having to go through the motions.

I wonder why people think you are a control freak?
Oh, kill me, please. (*face/sigh/resignation/peril/defiance*)

Because you've been known to mouth off now and then, it's thought that you might spark off turf wars across the celebrity landscape with Jordan, or Posh and Becks, or Pete Burns . . . that you are the kind of opinionated celebrity who was originally obsessed with celebrity, and who might have a take on the whole thing.
And if I do or don't have an opinion about Jordan or Posh and Becks, how in the end is that really going to change people's day? And if I have the most startling opinion about Posh and Becks or Jordan, how is that going to alter the course of the universe? It isn't going to. I was interested in intelligent celebrity. The word now is so base and disgusting and seems to apply to anybody that is anything but a celebrity. So . . . what would I be saying? Use your imagination to decide what I might say about these people.

This will disappoint those people who rely on you as a wit in all situations.
Because they expect me to insult such people. And controversy ensues. (*sigh*) Well, I will leave it to the imagination of the reader to make up their own mind as to my feelings towards the people that would be on a list that I might be expected to have an opinion about, in this day and age.

Pete Doherty will be on that list.
I think it is unfortunate that he is more associated with the media and the press and hoo ha and the silliness than he is with music. It's a terrible trap and he's jumped straight into it. And Kate Moss has just dragged him down to her level. I don't hon-

estly have an opinion on him, to be honest. I don't care. That's my opinion. I don't care. I'm sorry to disappoint everyone, but in the end, I can't be expected to have something to say about these things just because people expect me to. I don't have to believe in all the fuss that's generated. In truth, I mean, I don't care about Pete Doherty, and why keep feeding the situation and making it out to be extraordinary, because when you come to think about it, what is it? What is it? What? I'm asking you. That's a question. To you.

Sorry, I thought you were being rhetorical.
Not this time.

The phenomenon around it is the phenomenon – the Smiths could not have functioned as they did under such circumstances, instantly being hurled into the mainstream to be consumed as playthings before they had worked themselves out.
I was always concerned simply with the songs and the singing. We didn't have to contend with any kind of celebrity community, either to join or rebel against. I have never tried to be part of a celebrity community, and the very idea of being in gossip columns is horrific to me, regardless of what is written. I am principally interested in music and nothing else. I don't want awards and I don't want to be someone whose work is defined by awards.

You've been turning down awards?
A few. I find the entire award culture appalling and destructive . . . never mind the celebrity culture. I think the award culture is destroying music and possibly every other form of entertainment. It's so ludicrous and it's so pointless. You might as well become a travelling salesman. The Brits are ghastly, and there has never been a time when they haven't got it wrong. For me to ever accept a Brit, well, I never would, it would be like Laurence Olivier being happy getting a *TV Times* award. And now of course, in order to get an award in music, awards of the highest magnitude, all you have to do is turn up. All you have to do is make one reasonably OK album, and you have awards, flowers, gold medals, the whole world at your feet. If you accept such an award you are, of course, joining in with the mediocrity of it all, but everyone has started to think that it's all about awards, and that if you don't want to accept one there must be something wrong with you.

The ecstatic obsession with pop culture has travelled almost from deep inside your teenage bedroom and taken over the world – everyone reacts to pop and fame in the way you did locked inside your gloom.
What makes it different is the easy access to every aspect of pop music now, so there is no effort involved. There's no strain or risk involved for the listener. There's nowhere to hide, or to find the hidden and the forbidden for yourself, it's all on vulgar display. Certainly, when I was younger than I am now, it was very unusual to come across any other living human who actually heard the records that you heard, and it was very unusual to discuss lyrics with somebody. But these days, of course, with the internet and so forth, and the obsession with knowing as much as possible,

it's all become meaningless, where everyone knows everything instantly.

Are all the bloggers – with their emotion, passion, narcissism, their endless sniping, snobby appetite for recording, marking, organising, celebrating, condemning, loving, hating, gossiping, metaphorically wearing odd shoes – weird descendants of yours?
Yes . . . they are the modern me, because of course I am not. Nor do I want to be.

You have an iPod?
Is that a trick question? Yes.

What's on your iPod?
Oh, you know what's on there . . . the usual suspects, and a few less so . . . I cast the net quite broadly . . . I'm like a very obese person who eats food but doesn't enjoy it. I listen to a lot of new music but I don't enjoy it.

What about any of the new stuff reminding people so solidly of 1983?
You can anticipate the reply. There is very little that I haven't heard before. I think it's ludicrous that certain things are considered to be revolutionary and new when there is absolutely no way that they are.

Why does that bother you so much?
It bothers me because I can think of so many people down the line, in the Seventies and the Eighties, who were very prolific and had no attention and no success, and now so many groups and artists are simply mimicking the independent charts of the Eighties, and running away with gold awards and tiaras and flowers – simply because there are enough people around that don't remember the first time it all happened, or didn't allow it to happen then.

Is that inevitable?
Not necessarily, because who would have thought that the independent charts would have flipped over into the mainstream? There were so many great groups and sounds back then, and all of those people were on the dole then and they're on the dole now, if they're still alive . . .

Who are you thinking of?
Oh, all of your friends. [*I think he's referring to the likes of Magazine, Josef K, Fire Engines, the Monochrome Set, etc, etc – PM*] So the modern copyists, the bands that take the leaves out of the early Eighties pages, are considered to be prophets. It isn't enough these days for a group or an artist to be just successful, they have to be prophets leading us all, which is also ludicrous. Everybody has to be a phenomenon. I think it comes from the print media, who need to survive, and they have to convince themselves and their readers that things are moving in a culturally sensational way. The past came back in a big way in the Nineties, which is all very nice and interesting, but the press needs to convince us that everything is throbbing with revolution and not just echoing the past.

Arctic Monkeys – their album title, **Whatever People Say I Am, That's What I'm Not,** *seemed very Morrissey, and is in fact from one of your favourite books/films, Alan Silitoe's* **Saturday Night and Saturday Morning.**
The album title reminded me of when Jools Holland introduced me on *Later* by saying whatever people say I am, that's what I am not . . . I'm not so possessive that I would assume that everything I enjoyed in the past belongs only to me . . . I'm very pleased that they show that degree of taste . . . beyond that, I don't really know that much about them.

Have you heard them?
I saw them once on television. I thought it was very pleasant in the way that Jasmine Minks were pleasant.

Are the Arctic Monkeys leading a vindication of those early Eighties ideas? This entering into the mainstream of a smarter, louder, more local music . . .
Well, it was all bound to happen eventually, but that doesn't mean it happens in the right way, at the right time.

It's created a scene where you fit perfectly . . . still on the cover of the NME *at your age – why is that?*
Because people aren't entirely bored of the subject yet. As a living, breathing human being I am, when all is said and done, not that offensive. I haven't stepped into the world of *Hello* and *Richard and Judy*. I have not made life easy for myself by disappearing into the celebrity world. I think people somehow acknowledge that. Some people in my position wobble. They wear the wrong clothes and allow themselves to be photographed with the wrong people. Of course, I've never even met the wrong people. Here's hoping I never do.

How can you manage to not meet the wrong people?
Well, there's been a couple of close calls. There have been a few people who have shunned me. Keith Richards. Buffy St. Marie and . . . somebody else who just completely blanked me in a shocking way, who just completely wiped me out of history. I can't remember who it was.* They simply smile hello and then quickly turn their back.

Perhaps Keith Richards doesn't know who the hell you are.
You see, you're wrong. He knew me. But he didn't actually like me. But I pick up the pieces and I crawl on with my life and live to see another dawn.

What do you make of the iPodification of the world?
It's part of the watering down, as far as I can see. It's part of the door closing on this great, wonderful thing. I wouldn't listen out of preference. I still prefer to listen to the old rusty CD player . . .

Vinyl?
It's so difficult to get the needles. (*snigger*) Do you? Isn't it such an anachronism?

Yes, I don't care anymore about whether that dates me.
Well, that's what middle-aged people always say.

Your songs are based on a vinyl idea of song, and the story, and the mystery . . .
Of course it is. For years I was fascinated by the fact that the needle could simply land on this lumpy piece of wobbly plastic, and suddenly this great orchestration would appear. I spent years trying to work this out, and I still haven't worked it out. It's such a great mystery. But it really doesn't do to talk about such things . . .

Why not? Are you worried about what people will think, us sitting around talking about the good old days? . . .
Yes, because it's really like talking about Gracie Fields' 78's . . .

You're worried about disappearing into the past?
What, worried about being seen as a specimen of a bygone age? No, that's not something that concerns me really. To be honest, I don't think it's a problem. I feel startlingly now-ish. It isn't 1957 any more. It can't be 1957 any more. Are you surprised to hear me say that? I'm very much living in the swill of modern life.

Do you take yourself too seriously?
If I don't, who will?

I might.
But I don't know that. You fluctuate.

[John] Peel felt it had all gone to your head and you'd gone a bit stuck up, a bit Duke of Edinburgh.
(*face*) . . . (*grimace*) . . . I honestly don't think I ever really changed from those early smelly days in the back of a smelly van.

Do you think you there might be a tendency for you to take yourself too seriously? . . (*face/warning/agony*)

. . . because people in situations like this will ask, in all seriousness – if you were Prime Minister, how would you fix the country?
If I'm asked, it seems impolite not to reply . . . Well, I'll never be Prime Minister, because I'm not corrupt. You cannot really believe anything Tony Blair says. I don't like his face. I don't like his expression. I don't think anybody else does. And I can't stand Cherie Blair's face, and I just wonder if there can ever be a photograph of her where she has her mouth shut. Unfortunately, politicians are never poets and politicians never give up power. What Tony Blair tells you is happening in Iraq and what actually is happening in Iraq are, of course, two completely different things. So I could never see myself in politics, because it strikes me that to be successful in politics, or to even be in politics, you have to be completely corrupt. I can't see anyone in politics the world over who is sane. Politics to most people is horrific.

The royals. . .
Why would you say that? Are you asking if I have an opinion about them? If anybody has an opinion about them? What about them? You see, this is such an example of lazy journalism. I mean, I know who they are. I'm not that out of touch.

Do you share the same fate – having to live out your life as a construct, trapped inside being Morrissey until the day you die?
We're all heading for the same swill bucket, and there are very few people who can change horses in midstream. We're all trapped inside our own identities, whatever they may be. The monarchy is a memory. It doesn't exist any more, and quite rightly so. You can see the terror on the Queen's expression whenever she has to open a hospital. She's horrified because she can see the whole ship slip away, like the Titanic under the waves. The arrogance of Charles and Camilla is unspeakable. Nobody likes them. Nobody wants them. With the television coverage of their wedding you could see that there was nobody there. So it's not for me to sit here and say that the monarchy is a memory and no one cares any more, because it's obvious. Everybody knows the show is over. The very idea of Charles being king is laughable. You might as well say that Ronnie Corbett will be king one day. I think that would give people more pleasure.

Do you want to be king?
(*face*) . . . (*cringe*) . . . (*hallelujah*) . . .

You're trying to find the lost continent of Presley.
Well, I'm swimming as fast as I can. The final years were reasonably grotesque and they are willingly forgotten by everyone, and they concentrate on the years of strength and beauty and grandeur. That's not such a bad continent to reach, all things considered.

Do you really want that mad level of iconic presence?
Why do you think I'm wearing my water wings?

Is there a dichotomy between your nostalgia for certain elements of entertainment and society, and the fact that you're interested in music and ideas that were about remaking the world, wanting the world to move forward, about creating a better future?
Oh definitely. But it would be nice to have things both ways. There's a cosy side of the brain that needs to be comforted and there's a side of the brain that needs to be pushed and pulled. That's your article right there . . . (*snigger/sneer/sigh/face/glance to the heavens and the hells*)

Do you like people?
Not really. (*sigh*) . . . (*damn*) . . . I can't think of any reason to like them. Human beings are not, by nature, interesting.

Why do you want to get involved then?
Because I'm on this planet and they are all around me, and the alternative is to sit incarcerated in a tomb.

But you entertain everyone – why bother becoming such a great entertainer?
Oh God, you make me sound like Sid Fields or Charlie Drake. Well, I don't bestow it
on people as a gift . . . I sing for my own reasons, and happily there are people to listen.

*Where do you put yourself in the developing canon – Devoto and Shelley, Reed and
Cale, Yorke and Martin, Dylan and Young, Robert Smith and Curtis, Brecht and
Sondheim? . . .*
(*puzzled frown coexisting with deep amusement*) I can only imagine. . . .

Was The Smiths *the greatest debut album in the past 25 years?*
What an extraordinary question . . . (*face*)

How much money would it take for the Smiths to reform?
(*face*) . . . (*sigh*) . . . (*twitch*) . . . (*snort*) . . . (*feels for dagger or handkerchief in breast pocket*) . . . (*stands up in an act of sudden aloofness*) . . . (*sheer dishevelment of the mind*) . . .

*You must understand why there is such interest, and therefore the asking of the ques-
tion is inevitable.*
I understand in an oblique way, but the implication is that I am just waiting for a big
fat cheque to arrive and I will wobble onstage . . . there is no point. It has been eighteen years since it ended, I don't know them, they don't know me, they know nothing
about me, I know nothing about them. Anything I know about them is unpleasant,
so why on earth do we want to be onstage together, making music?

*Is it flattering? This natural kind of nostalgia for a splendid past that you always
demonstrated for your pet loves?*
No and no. It's a question that is applied to almost all important groups in a similar
situation, but – and this is not a rehearsed answer – I would rather eat my own testi-
cles than reform the Smiths, and that's saying something for a vegetarian.

You're happy to sing the songs . . .
That's a different matter, and I do sing the songs, and I will sing the songs. They stand
the test of time. Taste has shifted, what seemed a little marginal back then is now
much more mainstream, the songs work now because they weren't written just to be
heard then. The Smiths were in the pop charts but they were also ahead of their time,
which was a little freakish.

You talk a lot about keeping your integrity.
Not many people have it.

What is it?
It's avoiding social embarrassment in all ways. It's trying desperately not to answer the
telephone at the wrong time. It's trying desperately not to be in the wrong place at the
wrong time. It's trying not to be seen doing something ridiculous. It's not wanting to be
trapped or engineered into doing or saying and being something that you don't want to.

But does that make it difficult getting through the day?
Not at all. (*face*) . . . (*agitated sluggishness*) . . .

The myth is that it does, that you're too sensitive to live, that no one can imagine how you function, that you're just far too awkward and too bothered by perceived slights . . .
Well . . . that isn't the case. I can only promise you that this is not the case.

But the perception is that this is the case, hence the incandescent nosiness, and then the nosiness and prurient wonder is provoked by interviews like this, where you slip into grimly playful interview mode. People want to know, does he have a good time, does he watch telly, what's he laughing at, who are his friends? . . .
What's it matter? The truth is in the songs. So much is in the songs. No one is so interested in those questions in relation to a champion ice skater . . . they either succeed or they don't succeed . . .

But your songs and where they go, what they do, tempt us to find out more, or to find out how and why they appear.
It's all in the songs.

The interest suggests then that maybe you haven't succeeded . . . because we're not quite sure who you are.
I'm very sure about myself . . . (*exhaustion*)
But no one else is.
I can't help that. Why should I care about that? It's just not my problem. I can't issue daily newsletters about my behaviour to help everyone figure me out. It's just simple pop music. I just wanted to be Bobby out of the Righteous Brothers.

You just wanted to be Bobby out of the Righteous Brothers, and we're all looking to you to be a combination of Wittgenstein, Dorothy Parker and Oscar Wilde.
Well, I am that as well.

You have said that you'd be the first to criticise yourself, and the first to notice something about yourself before the critics.
Well, I self-edit and self-flagellate ridiculously, so there's absolutely no point in anyone criticising me, because I've really done it already.

What do you criticise about yourself?
Everything . . . everything! To get where I get, do you not think I have some kind of perspective on my own behaviour? It's all part of the search for perfection and the search for beauty, and to make sure that you make an album that people jump out of bed at night to listen to . . .

Which you've done. It makes me think it really would be a poorer world without you.
Well, you say that now, but you won't say it in print.

Did it take a certain kind of willpower, courage, heartache and bloody-mindedness to make this particular record?
Well, I don't want to be too me, me, me about it all. For now, let's just bask in the kindness of your thoughts.

Any last words?
It's too late to change now.

A couple of days after the interview, Morrissey sends me a message regarding the third person to have shunned him. It was Eric Cantona.

A truncated version of this interview appeared in *Uncut*, May 2006.

THE UNBEARABLE LIGHTNESS OF BEING MORRISSEY

—••— BY PETER MURPHY —••—

Stephen Patrick Morrissey will reach the milestone year of 50 this May, but rather than slink quietly into dotage (as if!), the singer has delivered an album, *Years Of Refusal*, that is both strident and defiant. Produced by the late Jerry Finn (Blink 182, Green Day, Rancid, Sum 41, the Offspring), who died of a cerebral haemorrhage last summer, Morrissey's tenth solo album is amongst the most committed (and certainly the *heaviest*) of his career. The apparently oppositional forces of Finn's production, which at times verges on the Pistols-ian, and the singer's vocal range – sometimes vulnerable, sometimes shockingly full-blooded – make for a collection of songs that are impressive in their scope, ranging from the despair of 'Black Cloud' to the tenderness of 'Mama Lay Softly On The Riverbed' to the classically Morrisseyonian sweep of 'I'm Throwing My Arms Around Paris' ('Only stone and steel accept my love'). There are even a number of widescreen epics ('When Last I Spoke To Carol') embellished with Mark Isham's gallant trumpet. In short, the man's never sounded so flamboyant or fearless.

Here, in an exclusive interview with *Hot Press*, the singer reflects on working with Finn, his childhood in depressed '70s Manchester, why he'll never inflict parenthood on an innocent child, his thoughts on the US presidential election, his love of post-war LA film icons, and how you learn to forgive yourself with the onset of age.

You've gravitated towards a more and more muscular sound with each successive album. Did the forceful arrangements on Years Of Refusal, *plus the predominantly live sound, push you as a singer?*

Yes, it did. I moved up several notches with tracks such as 'It's Not Your Birthday Anymore', 'I'm OK By Myself' and 'Sorry Doesn't Help'. I wasn't sure if I'd make it. But I did. There's a natural timidity about pushing the voice too much just in case you begin to sound rockist. *Spin* magazine reviewed the album and said, 'Morrissey's vocal range has narrowed with age,' which is laughable since the opposite has happened. The comments we're forced to put up with . . .

Can you remember your state of mind as you were putting those songs on tape?

I was a bit frightened because, in any circumstance in life, I never shout or even raise my voice. So it takes a lot for me to let myself go. The closing minute of 'I'm OK By Myself' was especially nerve-wracking because it was time for me to become so completely absorbed that I almost start to ignore the backing track. I had done two run-throughs and felt particularly proud, but Jerry Finn the producer stepped in and said, 'I don't actually like this song,' and I thought, 'Oh dear God!' – but I pushed on, which was difficult because as I was singing I was then aware that Jerry was sitting there with his hands over his ears. It was obviously wrong of him to say that whilst I was standing behind the microphone, because, win or lose, it takes a lot for a singer to let the horse off the reins, as it were, and when I walked into the control room he was sitting away from the desk instead of leaning over the desk engaged, which was his way of saying that this track was not for him. So this became the indication that what I was doing was just too much. But I didn't care. I love the track. It's my favourite on *Refusal.*

It must be upsetting when the producer tells you he doesn't like the song you're working on . . .
The people who are directly involved can often be the hardest to convince, but the voice is such a personal instrument. It has more reality to people than a guitar or a trombone. It has to be treated with special consideration. The sexual components of singing are enormous, even if you sing a song that isn't especially sensual. We therefore judge the singing voice in a very intimate way, because we all have one, whereas no one responds erotically to, say, the bass guitar. The worst thing you can do when you sing is to try to attempt to be interesting. It doesn't work. And the most important parts of the vocal can be how you rest or pause your voice for the gaps. The most tender gestures require more energy than the great big yelps.

Certain of the new songs – 'Black Cloud', 'When Last I Spoke To Carol', 'One Day Goodbye Will Be Farewell' – have an almost Saturday matinee daredevil bravado, suggested in part by Mark Isham's trumpet.
We had been listening a lot to Herb Alpert, and he agreed to come in and play on three tracks, so we were hugely excited. In the event, he cancelled and cancelled and then ultimately backed off. We cried. But Mark was terrific, and had played with Herb, and he caught that swirling Los Angeles midday sun gallop perfectly.

'Something Is Squeezing My Skull' describes a state of some despair or isolation, set to paradoxically driving music. Does the song pertain to a specific episode or period in your life, or does it refer to a more general disquiet?
I was enormously influenced by film as a child, and I made the assumption at a very early age that whatever you see in feature film is what will eventually happen when you grow up. When I became a teenager it was strikingly obvious that feature films – especially Hollywood films – were the biggest lie of all. And still are. This, coupled with the realisation when I was around ten or eleven, that abattoirs existed, was too much for me and I slipped from being quite a noisy and yappy child into an intense and withdrawn thirteen-year-old. Further on, the direct result of this was the inevitable anti-depressants. If you can't shoulder the burden of living in a society which is less than civilised then you don't quite fit into the community and too much is going on in your head. When I was fifteen I was under no illusion that

life was a terrible thing. My view has never changed. I think this is why we all love to sleep – because it's the only way we can get away from life. Well, of course, there is another way . . .

With regard to 'Mama Lay Softly On The Riverbed'; I've read that your mother was a librarian. Did she influence your reading as a boy?
No, not really. My mother has masses and masses of books on Irish politics and Irish history, which I was never responsible enough to examine too deeply. When you're a teenager you want to read about people in your own situation because you need to compare whatever is happening to you with how other people manage when faced with your, uh, limitations. I went to a working-class school in Manchester so naturally there were never any books and no one ever suggested to us that we might want to read anything.

Do you favour either of your parents in temperament or appearance?
Both equally, both uncannily.

In 'All You Need Is Me' you sing, 'I was a small fat child in a welfare house/There was only one thing I dreamed about/Fate has just handed it to me.' Was a nine-to-five always out of the question?
With what was available to me in the mid-'70s, yes. When your background is one without money, you are forced to accept your lot in life. I never could. The economic climate was vastly different in the '70s – except the so-called Royal family, of course, and all of that money belonged to the British working people. I recall one defining incident when I was seventeen and I went along to the Job Centre and I sat in front of this fat and hairy little woman whose face and general countenance were as ugly as sin, and she told me I had claimed unemployment benefit for 'quite long enough' and she handed me a small card with a job interview appointment and she explained that *if* I was accepted I'd be required to keep canal banks tidy of any discarded rubbish. I looked at her and laughed. She said, 'You think you're too good for this, don't you?' and I stood up and walked out.

They were pathetic times. Manchester in the 1970s was centuries ago.

As well as being a New York Dolls devotee in your youth, you also founded the Legion of the Cramps fanclub. Did the recent passing of Lux Interior give you any pause for reflection?
No, not really. It's inevitable that they'll all pop off over the next decade. Bowie has had a triple bypass, four New York Dolls have died, three Ramones are dead, three T. Rex members have gone. It's interesting how, if you make music at an early age, you remain that age for eternity, long after the pull of the earth. You will always be as you were on that recorded song. To the listeners, anyway.

Years Of Refusal *has been referred to in several quarters as a 'grudge-settling' album. Fair comment, or does that diminish the emotional scope of the work?*
It doesn't strike me as a grudge-settling album. My grudges are all settled.

If you listen to almost any great album in your personal collection you'll find that the principle motivation is anger, and this can be greatly indulged when you record because you are in the world of the art of noise. There are no boundaries and we are lucky when anyone gets it right as, say, Iggy and the Stooges did with 'Raw Power'. Art is a miracle. The music that most affects us usually has dramatic shock. Usually, but not always.

Your partnership with the late Jerry Finn seemed, on the face of it, an unlikely one, given his production background, and yet it has resulted in some of your best work. Could you describe the creative chemistry you enjoyed?
We had great fun together and got on very well. He loved the band and every session became a battle of wits – which was always quite funny. But if he didn't care for a song then he'd mix it dispassionately. This happened with the songs 'I Like You' and 'How Can Anybody Possibly Know How I Feel' on *You Are The Quarry*. He would step back and relish his own judgement too much. He wouldn't bend. Neither would I. I always won. His death was just terrible. I thought the British music press might salute him for his last and final work, but I must have been drunk when that crossed my mind – they were as petty and skanky as ever. *Rolling Stone* magazine said that Jerry had died during the recording of *Years Of Refusal*, but they knew very well that this was not the case because the writer was given the full facts. I think they were scrambling for a cheap joke at my expense – you know, 'Morrissey Kills Producer'. It's the only thing I haven't been accused of.

How crucial is a producer as collaborator, de facto A&R man, psychiatrist, friend?
Oddly, very. Jerry was a friend, foremost. We got on from the second we met, as if we were meant to. I'm a non-musical person so a bit mentally constipated in the studio – it's hard to find the right words to explain sound. When we first did the track, 'Irish Blood, English Heart', there was nothing much happening behind the line 'I've been dreaming of a time when . . .' and I asked Jerry if he could give Alain's guitar a Nordic retch – as if rising from the ocean bed – and eleven seconds later there it was.

Moments like this would justify Jerry's indifference on other tracks. I think a producer's role is to create order – even chaotic order, but order nonetheless. There are so many considerations flying around a studio during the time of recording – vanity, inferiority, ambition, the practical approach, anxiety, and the producer is the link to making all of these considerations unified, otherwise everyone is more or less just making their own solo album in their head.

The album cover features a photo of you holding a small child, who I believe is Sebastian Pesel-Browne, son of your assistant tour manager. Have you ever considered parenthood?
I wouldn't have the gall to assume that any living thing would want me as a father. What a burden to place on a small, innocent child.

Many performers reach a stage where they start to feel self-conscious about working in the realm of popular music and cast about for some way to keep doing what they're doing, but with a dignity that befits age. How do you negotiate this?
I think it's important to ignore praise. If you ignore praise then you naturally ignore criticism. If you let criticism in, then you're done for.

You live, in any case, in a situation whereby the music writers who are inclined to criticise you have never actually themselves attempted to do what it is you are doing, so you wonder how they can fault you for doing something that they themselves have never mastered. It can all very easily unbalance you, especially when most pop journalism is so consistently inaccurate, yet relishing their own wit and their own place within the review of your recording. My own position, therefore, is to lethally disregard anything at all that is said – whether good or bad. It isn't the gluttony of the self-engrossed, but a form of protection. It's true that once you make a recording you then hand it to the appraisers, but your own instinct is the best judge of whatever it is you do. When you first begin, before you've ever recorded, you don't write to music critics to ask them what you should play if and when you finally get a chance to record, so why on earth you should listen to them once you've made your record is baffling to me . . .

Hot Press, April 2009

BIG MOUTH STRIKES AGAIN
—— BY SIMON ARMITAGE ——

It's a bit like being on a date. It's not a blind date exactly; poet meets songwriter seems to be the general idea. But I've no idea if he knows who I am, and for all that I've stalked the man and his music over the years, I can't say with any confidence that I know who Morrissey is either. Can anyone? So when the door opens and he strides into the room, neither of us seems sure of the protocol. I am meeting him of course, that's a given, but is he meeting me? I shake his hand, a square and solid hand, more in keeping with the mobster and bare-knuckle boxer image he's cultivated of late than the stick-thin, knock-me-over-with-a-feather campness of yesteryear. Then he gives a little bow, a modified version of the one I've seen him give about a thousand times onstage, one foot forward and the other behind, head low, eyes to the floor. It's a bit like being greeted by a matador: the gesture of respect is genuine, but we all know what happens to the bull. I cast my eyes downward as well, and notice that he's wearing cute gold trainers, like those football boots reserved for the world's greatest players. They look like they should have wings on the side.

We're in the ballroom of a swanky hotel in a swanky street near London's swankiest department store, and while he's ushered away in the direction of an ornately upholstered chair for a portrait photograph, I head towards the hospitality trolley. Rock'n'roll riders are famously lavish or idiosyncratic, but I am in the company of a man who is famously abstemious. So where there might have been gallons of Jack Daniel's and chopped pharmaceuticals offered on the bare breasts of Filipino slave girls, it comes down to a straight choice between hand-stitched tea bags and several cans of Fanta orange, Morrissey's fizzy drink of choice.

I sidle over to the action. Morrissey is swivelling his head as instructed, registering one pose, then another. The light falls on his rugby-ball chin, then picks out his quiff, somewhat thin these days but still capable of standing a couple of inches above his scalp when given a bit of a finger-massage. He wears a red polo shirt, knuckle-duster rings and the general high-definition radiance of his celebrity. When the camera flashes, there's the occasional glimpse of the younger man within the 51-year-old face, then it fades. Somewhat implausibly in these decorous surroundings, I notice a push-bike leaning against the wall behind the photographer's screen, so I wheel it out and suggest we could do a remake of the 'This Charming Man' video.

'It's been done,' he says, with a kind of theatrical dismissal.

I was only kidding.

'Now both of you together,' says the photographer.

'Cameron and Clegg,' quips Morrissey.

'Which one am I?'

'You're Vince Cable.'

The photographer positions us in front of a full-length mirror, not more than three feet apart. It's a me-looking-at-him-looking-at-me-looking-at-him sort of idea.

'Bit closer, please,' says the photographer, so I edge a little nearer.

Morrissey: 'Am I looking in the mirror?'

Photographer: 'Yes, please.'

Morrissey: ''Twas ever thus.'

Photographer (to me): 'A bit closer.'

I do what I'm told, until my nose is no further than six inches from his cheek. I can't remember the last time I got within this range of another man's face, and this man is Morrissey, and we've only just met. I notice the grey hairs in his sideburns, his indoor complexion, the cool quartz of his eyes. I inhale the atomised confection of what I assume is an expensive cologne.

For me, this close encounter could be described as the arrival point of a journey that started over a quarter of a century ago. I won't go into the exact circumstances, except to say I was lying in a bath in a house on the south coast of England shared with five geography students and several members of the Nigerian navy. On the windowsill was a battery-operated transistor radio, and out of its tinny speaker, John Peel was talking about a band called the Smiths. Peel was never one for hype or eulogy, but somewhere within the lugubrious voice and deadpan delivery, I thought I heard a little note of excitement and perhaps even an adjective of praise. I dipped below the waterline to rinse the last of the Fairy Liquid out of my hair, and once the water had drained from my ears, I found myself listening to 'Hand In Glove'. And to a homesick northerner honed on alternative guitar music, it was love at first hearing: everything came together with the Smiths, a band whose very name suggested both the everyman nature of their attitude and the fashioned, crafted nature of their output. When Morrissey sported Jack Duckworth-style prescription glasses mended with Elastoplast I went looking for a pair in the market. When he wore blouses and beads, I waited until my mother had gone to a parochial church council meeting then had a flick through her wardrobe and jewellery box. And once he had appeared on *Top Of The Pops* with a bunch of gladioli rammed in his back pocket, any garden or allotment became a collection point on the way to the disco, and the dance floor, come the end of the night, would look like the aftermath of the Chelsea Flower Show. The Smiths split up in 1987 but Morrissey threw himself into a solo career, going on to produce – in my estimation – an unrivalled body of work, one that confirms him as the pre-eminent singer-songwriter of his generation. I listen to the albums ceaselessly. Despite which, I have never particularly wanted to meet Morrissey. A high court judge famously branded him as 'devious, truculent and unreliable', and in interviews he has always appeared diffident, a touch arrogant and always uncomfortable. In fact, I've always wondered why someone who seems so painfully awkward in the company of others would want to punish himself with the agonies of public performance?

'Because as a very small child I found recorded noise and the solitary singer beneath the spotlight so dramatic and so brave . . . walking the plank . . . willingly . . . It was sink or swim. The very notion of standing there, alone, I found beautiful. It makes you extremely vulnerable, but everything taking place in the hall is down to you. That's an incredible strength, especially for someone who had always felt insignificant and disregarded. Coupled with the fact that you could also be assassinated . . .'

We're now sitting in diagonally positioned chairs with a table between us, Morrissey with his stockpile of Fanta, me with my list of questions.

'Where's home?'

'I'm very comfortable in three or four places. When the world was a smaller place, Manchester was the boundary. But it's a relief to feel relaxed in more places than just one. I know LA well, but it's a police state. I frequent Rome and a certain part of Switzerland. And I know this city very well.'

'And presumably it would be a problem now, walking down Deansgate. Because of the fame?'

'Yes, but I don't really do all the things that famous people do.'

'You don't dip your bread in, you mean?'

'Yes. That's very well put. I can see why Faber jumped on you.'

It's quickly apparent that Morrissey's wit, articulacy and all-round smartness is always going to mark him out as an oddity in the music business. It's also clear that the sharpness of his tongue will make him more enemies than friends, and his list of dislikes is long. Morrissey on other singers: 'They have two or three melodies and they repeat them ad nauseam over the course of 28 albums.' Morrissey on people: 'They are problems.' And on the charts: 'Nothing anymore to do with talent or gift or cleverness or originality. Every new artist flies in at number one, but in terms of live music they couldn't fill a telephone box.' And shockingly, on the Chinese: 'Did you see the thing on the news about their treatment of animals and animal welfare? Absolutely horrific. You can't help but feel that the Chinese are a subspecies.' Neither is he impressed with Arctic Monkeys' Alex Turner ('an *NME* creation') or George Alagiah (an unspecified complaint signalled with a roll of the eyes), and his views on the royal family would have seen him hanged in former times. He even has a low opinion of our poet laureate, and when I refuse to be drawn into the sniping, pointing out that she happens to be a friend of mine, this seems to encourage his desire to disparage. Like many who've gone before me, as the conversation rolls on I find I can't unpick the contradictions. The charm, but also the barbed comments. The effeminate gestures, then the surly machismo. The desire to be centre stage coupled with the lack of social ease. The obvious trappings of success, fame and fortune, but the repeated complaints of victimisation and neglect. What I am certain of is that nobody is more aware of being in the company of Morrissey than Morrissey himself. Call it self-consciousness, call it self-absorption, call it self-defence, but every gesture seems carefully designed, and every syllable weighed and measured for the ripples it will produce when lobbed into the pond. Sometimes it's in the form of a brilliant, Wildean retort, sometimes it's a self-deprecating comment of suicidal intensity, sometimes it's a shameless remark about the indisputable nature of his own brilliance, and sometimes it's a claim so mystifying that at first I think he's taking the piss.

'I'm cursed with the gift of foresight,' he says. Then a few minutes later, he says it again.

'You don't mean in a crystal ball kind of way, do you?'

'That's exactly what I mean. Cross my palm with silver.'

I smile at the thought of one of life's renowned social realists staring into the tea leaves, and I'm on the point of asking him to prove his assertion by forecasting the winner of this afternoon's 3.30 at Market Rasen when I notice he isn't joking.

'Do you find that you've accumulated cash?' he asks me, apropos of nothing.

'I get by.'

'Is that a way of saying you've got loads but you're too embarrassed to admit it?'

'How would you like it if I asked you how much you earned?'

'Not an answer.'

'I earn more than I thought I would when I became a poet.'

'When did you know you were a poet?'

'Not until other people said I was.'

Referring to his own experience, he tells me, 'Once you feel it and other people feel it, too, you stand and are authorised as a poet. I was the boy least likely to, in many ways. I was staunchly antisocial. It was a question of being a poet at the expense of being anything else, and that includes physical relationships, strong bonds with people. I think you discover you are a poet; someone doesn't walk up to you, tap you on the shoulder and say, "Excuse me, you are a poet."'

In fact, Morrissey isn't a poet. He's a very witty emailer ('Bring me several yards of heavy rope and a small stool,' he wrote, when I'd asked him if he'd like anything fetching from the north), and a convincing correspondent, especially on the subject of bearskin hats, as his recent letter to *The Times* testified ('There is no sanity in making life difficult for the Canadian brown bear, especially for guards' hats that look absurd in the first place'). He has also penned an autobiography, which he assures me is 'almost concluded'. But poets write poems, requiring no backbeat, no melody, and no performance. Being the author of 'There Is A Light That Never Goes Out' and other such works of genius doesn't make him W.H. Auden, any more than singing in a band called the Scaremongers at weekends makes me an Elvis Presley.

'Are you a violent person?' I ask. 'You flirt with violent images in your work. Guns, knives . . .'

'All useful implements. As you must know, living where you live. Do you go out much, into those Leeds side streets?'

'No.'

'You're missing everything.'

I say, 'At this moment in time you have no contractual obligations, do you?'

'That's right.'

'I thought labels would be queuing to sign you.'

'Believe me, there is no queue.' Surprisingly, a rant about the music industry develops into a very touching statement about his band, talking almost paternalistically about his responsibilities and loyalties. The tone of voice reminds me of a recent email he posted to a Mozzer website, a tender and poignant citation for a girl who wasn't much more than a regular face in the crowd at his concerts, but whose devotion and death had clearly touched him. In fact, he talks movingly about all his fans, as if they were blood relatives, or even something more intimate.

Which, rightly or wrongly, I take as my cue to ask him about his love life, or his alleged celibacy. Not because I want to know if he's gay or bi or straight, but because I can't understand how a man who apparently shuns emotional involvement and physical proximity of any kind can write with such passion and desire. If it isn't personal, is he simply making it all up?

'Well, it is personal because I have written it. But I don't believe you need to be stuck in the cut and thrust of flesh-and-blood relationships to understand them. Because if that was the case, everyone on the planet who had been married or in a relationship would be a prophet of some kind, and they're not. You don't need to be immersed to understand. And if you do take on a relationship you have to take on another person's family and friends and it's . . . really too much. I'd rather not. You find yourself working overtime at a factory to buy a present for a niece you can't stand. That's what happens when you become entangled with other people.'

'But aren't you lonely?'

'We're all lonely, but I'd rather be lonely by myself than with a long list of duties and obligations. I think that's why people kill themselves, really. Or at least that's why they think, "Thank heaven for death."'

'How would you describe your level of contentment?'

He muses on the question for a moment. 'Even.'

'Does that mean your writing is a cold and clinical activity?'

'No, never clinical. I feel I don't have any choice. It's constant and overpowering. It has to happen. Even at the expense of anything else. Relentless. I know it's . . . insanity. An illness in a way, one you can't shake off.'

'Will you keep on doing this till you fall over, or will there come a time when you decide to pack it in and paint pictures or plant an orchard instead?'

'The ageing process isn't terribly pretty . . . and you don't want yourself splattered all over the place if you look pitiful. You can't go on forever, and those that do really shouldn't.'

'Any names?'

'No names. Why mock the elderly?'

While trying not to lose eye contact, I glance at the list of remaining questions in my notebook.

'Do you own a valid driving licence?'

'What kind of bland, insipid question is that?'

'It's a good question, isn't it? Has anyone asked you it before?'

'No. But that's hardly a surprise, is it?'

'I thought it was a beauty.'

'Why? Because you consider me incapable of operating such large and complex pieces of engineering?'

'Okay, how about, "Do you have any pets?"'

'Yes. Cats. I've had lots of cats. But also many bereavements.'

A prescient remark, as it turns out, and one that suggests I should have taken Morrissey's powers of prediction more seriously. Because a week or so later I get a message to say he hates the photographs so much he has insisted they will never see the light of day. The bereavement, it seems, is mine, in the sense that he won't be seen dead with me. And I am to be replaced in the images by a cat. Thirty years of admiration bordering on the obsessive, then a date, then dumped. Jilted for a fucking moggy.

Back at the hotel, he doesn't seem to be in any sort of hurry, but the conversation has run its course, and as a way of winding things up I embark on some ill-conceived sentence that begins as a heartfelt compliment but escalates into some lavish toast of gratitude on behalf of the nation. With no obvious end to the burgeoning tribute in sight, I cut to the chase and simply say thank you.

'And I have a little gift for you,' I add, pulling my latest slim volume out of my bag.

'Will you write something in it?'

'I already did.'

'Two r's and two s's,' he says. And I think, don't worry, Morrissey; if anyone knows how to spell your name, it's me.

He spins around on the thick carpet and walks towards the staircase. Except half way down the corridor he opens the book of poems and pulls out – forgive me, people, but who wouldn't have? – a Scaremongers CD.

'Did you know you'd left this in here?' he asks.

'Er, sort of,' I admit.

His eyebrows lift and fall, uncomprehendingly. Then the little wings on his golden shoes flutter about his ankles, and he ascends into heaven.

The Guardian, 3 September 2010

CONTRIBUTORS

Simon Armitage is a British poet, playwright and novelist. His poetry books include *Zoom!* (1989), *Kid* (1992) and *CloudCuckooLand* (1997). In 1993 he won *The Sunday Times* Young Writer of the Year Award, and later published two novels, *Little Green Man* (2001) and *White Stuff* (2004). He has worked extensively in film, radio and television, and is currently a senior lecturer at Manchester Metropolitan University. In 2010 he was awarded a CBE for services to poetry.

Stuart Bailie is a freelance journalist and broadcaster. He worked in London from 1985-96, and was assistant editor of *NME* before returning home to Belfast. He has written for *Mojo, Q, Uncut, The Times* and *Hot Press*, and has scripted a series of BBC Radio 2 documentaries on U2, Elvis Costello and Glen Campbell. Since 1999, he has presented a BBC Radio Ulster music programme on Friday nights, and now heads a music centre.

Max Bell is a veteran music journalist, from the same generation of classic 1970s *NME* writers as Charles Shaar Murray and Nick Kent. In the 1980s, he launched the world's first C60 tape mag featuring music and interviews, *SFX*, diversified into writing for style magazine *The Face*, teenypop mags *Smash Hits* and *Number One*, and *The Times*, and became the rock critic of the *London Evening Standard* for two decades. Today, Max is a regular contributor to *Uncut* magazine.

Ian Birch has been around. He cut his writing and reporting teeth in the late seventies on *Time Out* and *Melody Maker*. In the eighties he helped turn *Smash Hits* into a phenomenon (the Neil Tennant/Mark Ellen/David Hepworth era), moved to a newly launched *Elle* (as the token man), and ended the decade by launching *Sky* magazine. In the early nineties he worked for Jann Wenner in New York, editing *Us* magazine, before returning to London and EMAP as editorial director, launching *Red* and *Closer* (with Jane Johnson), re-launching *Heat* (with Mark Frith) and working with Fiona McIntosh on the UK version of *Grazia*. Then it was back to America – as editor-in-chief of *TV Guide* magazine, which has 21.3 million readers a week.

Lynn Barber has won five British Press Awards for her interviews, which have been collected in two books, *Mostly Men* and *Demon Barber*. For over a decade she worked for *The Observer* – preceded by work for *Penthouse*, the *Sunday Express*, the *Sunday Times*, *Vanity Fair* and the *Independent on Sunday*. She is also the author of *How to Improve Your Man in Bed* and the critically acclaimed memoir *An Education*.

Keith Cameron first saw the Smiths on 5 March 1984, in Edinburgh, aged eighteen. He's been recuperating ever since. A writer and sub-editor for *Mojo*, he lives in Hither

Green, south-east London – where if every day was like Sunday, it would be considered a bonus.

Steven Daly formed the Nu-Sonics with fellow Edinburgh boy Edwyn Collins in 1976, in his mid-teens. They became the classic post-punk band Orange Juice, for whom Steven was the drummer throughout their early 1980s singles and first album. After entering journalism, he relocated to the USA and became a writer on rock music and pop culture for *Rolling Stone*, and later an associate editor for *Vanity Fair*. Based in Manhattan, he is the co-author of two books: *Alt. Culture: An A-to-Z Guide to the '90s Underground, Online, and Over-the-Counter* (with Nathaniel Wice, 1995) and *The Rock Snob's Dictionary* (with David Kamp, 2005).

Adrian Deevoy is a freelance writer living in west London. He first met Morrissey in May 1983, and has remained in touch ever since. Shared interests include the Ramones, quality knitwear and murder.

David Dorrell wrote for *NME* in the early to mid-1980s. He is widely credited as christening the Batcave club crowd 'goths', but his own tastes lay in the direction of dance music. As a DJ and the founder of M.A.R.R.S., he had a UK number one hit with 'Pump Up The Volume'; he also remixed such popular 1980s dance acts as Janet Jackson, Snap and De La Soul. Since then, he has founded Dorrell Management, who were instrumental in breaking the band Bush in the USA, and boast the Pet Shop Boys as long-term clients.

Simon Garfield is an award-winning feature writer on *The Observer*, and the author of eight works of non-fiction – including *The End of Innocence: Britain in the Time of Aids*, *The Wrestling*, *The Nation's Favourite*, and the best-selling *Mauve* and *Our Hidden Lives*. His favourite Smiths song is 'There Is A Light That Never Goes Out'.

Andrew Harrison was editor of *Select*, the magazine that identified and named Britpop, between 1991 and 1995. Since then he has been music editor at *Details* in New York, and has edited *Q* and the award-winning dance title *Mixmag*. He has written for *Mojo*, *Rolling Stone*, *The Face*, *Spin* and *Blender*. Andrew is presently associate editor of the acclaimed *Word* magazine – for which he interviewed Morrissey for a second time, in 2003, visiting the singer at his Los Angeles home.

Tom Hibbert is a respected British music journalist who's published a number of rock-related books, including *Rare Records*, *Rockspeak: A Dictionary of Rock Terms*, *Electro-Rock* and *Encyclopedia of Rock/Pop Stars*. He made his name on *Smash Hits* in the mid-eighties and was a mainstay of both *Mojo* and *Q*, for whom he filed a legendary monthly profile entitled 'Who the Hell Does [insert name] Think S/He Is?' For several years he wrote the Pendennis column for *The Observer*.

Dylan Jones is the editor of British *GQ*. He studied at Chelsea School of Art and St Martins School of Art before editing the groundbreaking style magazine *i-D* from

1984. In the 1980s he was also a contributing editor at *The Face*, before becoming editor of leading men's magazine *Arena* in 1988, winning the Editor of the Year award in 1993. During the 1990s he was an associate editor on the *Observer* and *Sunday Times* magazines. Since 1999 he has been *GQ* editor, during which period it has won the Men's Magazine of the Year award three times. Dylan Jones is also the author of *Dark Star* (a best-selling biography of Jim Morrison, 1991), *True Brit* (a monograph of fashion designer Paul Smith, 1995), *iPod, therefore I Am: A Personal Journey through Music* (2005), and *Mr. Jones' Rules for the Modern Man* (2006).

Biba Kopf is the penname of Chris Bohn, after the character Franz Biberkopf in Alfred Doblin's novel *Berlin Alexanderplatz*. He began writing for *NME* and *Melody Maker* in the late '70s, and in the early 1980s was among the first writers to extensively cover bands such as the Birthday Party and Einstürzende Neubauten. In 1997 he became reviews editor of *The Wire*, taking over as editor in 2004.

Eleanor Levy was inspired to write about music after seeing the Clash at the Music Machine in Camden, three days before her fifteenth birthday. She joined *Record Mirror* as a writer straight from college, eventually becoming editor. She then turned to her other great love at the weekly satirical football magazine, *90 Minutes* – first as deputy, then editor. She is now deputy editor on a weekly women's magazine.

Stuart Maconie gave up teaching during the late 1980s and began writing for *NME*, as detailed in his *Cider with Roadies*. He wrote *3682 Days*, the official history of Blur, and *Folklore*, the official James biography, and wrote and starred in *Lloyd Cole Knew My Father* on radio and stage. He was the 2001 Sony Radio Academy Gold Award Broadcaster of the Year for his music shows on Radio 2; as a TV broadcaster, he wrote the BAFTA-nominated *After They Were Famous: The Sound of Music* for ITV, and was a stalwart of BBC2's *I Love the 1970s/1980s* and Channel 4's *Top Ten* and *100 Best/ Worst*. He currently appears on Radio 4's *Saturday Review*, his own Radio 2 show and BBC2's *The Cinema Show*, has a column in *The Radio Times*, and writes for *Word*. Stuart's latest book is *Hope and Glory: The Days that Made Britain*.

Andrew Male is the deputy editor of *Mojo*. He lives in Walthamstow, east London, where he is very happy. He first saw the Smiths at Edge Hill College, Liverpool, on 18 November 1983, and is currently the proud possessor of Morrissey's personal e-mail address – although it doesn't seem to work anymore.

Neil McCormick is a well-known UK music critic, a syndicated columnist in *The Daily Telegraph*, and a regular guest on the BBC. He began work for *Hot Press* in Dublin in 1978, at seventeen; after interviewing Morrissey in 1984, he became convinced the apparently suicidal singer wouldn't last another year. He is delighted to be proven wrong. In another life, Neil was allegedly the first person to leave U2. A schoolmate of Bono, he misspent his youth as a singer in obscure bands like Frankie Corpse and the Undertakers, the Modulators, Yeah!Yeah! and Shook Up! His musical misadventures are recounted in painful detail in *I Was Bono's Doppelganger* (US,

Killing Bono). Neil is also the co-author of *U2 by U2*, and continues to make music under the alias The Ghost Who Walks.

Dave McCullough came to the now defunct music paper *Sounds* in 1979, after writing as 'Dave Angry' for the Northern Irish punk 'zine *Alternative Ulster*. Until the mid-1980s, he was *Sounds'* champion of such post-punk luminaries as Magazine, Joy Division, the Fall, Subway Sect, the Scars, Scotland's Postcard label – and the Smiths, who he was the first to interview for the national music press. After this time, he put his faith in the 'new pop' of eighties bands like Scritti Politti and ABC, and moved to London listings magazine *City Limits*, now also defunct. His current whereabouts are unknown.

Paul Morley saw 'minor local legend' Morrissey sing with Ed Banger and the Nosebleeds in 1978. 'A Front Man With Charisma,' he instantly noted in the *New Musical Express*. 'He is aware in his own way that rock and roll is about magic, and inspiration.' Morley has written about Morrissey over the years for *NME*, *Blitz*, *Uncut*, *The Observer Music Monthly* and *The Sunday Telegraph*, and has also talked about him on various radio and television shows. Whatever he writes or says about Morrissey always seems to come down, in one way or another, what with one thing and another, to the same thing – charisma. While Morrissey has moved on from the Nosebleeds to become a major international legend, Morley has become one of Britain's leading cultural commentators, and an acclaimed author of books including *Ask*, *Nothing, Words and Music*, and *Joy Division: Piece by Piece*.

Peter Murphy is a novelist and journalist based in Dublin. A senior writer for *Hot Press* magazine, he has contributed articles to publications including *Music Week* and *Rolling Stone*. His first novel, *John the Revelator*, was published by Faber & Faber in 2009.

Jennifer Nine has been, variously, a record label dogsbody and marketing manager; a publicist for bitter middle-aged poets; a late-night radio host, and an anxious tour manager. She left Canada in 1994 as an economic migrant to the UK, where she made a modest pen name for herself as a music writer for *Melody Maker* – and whoever else would let her. She lives in Bethnal Green.

Shaun Phillips was a contributor to *Sounds* in its latter years, before it folded in 1990. In the ensuing decade, he wrote for *Vox* and was mooted as the editor for *Blah, Blah, Blah*, an intended British counterpart of US music/lifestyle magazine *Raygun*. His current whereabouts are unknown.

Will Self has earned his reputation through a body of innovative work: there's nobody quite like him writing today. He is the author of five novels, four collections of short stories, three novellas and four non-fiction works. As a journalist he has contributed to a plethora of publications over the years; he is also a regular broadcaster on television and radio. He lives in London with his wife and four children.

Mat Snow is the former award-winning editor of the magazines *Mojo* and *FourFourTwo*, who now writes and broadcasts about music, football, literature and workplace issues. A near-contemporary of Morrissey, he started his journalistic career writing for the Manchester fanzine *City Fun* in 1979 and, a few years later, was one of the Smiths' early champions in the pages of *New Musical Express*. In 1986, he was immortalised by his former flatmate Nick Cave in the song 'Scum' – every word of which is true. Mat has also edited a collection of interviews with Cave entitled *Nick Cave: Sinner Saint: The True Confessions*.

Elissa Van Poznak was a regular contributor and interviewer on seminal 1980s style magazine *The Face* – her interviewees ranging from Morrissey, to young 'Brit Pack' actors Tim Roth and Colin Firth, and legendary boho balladeer Tom Waits. In the late 1980s and 1990s she wrote for the UK edition of *Elle* magazine. Her current whereabouts are unknown.

ACKNOWLEDGEMENTS

The following articles appear by courtesy of their respective copyright holders:

'Morrissey Needs No Introduction' by Paul A. Woods, copyright © 2007 by Plexus Publishing Limited. 'Morrissey Answers Twenty Questions', from *Star Hits Collection*, 1985. Copyright © 1985 by *Star Hits*. 'The Morrissey Collection' by Ian Birch, from *Smash Hits*, 21 June-4 July, 1984. Words: Ian Birch/*Smash Hits*. Reprinted by permission of Emap London Lifestyle Ltd. 'Handsome Devils' by Dave McCullough, from *Sounds*, 4 June, 1983. Copyright © 1983 by Dave McCullough. 'The Smith Hunt!' by David Dorrell, from *New Musical Express*, 24 September, 1983. Copyright © 2007 by David Dorrell. Reprinted by permission of the author. 'All Men Have Secrets . . . ' by Neil McCormick, from *Hot Press*, 4 May, 1984. Copyright © 1984 by Neil McCormick. Reprinted by permission of the author. 'Morrissey Interviewed by Elissa Van Poznack', from *The Face*, July 1984. Copyright © 1984 by Elissa Van Poznack. 'A Suitable Case for Treatment' by Biba Kopf, from *New Musical Express*, 22/29 December, 1984. Copyright © 1984 by Chris Bohn. Reprinted by permission of the author. 'Meat Is Murder!' by Tom Hibbert, from *Smash Hits*, 31 January, 1985. Copyright © 1985 by Tom Hibbert. Reprinted by permission of the author. 'This Charming Man' by Simon Garfield, from *Time Out*, 7-13 March, 1985. Copyright © 1985 by Simon Garfield. Reprinted by permission of the author. 'Bigmouth Strikes Again' by Max Bell, from *No. 1*, 28 June, 1986. Copyright © 1986 by Max Bell. Reprinted by permission of the author. 'The Boy in the Bubble' by Stuart Bailie, from *Record Mirror*, 14 February, 1987. Copyright © 1987 by Stuart Bailie. Reprinted by permission of the author. 'Mr. Smith: All Mouth and Trousers?' by Dylan Jones, from *i-D*, October 1987. Copyright © 1987 by *i-D*. Reprinted by permission of the publisher. 'Wilde Child', by Paul Morley, from *Blitz*, April 1988. Copyright © 1988 by Paul Morley. Reprinted by permission of the author. 'Private Diary of a Middle-Aged Man' by Shaun Phillips, from *Sounds*, 18 June, 1988. Copyright © 1988 by Shaun Phillips. 'Playboy of the Western World' by Eleanor Levy, from *Record Mirror*, 11 February 1989. Copyright © 1989 by Eleanor Levy. Reprinted by permission of the author. 'The Soft Touch' by Mat Snow, from *Q*, December 1989. Words by Mat Snow/*Q*. Reprinted by permission of the author/Emap London Lifestyle Ltd. 'Lyrical King' by Steven Daly, from *Spin*, April 1991. Copyright © 1991 by *Spin*. Reprinted by permission of the publisher. 'Morrissey Comes Out! (For a Drink)' by Stuart Maconie, from *New Musical Express*, 18 May, 1991. Copyright © 1991 by Stuart Maconie. Reprinted by permission of the author/Amanda Howard Associates. 'Ooh I Say!' by Adrian Deevoy, from *Q*, September 1992. Words by Adrian Deevoy/*Q*. Reprinted by permission of the author/Emap London Lifestyle Ltd. 'Hand in Glove' by Andrew Harrison, from *Select*, May 1994. Words by Andrew Harrison/*Select*. Reprinted by permission of Emap London Lifestyle Ltd. 'Do You F*@kin' Want